Art in Question

Art in Question

THE
ARTS
COUNCIL
OF ENGLAND

continuum
LONDON · NEW YORK

Continuum

The Tower Building   370 Lexington Avenue

11 York Road   New York

London SE1 7NX   NY 10017–6503

First published 2003

Cover image

Bill Viola *The World of Appearances* (2000) Video/sound installation.

Collection: Helaba, Landesbank Hessen-Thüringen, Main Tower, Frankfurt.

(Photo: Kira Perov)

British Library Cataloguing-in-Publication Data

A catalogue record for this book is available from the British Library.

ISBN   0–8264–6181–6 (hardback)

        0–8264–6182–4 (paperback)

Designed and typeset by Ben Cracknell Studios

Printed and bound in Great Britain by MPG Books Ltd, Bodmin, Cornwall

Contents

List of Images

Acknowledgements

Above all, I am grateful to the individuals represented here who gave their time and thoughts so generously. The book is built upon their reflections, which represent decades of thinking, making and scholarship. Doing the interviews was a fascinating and at times humbling experience. It was a privilege to be able to ask questions of people whose work I admire, and to try to follow their lines of thought in a live conversation. It was a challenge to keep the conversations open enough to ask big questions, yet focused enough to be of more specific interest. After each interview I was left with a sense of excitement and optimism. This came in part from the exciting nature of the ideas, and in part from talking with people who are passionate about their subject and committed to going where it takes them. I hope these qualities come through the interviews in their written form.

After the interviewees, primary thanks goes to Viv Reiss of the Arts Council of England, without whom this book would not have come about. She co-directed the visual literacy project at Middlesex University; *Art in Question* was one of its final outcomes. She has persisted, with great humour, energy and vision through the book's many phases and reincarnations, and she has had a large hand in its finished form, particularly the logic of the images.

Tristan Palmer of Continuum supplied the enthusiasm, wit and patience needed to see the project through, as well as help in opening out the scope of the book and keeping it focused. Marjorie Allthorpe-Guyton, Director of Visual Arts at the Arts Council, provided support for the enquiry as a whole. Sarah Hopper was an efficient picture researcher. I am grateful to Pam Meecham and Fran Lloyd, whose close reading of the manuscript in its later stages identified gaps and helped me to draw together the many threads of the interviews.

Thanks are due to Richard Andrews, co-creator of the 1996 visual literacy project, and to other colleagues at Middlesex University who supervised and supported it: Howard Hollands, Claire Pajaczkowska, Lola Young and Sally Mitchell. I would also like to thank other people interviewed in relation to the project over the years, whose thoughts have contributed to my own. They are: Dave Allen, Cary Bazalgette, Sara Bowler, Michael Buchanan, Pauline van Mourik Broekman, Christine Burton, Ian Cole, Alison Cox, Miranda Cox, David Dabydeen, Howard Hollands, Martin Kennedy, Gunther Kress, Sarat Maharaj, Peter Medway, Virginia Nimarkoh, Andrea Nutter, Michael O'Pray, Colin Painter, Maureen Paley, Alistair Raphael, Victoria de Rijke, Veronica Sekules and Rebecca Sinker.

My friends and family have contributed indirectly to the book with their impromptu reflections and challenging questions, as well as encouragement of a more general nature. I would like especially to thank Marion Raney, Leanne Jackson, Dave Raney, Paul Raney, Diana Wolzak, Teresa Thornhill, Isobel Stevenson, Marjorie McDaid, Nick Manning and Dave Tebbs. The biggest thanks in this respect, though, must go to my partner Greg Morter for his spectacularly good-humoured support over the course of a long and at times trying project. The book is dedicated to our daughter Kelly, who questions everything.

Karen Raney

2002

Foreword

The quest to understand the nature, value and place of art now has been a central concern in the development of this book. *Art in Question* points to some of the conundrums, contradictions, revelations and pleasures inherent in this vast field of enquiry. The way in which contemporary artists think about 'medium' and aesthetic production is in constant flux. The convergence of disciplines, the performative nature of some art, and the opening up of different spaces to show and talk about art, present complex and sometimes conflicting pictures. As the territory of art itself is being redefined, so are the boundaries between histories and theories of art, art production, visual education and curatorship. The Visual Arts Department at the Arts Council of England commissioned the book in order to build a picture of this changing field and to ensure that funding policies keep pace with current thinking and practice. The idea was to seek the views of key contemporary practitioners and theorists in the art community whose roles are multiple and overlapping. Some of the thinking behind the book lies in an earlier publication *Visual Literacy: Issues and Debates*, which was a collaborative project between the Arts Council and Middlesex University. It was not possible to publish all the interviews but these thoughts and voices have informed the final text of *Art in Question*.

The hybrid term 'visual literacy' has been used as a starting point in some of the interviews. Response to the phrase has offered insights into current thinking about the use of linguistic models to understand art. It led to discussion about the many kinds of interaction between word and image, and called into question the idea of 'word' and 'image' as fixed categories. What emerges is a sense of how artists and viewers 'work in the gap' between word and image, and this carries over into accounts of artists' working methods.

One strength of the book is its 'thinking aloud' quality, as interviewees bring examples from personal as well as professional life to bear on the questions. This gives the material a more raw and informal feel than published essays tend to have.

They discuss their approaches to the study of visual culture and the practice of art, and differences and commonalities are highlighted through the editor's introduction. There is a sense of the conversations crossing over one another. Sometimes contributors independently mention the same artwork or exhibition, or one interviewee may refer to another. At other times it is the interviewer who imports ideas from another conversation and asks directly for comment.

We are indebted to each contributor and to Karen Raney whose curiosity and clear thinking has kept such a wide-ranging enquiry in focus. She enables the interests of each person to guide the conversations without losing sight of core concerns which link them together, giving an extraordinary insight into their thinking and practice.

Vivienne Reiss, Senior Visual Arts Officer
Marjorie Allthorpe-Guyton, Director of Visual Arts,
Arts Council of England

Introduction

The title of this book – *Art in Question* – draws attention to the uncertainties which surround the study and making of art. 'Art', says Okwui Enwezor, 'is no longer something that is handed down by the Academy, which has laws about how you must see and experience it.' How, then, is art being thought about now, in the absence of such standards and laws, and given the wider visual culture of which it is a part? This is the question which, through different routes, the interviews try to answer. My aim in this Introduction is to sketch out some of the emerging themes and to place them within recent, and not so recent, changes in how art is practised and understood.

Changing vocabularies

One sense that comes across is of uncertainty about the vocabularies used to talk about art. This uncertainty suggests that categories are being reconsidered and reformed. People are feeling their way toward new patterns of ideas whose edges are still blurred.

While this may be true of transitional periods in any field, in the study of art uncertainty about vocabularies has some specific origins. Changes in art history since the 1970s have aimed to make its methods and biases more transparent. In the course of this, the languages used to discuss art have come under scrutiny. Uncertainty about terms, then, may be in the spirit of self-examination of the so-called 'new art histories'.[1] In some universities, art history has itself been renamed or placed in a broader subject area such as 'visual histories' or 'visual culture', of which art is seen to be just one part.[2]

The opening out of the study of art to other disciplines has implications too, as specialist terms are imported from fields as diverse as linguistics, psychoanalysis, semiotics, anthropology, philosophy, psychology and political theory. Such terms are sprinkled throughout the interviews. Bill Viola refers to the 'indexicality' of a photograph (semiotics); Griselda Pollock refers to 'the Symbolic' and 'the Real' (Lacanian psychoanalysis); Okwui Enwezor refers to 'exchange value' and 'use value' (Marxist theory). Words which had a specific meaning in one context cannot simply be imported intact into another; they must be refashioned and reunderstood.

As well as managing foreign terms, people have reshaped the traditional art vocabulary in order to shed unwelcome associations and give a new emphasis. Pollock talks of the 'singularity', as opposed to the 'individuality', of an artist's practice. By singularity she means 'an embodied subject working within his or her moment' whose artwork will bear the stamp of larger historical forces. Individuality evokes ideas of individualism and genius which she wishes to avoid. For similar reasons, she talks of artists being 'productive' rather than 'expressive'.[3] Enwezor favours the phrase the 'economies of art', because it places art into a relationship with different sorts of values – exchange, use and exhibition value, as well as aesthetic and ethical values.

New words are sometimes coined to carve out a space for developing ideas. Hani Rashid talks of 'spatiality' instead of 'architectural space'. We need the word spatiality, he says, because we need a new way of thinking about the total set of conditions – including sound and the flow of time and information – that make up the built environment. The word 'visuality' is similarly inclusive. It suggests the sum of social discourses which attend and shape human vision, something not wholly catered for by the idea of 'visual perception'. W. J. T. Mitchell invents the terms 'imagetext', 'image-text', and 'image/text' in order to make distinctions as to how images and words interact on specific occasions.[4]

Finally, words can slip out of use and then return, having undergone a change in meaning. Words like creativity, imagination and quality have been suspect because of their association with elitist assumptions about the (white, male, European) artist and a received canon of great art. Now perhaps we are in a position to re-examine these ideas, in light of the changes over the past 30 years which have called them into question. Griselda Pollock describes the way her attention has shifted back from the circulation of discourses in visual culture toward an interest in how the visual is articulated in different art practices. A refocus such as this needs some concept of 'creativity', or a related notion like 'aesthetic intelligence' which she offers as a way of talking about the nature of artistic decisions:

> I think one can go back to that concept now, which was, in the past, so romantically overloaded that it sank into mystical mud. But I would now use the term 'creativity' with an entirely different set of possibilities. We've cleared some space, reclaimed the productivity of art from connoisseurial mystification.

The generation that went through this ground-clearing process will have a different, perhaps more embattled, perspective than those who came of age in a postmodern world and can take its challenges and uncertainties for granted. 'If the field has been cleared', says Hani Rashid, 'the next radical procedure is to build on that field.'

New laboratories of art

A primary source of doubt about categories and vocabularies comes from changes in art practice itself, which have preceded or run in parallel with changes in its study. Griselda Pollock explains that it was precisely her engagement with contemporary art – with 'living artistic cultures' – which led to the need to break the moulds that art history had established.

As art history has widened its scope to take in the whole of visual culture, marshalling the languages and resources of other disciplines, artists have worked across the categories of performance, document, art, craft and design. They use still and moving images, object-making, text, photography, sound, digital media, and a host of other means of exploring their subjects. Moreover, the setting for art is no longer just the studio and the gallery, but the highway, the book, the department store, the internet. Barbara Kruger's art practice has included writing, curating, architectural projects, designing posters, billboards, T-shirts, mugs and matchbooks, as well as making photographic works, audio and video installations and sculpture. These varied endeavours are not divided into 'artwork' and activities which support it; they are all part of what has been called a 'splintered' practice, that 'begins elsewhere, outside the artistic frame'.[5] This approach to art can be seen in terms of the impulses of modernity which Stuart Hall identifies in postmodern practice: modernism in the streets, the aesthetization of daily life, and the proliferation of the media, sites and means of signification.[6]

By and large, contemporary artists work differently with a medium than painters traditionally work with paint, or sculptors with clay. Martin Kemp talks about medium initially as a matter of taxonomy: a medium can be defined in terms of what it is made of (bronze, paper) or how the institutions of art classify it (fine art, applied art). In the end, though, 'medium' has to be seen as an idea which itself has undergone a change. Richard Wentworth is an artist who makes photographs, and constructs objects from everyday things – wood, plates, string, books, brooms, light bulbs, buckets. Wentworth's response to the question 'what is your medium?' is telling:

> I think my medium probably is the ability to think about things. It's thoughtfulness. If I want to do something about that thoughtfulness, if I want to put it into the world or I want to de-privatize it then there are various mechanical methods or procedures which are to my taste and pass a kind of philosophical muster. I can argue for why they are done that way. But that isn't to say they couldn't be done another way.

This approach is resonant with Rosalind Krauss's famous account of postmodern art practice: '[W]ithin the situation of postmodernism, practice is not defined in relation to a given medium – sculpture – but rather in relation to the logical operations on a set of cultural terms for which any medium – photography, books, lines on walls, mirrors, or sculpture itself – might be used.'[7] Bill Viola is an artist who has concentrated mainly on one artform – video. With others in the field, he has created the conventions of this new medium; yet his view echoes Wentworth's: the contemporary artist is someone who thinks well.[8]

If the notion of medium is a moveable thing, so is the line between art and other activities. The interviews with Hani Rashid and Okwui Enwezor call attention to the blurring of boundaries between architecture and art. Some artists are working in an architectural space. Barbara Kruger, who considers architecture 'one of the predominant orderings of social space',[9] collaborated with architects on a permanent, outdoor installation in North Carolina (*Imperfect Utopia 1987–96*). Conversely, some architects choose to work in an artistic space. The conceptual experiments run by the Asymptote architects – *Writing Space* for instance – function very like some kinds of performance art. Okwui Enwezor, the artistic director of the international art exhibition, Documenta 11 (2002), included the Asymptote architects amongst the artists. 'Staging this convergence', says Enwezor, 'will help us to make proper distinctions between different categories of aesthetic production.'

'Research' has to a large extent replaced 'expression' as a model for art practice. In Britain and the United States this may have to do with the absorption of art schools into the degree-awarding system, thus reframing art as an academic rather than a vocational – or anarchic – pursuit. But the deeper reasons for the research model have to do with art's opening up to the methods, imagery and structures of thought of other fields. Art practice has reframed itself as one branch of a vital and varied visual culture. Projects which look across disciplines are now commonplace, and research provides a concept to link the activities taking place in different fields. Martin Kemp's research has been into relations between art and science. He speaks about the 'researching' artists he works with 'who are interested in sustained investigation in relation to what they produce . . . in relating to bands of imagery, historical and contemporary, and who do a lot of cannibalizing of images, drawing upon a wide range of visual culture'. An exhibition about the brain at the Science Museum in London ('Head On', 2001) paired artists with scientists to investigate their different purposes of looking and ways of approaching visual material.

The research model hovers as well over curation. Enwezor, Pollock and Kemp all talk about curating as a form of research, and the word 'laboratory' crops up often. Research suggests an endeavour that is exploratory, collaborative, dynamic. Research suggests intellectual engagement and some degree of objectivity. And not only artists and curators but audiences as well are assumed to be carrying out research. Viewers are no longer enrapt contemplators or appreciators; they are consumers, participants, students of art. Wentworth described his exhibition 'Thinking Aloud' as something between a library and a shop, where 'there's the possibility of research, of each person exploring it in their own way'.[10]

One would expect artists to have a less sytematic, more 'lived' approach than those who theorize about art at one remove. In the interviews with practitioners, uncertainty seems to come not only from postmodern dilemmas, but from the imprecise, exploratory, immersed nature of making itself. Wentworth alludes to a chaotic way of working based on hunch and instinct. He is not sure where his artwork begins and ends. 'This current exhibition we're hanging at the Photographer's Gallery, I don't quite know what I'm doing, and I'm extremely anxious about it. I don't know even how I want it, I just know it's got to be right.' Barbara Kruger talks about her work in concrete terms: 'I've never worked in advertising, but I did work in editorial design. Everywhere you look there are pictures and words, pictures and words. That's where I developed my fluency. It was not a strategic development, it's just how it happened.' Sadie Plant speaks of the mysteriousness of the process of writing.

> [P]erhaps that's why other media are inspiring to your own, because you can look at them almost innocently. You can take what you need from them. To be honest, a lot of these processes are entirely mysterious to me. I don't know how any of it works. I don't know why I do what I do and I don't know what it's for. That's the real truth. You just have to trust it and do it.

This is not to suggest that artists stand outside of theoretical debates. It is to recognize the often anarchic, foraging, trial-and-error quality of what they do.

Theorizing with uncertainty

The people interviewed here live and work in a world where ideas about culture and art's place within it have undergone seismic shifts. Once it seemed that there were artworks whose meaning was put there by their creators in the process of expressing themselves. The art object was in a separate category superior to advertising, craft, fashion, decoration. The quality of individual artworks could be decided, and they could be placed, by those who knew enough, into a hierarchy of great achievements. The meanings of artworks, the intentions of artists, and historical facts themselves — what really happened — were seen as fixed in that they could be divined with effort and careful scholarship by a sensitive, suitably informed observer.

What interfered with this model was one in which culture came to be seen not so much as a collection of great works, but as a set of language-like systems of meaning. All kinds of representations were equally worthy of attention. Images and objects were texts to be deciphered or a meeting ground where ideas and identities form. Perception was a social and cultural question, not a matter of the individual's eye and mind. Things which had previously been understood as natural, biological or universal, came to be understood as the product of a particular set of circumstances, thrusting into the foreground the social functions of art. The idea of 'intention' came under question in the general unease about whether and how artistic meaning could be determined.

Both models have provided insights and deepened and complicated our understanding of art. The second approach worked as a corrective to the first. Many theorists, however, have grown dissatisfied with the reductionism inherent in the extremes of both models. An overemphasis on the object and its archeological details leads to a blinkered view of art as untouched by the social world. An overemphasis on the social framework causes the object to disappear; art becomes a mere symptom of social facts. The first approach runs the risk of becoming unresponsive to change, passing off a particular world view as universal; the second approach can lead to an extreme relativism where all distinctions of quality are levelled. How have those interviewed below tried to steer between the two extremes?

Firstly, while acknowledging the uncertainties, there seems to be a search for relatively fixed points, provisional certainties. Within this is a drive to reinstate the specificity of art practices. Martin Kemp is perhaps the least sympathetic to the idea that knowledge is negotiated or relative. He looks to perceptual psychology and cognitive science as more or less stable forms of enquiry, better able than the language-based theories to address visual experience and representation. Griselda Pollock's approach is to study what is peculiar to different systems of representation. These would be characteristics which are relatively stable and universal, but which are articulated differently through changing historical circumstances. Pollock uses 'specificity' here to refer to the fact that art practices have identifiable internal structures. Painting has different potentials for making meaning than installation or film has, and a Renaissance painter does not use these potentials in the same way as a painter in the twenty-first century.[11] Her approach is part of what has been called a 'new formalism' in the study of art, which seeks to look closely at the materiality, structure and content of works without abandoning social or historical perspectives.[12]

Secondly, theorists are concerned to locate themselves, rather than remain an invisible, expert voice. It is significant that each person sketches out a professional narrative to explain how their thinking has evolved over time. This autobiographical impulse may have been encouraged by the informality of an interview. Its deeper source, though, is the belief that interpretations are partial and partisan. The world is too complex and our instruments of enquiry too restricted for any one theoretical system to explain everything. Not only does autobiography shed light on what people say, but who is talking can be seen as an integral part of an argument. Interpretation, as well as artwork, is a product of 'an embodied subject working in his or her moment'.

Theorizing now is seen as a fluid enterprise in which we look backward and forward through the lens of a present which is itself constantly changing. Art history does not discover once and for all the way things really are or were. Instead, the values and languages of the present infuse our interpretations of the past and make them provisional. During periods of big change, it becomes more obvious the way that the present shapes our view of the past. Through the change we see what came before differently. Sadie Plant offers an example of this. Our preoccupation with 'interactivity' in the digital age allows us to see 'interactivity' in an older medium like a book, which might have been invisible before we had the vocabulary for it. She describes the sense of vertigo that comes from such retrospective insights. 'The rug does get pulled out from under your feet. It's not just that something changes now, it's that it changes how everything seemed in the past as well. Any big change rewrites history.'

Finally, there seems to be a growing acceptance of conflict and incoherence in the practice and study of art. The explosive pluralization of art, the merging of disciplines, the myriad stories being told through different voices and visual languages makes for a field of great turbulence. The tendency now is to want to preserve this turbulence and work within it – to see it as the point of departure – rather than prematurely to try to settle it. Enwezor describes the struggle as artists, institutions, curators and viewers 'go forward together to shape a theoretical field'. They do this often in a relationship of tension and subversion. Artists may subvert the project of the curator, curators may retaliate, and both agendas may be at odds with that of the institutions they are working within. 'We are beginning to see these folds and shadows that surround the practice of curatorship in very complex ways.' Mitchell speaks in a similar way about the subject area of visual culture. 'I prefer to think of visual culture as an *indiscipline*, a place of disciplinary turbulence, where media theory, art history, literary theory, philosophy, can come together and interact and produce interesting intellectual ferment.' Conflict is not to be deplored, but is seen as the very process through which ideas are tested, understanding is gained and meaning takes place.

Opposition and otherness

Oppositions arise in discussion throughout this book: observer and observed, high and low, male and female, black and white, theory and practice, image and word, reality and fiction, West and non-West. This is a commonsense way of talking; an entity is defined in terms of what it is *not*, or what it is assumed to be least like. The notion of 'binary opposition' (pairs of entities seen as polarized) and the critique of it has played an important part in theories about art and representation. As a consequence, many of those interviewed here are alert to the problems of binary opposition. They want to refuse simple oppositions, to argue that the two sides of polarized concepts live within and through one another.

Binary opposition was explored in the early twentieth century in structuralist theories of language. For Ferdinand Saussure, language as a system is based on the opposition of its units. Apart from instances of onomatopeoia, when 'sound echoes sense', words do not have significance in themselves, but only in relation to other words in the huge network of meanings of the language to which they belong. Difference is the basis of meaning, and difference will always be a matter of context. For two entities to be opposed, they have to be similar as well, that is, comparable along the same dimension. Man is only opposed to woman because both are human, adult and gendered, and gender is the category under scrutiny. On a scale which included animals and plants, man and woman would not be considered opposites. Similarity, then, is built into the very idea of difference.

Structuralism explored the logic of the oppositions that words create. A system of analysis was developed which could be applied to practically any social phenomenon – the arts, fashion, myths, literature – to reveal what were seen as 'deep structures' and more or less fixed meanings. Jacques Derrida and other post-structuralists challenged the idea that a stable relationship exists between a word – or any signifier – and what it refers to. The instability of meaning comes from two sources. One is that just at the moment of meaning, the signified turns into another signifier which points outward to other meanings; instead of closure on meaning there is an endless 'play of signifiers'. In this scenario, interpretation is more like game-playing than analysis. The second source of instability is the fact that every word suggests both what it means and its 'other' – what it does not mean. Derrida's critique is not only of structuralism but of Western philosophy itself and the central place that binary oppositions have held in it.[13] Not only is the world plural, paradoxical and continuously varying, but binary oppositions are inherently false. Because the two parts of a pair are defined in relation to one another, one side could not exist alone. The concept of 'high art' only gains meaning by being contrasted to 'popular culture'. The concept of 'primitive' only gains meaning by being contrasted to 'civilized'.

Part of the post-structuralist project was to link the polarities created by language with how they are used by the hierarchies that exist in a society. Distinctions of gender, ethnicity or class might become linked to oppositions between observer and observed, passive and active, word and image, or culture and nature. Visual distinctions between, for instance, light and dark will then become associated with these complex cultural pairings.[14] One of the terms of a binary opposition is almost always privileged over the other: male over female, white over black, culture over nature, true over false, centre over periphery. As these concepts live inside one another, the side that is suppressed or denigrated will find expression in oblique ways.[15] Derrida's method of deconstruction aims to dismantle oppositions and to expose them as arbitrary, to show that the 'lower' term of a pairing in fact has primacy over the privileged upper term.

Psychoanalysis offers an explanation of the human preoccupation with difference and the tendency to polarize difference into absolute opposites.[16] As a child gradually experiences him or herself as a separate entity, psychic mechanisms develop to retain control and to conceptualize the confusion about what is 'me' and what is 'not me'. As a consequence, difference tends to be idealized or demonized. Part of the power of visual representations is their readiness to embody and make concrete our fantasies about the self and the other.

Okwui Enwezor describes the way in which images of black people placed in the mostly white institution of an art gallery tend to be either underinterpreted or overinterpreted. In the first case blackness is seen as purely aesthetic, stripped of political charge. In the second case blackness is seen as something that needs special interpretation, in the way that whiteness does not. He gives an example of overinterpretation of the British artist Steve McQueen's video *Deadpan* (1997). In this piece a black man stands still while a wooden house topples around him, leaving him untouched. On its showing in the Museum of Modern Art in New York, one critic read into it images of sharecroppers' cabins (immortalized in Walker Evans' photographs *Let Us Now Praise Famous Men*) and slavery.[17]

In between and to and fro

How has oppositional thinking been explored by artists and how are theorists working with the concept? Barbara Kruger's photomontages make direct use of oppositions in order to trouble them. The word 'Perfect' appears over a grainy black and white photo of a woman's hands piously folded (*Perfect*, 1980). 'Not Perfect' is stamped across a pair of stained hands submerged in a bucket of water

(*Not Perfect*, 1980). *It's Our Pleasure to Disgust You* (1991), *We Won't Play Nature to Your Culture* (1984): the word-pairs evoke one set of clichés and stereotypes, the images another. Their clash or congruence blocks the comfort of our usual responses and presses on us, the viewers and readers, an ambiguous set of meanings. Directly addressed by the 'you' of advertising, we are forced into an unsettling space between what the words and the image seem to be saying.

An overriding theme of Okwui Enwezor's interview is the refusal of binary oppositions. The West and the non-West are not to be seen as fixed categories, as they are bound together in complex ways. His own Westernization did not come about from moving beyond his Nigerian 'origins' into another space, 'the West'. Rather the West was already contained within this so-called non-Western culture. He takes the same approach to ideas of the real and the fictive, interiority and exteriority, art and non-art. He seeks to constantly rework these categories, to find ways of inhabiting the space between them. It is a matter of 'to-ing and fro-ing' between zones which are themselves unfixed, in order to find a more mobile, complex understanding, a different ground from which to speak.

The idea of to-ing and fro-ing is more dynamic than the idea of the hybrid. In post-colonial debates about visual art, the idea of 'hybridity' is often used to describe the outcome of the meeting of cultures with different visual languages. Hybridity can be seen as the positive result of the effort to translate one culture's system of meaning into another's. A third identity is created in which the original ones are still discernible but neither dominates. This solution, though, is not without its problems. For one thing, it can work to deny and smooth out difference, to gloss over the very real conflicts of interest and inequities that operate in the international art world. If hybridity becomes the new standard, the risk is that this will polarize further the West/non-West distinction. 'Is there a danger', asks Sarat Maharaj, 'of hybridity . . . becoming the privileged, prime term, a danger of its swapping places with the notion of stylistic purity?'[18] Instead, the space between cultures needs to be charged with a 'volatile tension'. Enwezor speaks of an 'interspace' which is active, reciprocal, in flux, rather than a fixed hybrid product which can become a new orthodoxy.

Image and word

A major division which has structured the practice and theory of art is the division between image and word. There are a number of time-honoured ways of distinguishing an image from a word. One is that they exist differently in space and time. Words are apprehended in a linear sequence while visual representations are taken in all at once. Words and images are said to differ in their relationship to what they refer to. Words have a mostly arbitrary connection to their referent; they make meaning by conjuring up whatever the social world has linked them to. Images tend to replicate some of the features of what they stand for. Words and images are also said to differ in their analytic capability. Words can draw generalizations and state causality (how a situation came about). Images can vividly describe, but they can be analytic in only a limited way. Lacking explicit indicators of causality, and markers like 'not', 'never', 'always', 'usually', images tend to present a state of affairs whose interpretation relies heavily on context.[19] Hence the need to 'anchor' images with words, and the temptation of gallery-goers to spend more time reading labels than looking.

Insisting on a hard division between word and image on any of the above grounds may seem like common sense. However, when one tries to define 'image' difficulties immediately arise. Image is used to describe a bewildering array of things: pictures, marked surfaces, screens on which moving pictures are projected, diagrams, gestures, actions, performances – or any sight that is presented to the eyes. Image is also used to refer to visual experience that does not have a direct material basis – memories, hallucinations, dreams, as well as the mental representations that accompany thought. Part of the problem of dividing word from image, as with other opposed concepts, is that a definition of one concept always appeals to the other.

One approach to the word–image puzzle is to make it a problem of taxonomy and to devise a system whereby different kinds of image and word can be defined and translated into one another. This, crudely, is the project of semiotics. Verbal language tends to be used as the template for understanding all sign systems. 'Visual literacy', which acts as a trigger phrase in some of the interviews, suggests an affinity between the acts of looking and reading. It suggests that if one can learn the right alphabets, syntax and grammar, one can successfully read images and the visual world at large.[20] Part of the impulse behind using linguistic models to understand art was to counter the mystifying tendencies in modernism. In *Ways of Seeing* (1972, see note 1), John Berger urged us to think of pictures as being 'more like words and less like holy relics'. He was saying that at a time when the problems with treating pictures as 'holy relics' were as yet largely unchallenged. Seeing pictures as word-like was to make them continuous with everyday knowledge and capabilities, rather than something that requires an authorized body of knowledge to approach. More importantly, to say a picture or object functions like a word is to restore it to a field of social, political, cultural relationship. In any context in which art is felt to need demystifying and politicizing, linguistic analogies tend to be in favour.

However, in spite of our debt to semiotics, there is a recurring dissatisfaction in these interviews with the kind of language analogy built into it. If visual art and the visual world at large is seen as a text to be deciphered, what is distinctive about objects and images may disappear under a screen of codes and classifications. As Sadie Plant says:

> Your clothes are clothes, they're not a text. I think you can lose what is special about clothes, for example, by superimposing the concept of text onto them . . . What excites me about a city like Birmingham is that it's a convergence of different kinds of flows of material – the traffic, the pollution, the sewage system, the power supplies, the waste disposal, and all the images and the culture and the people. I think you need different approaches to each of those material processes, and that they are processes that are above and beyond, or below and beyond, our human perspectives on them. Sure, you can 'read' the sewage system but I don't think it's going to get you very far in understanding how it works or, more importantly, how it fits in with the composition of a city.

For Martin Kemp, the adoption of linguistically based strategies has been important, but in the end it has been damaging to art history and criticism.

Terms like 'reading images' and 'visual literacy', which were used as reasonable kinds of analogues, now play so much into a certain kind of theory — which simply sees the visual as subsidiary to a series of linguistic categories, objects as subsidiary to words, and the whole act of seeing as entirely articulated through verbal categories — that I am no longer prepared to use those terms because they stand no chance of getting towards the irreducibly visual nature of visual things.

Kemp's dissatisfaction with linguistic approaches inclines him toward the more concrete psychologies of perception and the cognitive sciences. The concern is with losing sight of the physicality of things, something behind recent calls for art historians to 'return to the object'.

In order to steer between the mystifying legacy of modernism and the tightness of semiotics, Griselda Pollock draws on the work of Julia Kristeva. She sees in both language and visual representation a potential to move between two terrains, one of fixity and clarity and one of ambiguity and contradiction. Rhythms and impulses deriving from the body constantly trouble and renew the system's will to make sense of the world and convey a specific message. Combining semiotics and psychoanalysis offers a way of speaking about, and moving between the two terrains. One ends up with 'a double sense of both the codedness of visual sign systems, and that which, as it were, nebulizes the codes'.

Working in the gap

As with other binary oppositions, is there an interspace between word and image that takes neither to be a fixed point? The search for such a space may start with the realization that we apprehend the world through a constant back and forth between verbalizing and picturing. 'There are no pictures within science or within art for that matter', Kemp writes, 'that operate outside an implicit or explicit dialogue with words, any more than there are theories about how things work that can ultimately resist our apparently irresistible desire to picture phenomena.'[21]

The hugely varied and fluid interactions that exist between what we call words and images also points to the need to rethink the two concepts. 'The varieties of their interaction across the range of media', says Mitchell, '. . . is truly amazing, and it provides an enticement to think beyond binary oppositions and essential categories, and to consider hybrid formations and dialectical structures. Words and images stop being the names of separate compartments, and designate a field of symbolic interaction and interplay in the arts and media.'

Mitchell asks not what is the difference between words and images, or how their sign systems mix and overlap. He asks what interests are served by the claims made on behalf of words and images. He looks at the usual divisions between the two entities in light of the values that motivate the divisions and become linked to them. An obvious example in Western culture is where the mute, concrete, ambiguous image has traditionally been identified with woman, and the articulate, abstract, rational word with man. Images in this view are not just a particular kind of sign, but something like an actor on the historical stage. The idea of imagery or the visual sign acts as a kind of 'relay' connecting theories of art, language and the mind with social and political values. How images and words are perceived and handled will provide clues to the conflicts within a culture at a given point in time. In Mitchell's view, fears and fantasies about the difference between words and images are deeply tied to fears and fantasies about the self and otherness. Because of this, the symbolic field of image and word is 'a space of intellectual struggle, historical investigation, and artistic/critical practice. Our only choice', he writes, 'is to inhabit this space.'[22]

How do artists inhabit this space? Art practice in the twentieth century has continually tested the boundaries between the visual and the verbal. Matisse played with a gap or rupture between image and word; Cubism turned the canvas into a screen of painted and written signs. Abstraction aspired to be 'purely' visual;[23] conceptual art attacked the primacy of the visual. Some artists turned words into painterly images; some made objects function like words. The artists included in this book inherit this legacy and position themselves in relation to it. Bill Viola's dislike of the term 'visual art' is in one sense a refusal of modernist notions of the 'purely visual'. Richard Wentworth's made, found and photographed objects have been described as 'dumb things encrypted in sentences, made to talk'.[24] Barbara Kruger's work plays directly with the conceits and deceits of words and images and the clashes between them. She says:

> When an image is stilled, or there's an image without a word, there's a sort of withholding, which is about coolness or muteness. The use of language over the picture, the declarativeness of that, was totally uncool, as opposed to the cool withholding of the image. So it was not a question of truth, but a flipping back and forth between different kinds of statements, cool and hot.

Enwezor talks about the interspace between word and image in the use of the moving image by different cultures. Traditional cultures like the Inuit, where the making of images has not been a main concern, are now using video and film to track what had previously been documented through an oral tradition.[25]

The space between image and word is inhabited by artists in another sense — through the process by which their work comes about. There are some fascinating accounts here of artists' working methods. Bill Viola does not do much of the preparation for his work in visual form; instead he prepares the ground by writing in words an experiential account of an image or series of images. 'What I'm after', he says,

> is not the visual aspect of images, but something under that surface, the place where the images are coming from and returning to . . . What I actually write about in the notebooks is usually not the literal facts — the color, the size of the image, the room, etc. These are the secondary aspects. What I'm writing about is the *feeling* of what it's like to experience the image. And, most essentially with my medium, writing is much better suited to dealing with the time form of the work, since it embodies the flow of time itself. What I'm getting clear to myself at this point is how this thing should feel, what the underlayers are to the experience, how the time will unfold . . . and not merely what it should look like.

Hani Rashid carries a digital video camera around to capture still frames. It becomes a 'notebook' in which to conceptualize his architectural projects. The video notebook may be visual, but he stresses that it is the 'abstract and fleeting spatial conditions' he is trying to capture, and this includes far more than visual information. It is more authentic, in his view, to structure a project conceptually, than to visualize it. The writer Sadie Plant, on the other hand, uses visual images – photographs – as starting points, or 'ladders' for writing, which she can throw off once she has positioned herself.

Subjective space and the invisible

In Bill Viola's *The World of Appearances* (2000) the smooth surface of a pool of water is shattered by a man diving in. His submerged body is seen at different angles from above and below. Gradually, the wobbling wave patterns of the disturbed water slow down and gather into a calm surface again. This then is split by another dive. The sequence is projected onto two screens, one on the floor and one on the wall; between them at 45 degrees is a pane of clear glass. The images of plunging and submergence, and the patterns created in the water are echoed, divided, multiplied and subtly varied by the interaction between the two screens and the glass. There is no clear reality of which this is an image; there is only layer upon layer of reflection and illusion. 'Everything is in motion, everything is a reflection of itself, and nothing is what it appears to be.'[26]

In Viola's view we are in a period where the relationship between subject and object – the 'in here' and the 'out there' of experience – is being reconceptualized. The shift is away from an objective, 'optical' view of reality toward a subjective one. He considers ours a period of transition analogous to that of the fifteenth century when the vision-centred world-view, and the optical model for making pictures, was being developed.[27] The skewed perspective of a Flemish painting represents this transition in its effort to make images conform to the way the world appears to the eye. Now the effort is to make images conform to the way the world appears to the mind. 'What's going on is that the basis of image-making is shifting from the visual to the conceptual. The material basis of the image is no longer founded on the behaviour of light; it is based on the behaviour of thought.'

The idea that our eyes are a window onto the world suggests a complete and clear transfer of information from outside world to inner mind – which are seen as two separate domains. One concern of philosophy and visual art in the twentieth century has been to trouble the opposition between mind and matter, something which, Viola reminds us, Eastern philosophies have never seen as opposed. The findings of twentieth-century physics have also called into question the model of ourselves as objective observers. If a fixed-point perspective picture stands for this idea of a clear window between observer and observed, a Cubist picture might stand for the idea that we are 'mixed up' with what we see, that, in the physicist Werner Heisenberg's words, 'what we observe is not nature itself, but nature exposed to our method of questioning'.[28] This rethinking of the relationship between subject and object pervades Viola's interview and animates much of his work.

The 'subjective' space that emerges is not one dominated by vision, but one in which the entire sensorium is addressed. Discussion moves away from the visual to include the haptic and somatic – touch and the body. Although Viola uses a medium reliant on light, he considers his real subject to be the invisible and unvisualizable – 'things you can't shine a light on'. Hani Rashid's notion of 'spatial' rather than 'visual' literacy speaks as well to this reorientation. His favourite architecture is 'Wall Street on a Sunday morning at 6 a.m. on a bicycle'. Spatial literacy uses all perceptual channels, is alert to the total set of circumstances and experiences which make up a 'spatial condition'. If one comes to understand this totality, it is possible to make an architecture which dissolves back into it, and becomes part of its collisions.

Griselda Pollock talks in a different way about the invisible, through the language of psychoanalysis.

Being in the womb is clearly not something of which we would have any visual memory. But you might be able to make paintings which, in a sense, translate that archaic sensory experience of contact, being carried, into an affect that can be perceived via a visual encounter with a painting . . . You could create, in the experience of painting, a visual scene which, through uncanniness, folds into the visible world, that which is non-visible, and never was in the order of the seen.

Artists working in a visual medium must believe that the means of representing the visible world are complex and subtle enough to stand for what cannot be seen. And this is by no means just a recent project. Martin Kemp points out that perspectival systems of drawing in the Renaissance stood for more than an attempt to make pictures conform to an outer reality. The larger aim was to represent what was invisible, what the eye cannot see. For Leonardo, one of the great aspirations of the artist was to portray the soul. The new system of drawing was exciting in part because it seemed to represent not only what was visible in the outside world, but the inner nature of the beholder as well.

Digital fictions

Moholy-Nagy's remark in 1935 that 'the illiterate of the future will be ignorant of the pen and camera alike'[29] suggests that new skills spring up alongside new technologies. What part might developing technologies play in our changing visual habits and even our conceptions of space? Visual signs appear to be more closely linked to technologies than sign systems such as speech or dance which are based on the human body alone. This means that different means of representing the visual will favour different kinds of meaning.[30] The photograph as a trace or footprint taken of the physical world has come to stand for an 'optical', objective model, where the image is assumed to refer to a reality outside of itself. The computer can synthesize different images and modes of representation and combine sound, text and visual image, or transform one into the other. This creates a non-optical or non-referential model, where an image is assumed to be a human-made construction rather than a trace of reality. Virtual reality is an extreme version of this kind of constructed world.

Soon, according to Viola, we will not be able to tell whether an actor or news-reader is a real person or a computerized creation – and what's more, the difference will cease in many circumstances to be significant. The virtual newsreader or the virtual Marilyn Monroe on the screen in his view is only a higher-tech realization of the virtual personas we carry with us in the form of personal or cultural memory. Hani Rashid is interested in spatial entities that have no analogy in the world, but are formed through digital tools which read and augment space. His work is beginning to explore what it means to inhabit a virtual world, in projects like the New York Stock Exchange and the Guggenheim Virtual Museum. The goal is to create totally hybrid spaces, where the virtual and the real exist side by side in a symbiotic relationship, neither privileged over the other.

Some people embrace these changes with more optimism than others. Viola concedes that the idea of the unfixed, constantly transforming or virtual image is 'disturbing to the older generation and very invigorating to the younger generation'. Enwezor makes the point that art has always staged a convergence of the real and the fictive, whether the medium is hand-drawing, or the newer imaging technologies. Pollock, though, sets traditional arts which are based on a bodily 'graphic' act (painter Lee Krasner thinking with her hands) against activities which seem to sever the link of body to image. She describes someone at a computer where 'the only thing going on is the visual scanning and the slight hand movement of the clicking mouse. I think that's quite new and different. It breaks the link between visuality, tactility and the body that has been so fundamental to what we have called art. I think there are going to be implications.' The implications extend of course beyond the frame of art. The artifically constructed visual world of the Gulf War made it a 'virtual' war which served to undermine our empathy with its bodily horrors. In Pollock's view, the dislocation afforded by technology is worrying; the visual arts are important precisely because they involve an 'embodied subject'.

Rashid, on the other hand, considers hand-drawing for architects to be, to a large extent, obsolete. Once reified as the central activity through which ideas form, it has become unnecessary for the architecture of the future, for the 'fluid, dimensionless territories of the post-information age', in which we 'navigate space, time and meaning through international travel, fax, channel-surfing, tele-conferencing'.[31] Although the hand-based arts are not likely to disappear, it is questionable whether visual art is any longer fundamentally 'graphic' in nature as Pollock suggests. Much of contemporary practice uses video, film, performance, assemblages, computers – forms which involve collaboration, staging, conceptualizing and overseeing rather than making marks.

The idea of surveillance comes up frequently in the interviews. Mitchell talks about the awareness of being watched as something which defines us at a deep level. 'Your identity is partly constructed by the fact that you are seen from outside, there is another person there. Otherwise, we would just be solipsistic beings. I think it goes right down to the moment when the human subject is constituted as somebody who is seen by someone else.' Viola uses the literal, dispassionate eye of the camera to allude to the non-literal dimensions of his subjects – birth, death, the nature of consciousness. The result is ambiguous. His work often forces us think about ourselves watching, and to consider the technology that enables us to be the detached eye – a 'dangerous instrument' in Viola's view which can distance us from moral responsibility toward others. Rashid speaks of embracing the technologies of surveillance and turning them to humanistic ends.

> Can we talk about what it is to be watched in some inspired and forward thinking way? It may be we can't, and then again it may be we can. We're doing a project now which is a showroom where we're using surveillance cameras everywhere. They're being used to celebrate the notion of people watching each other in a public space. If all goes well I think people will be fascinated. It's fascinating to see people watch each other in a space and be consciously under surveillance.

Well aware of the sinister ends to which a technology like the computer can be put, Sadie Plant finds it optimistic that we can never completely predict or control its use.

It is very much about unanticipated effects and unintended consequences. You can portray the whole digital enterprise as the epitome of a classically patriarchal dream of total control – now we can finally play God. And yet as we know, both in terms of theory and practical consequences, it has introduced far more chaos and disorder than control into the world . . . There are other processes going on that we just don't see until they actually happen. So it's another lesson about the limits of our ability to either comprehend the whole picture or to control it . . .

She gives an example of the revolution in the Philippines (2001) which was organized to a large degree through communication by mobile phone. Their use allowed a grass-roots process to develop without a centralized information source. 'When you see how people use technologies in ways that are so far from what the original intention was, I think it does give cause for enormous optimism.'

The changes in visual habits referred to in these pages have to do with speed and fragmentation – the ability to take in a series of rapid, fragmented images, spliced with words and sound. Pop music videos and television adverts are organized this way, channel-surfing creates the same conditions, and digital processes are by nature non-linear, transformative and multimodal. Those who discuss technology point out the subtle interactions between technological change, ideas, habits and social realities. In Martin Kemp's view, digital media are playing to capacities the brain has always had – for instance non-linear thinking – just as fixed-point perspective pictures played to our ability to see things arranged a certain way in our visual field. The fixed-point perspective picture was only invented when it became desirable – in a particular historical moment – to make a picture which had the illusion of space.

If I could make a historical analogy, what I could say now is that the new media are tweaking different proclivities in an analogous way, proclivities we've always had, but they're being newly articulated in a particular kind of a way. So I would see certain processes of conception and visualization as highlighted and extended, but I wouldn't see them as radically new at the deepest cognitive level.

Mitchell cautions too against seeing technology as a cause of fundamentally new ways of seeing. Rather than the technologies of vision shaping us, we shape technology according to what and how we want to see.[32]

Sadie Plant places more emphasis on the transforming and liberating potential of technological change.

> It's not that technology on its own makes things happen. But I do think that if you change the ways in which things are done in a practical way, then almost inevitably society does shift . . . if you change the processes of production or distribution or communication or whatever it might be – things crucial to a society – you will encourage and often accelerate certain social changes. If you look at what happened to the family and the role of women in the industrial revolution, or at any point after it, I think you can say that technology was hugely significant. And in terms of studying culture, it is a useful place to start – tracking the development of technology and the changes associated with it.

Social vision

'Buy me; I'll change your life.' 'Your body is a battleground.' 'Remember me.' 'It's our pleasure to disgust you.' 'Your moments of joy have the precision of military strategy.' When Barbara Kruger uses direct address – the implied or frank 'you' of advertising placed over an image – she immediately marks out the space of the image as a social one. Someone is speaking and someone is being spoken to, even if it is unclear who the parties are, or where we as viewers are located in the exchange. Kruger's work is inserted into public spaces – roundabouts, train stations, museums, magazines. The space in which they are seen, and the image itself, is treated not as an entity but as a relationship – a relationship defined by power.[33]

The idea of images defining a social, relational space, has been theorized through psychoanalysis. Here vision is seen as driven by fantasy, identity and desire. Psychoanalysis asks not how the brain allows us to see, but why it is we want to see in the first place, what we can't see or refuse to see, what passions and fears are aroused by seeing and being seen, and how these shape the making of images and objects. Psychoanalytic ideas trouble the notion of 'purely visual' experience by insisting that both vision and the body are social entities.

When we learn a language we inherit a vast network of signs that form the channels along which our thoughts can run. A similar thing is assumed to happen when we see. Rather than being a transparent window onto the world, vision is compared to reading, writing and speaking. It is as if we look through a screen of signs inserted between our eyes and world, consisting of all our culture's discourses on vision. In this view, vision is just as cultural as language is. Both have to follow paths already laid down, paths which are not made by us or under our control. Because we automatically internalize the conventions of our society, the way we see seems natural, unmediated, transparent. This idea of social vision is represented by the term 'the gaze'. The gaze keeps open a space for questions which the idea of 'perception' closes down. These are both interpersonal questions – about looking and being looked at – and intrapsychic ones about the relation between different parts of ourselves. Lacan's idea of the gaze, for example, is not so much that of a real person looking at us, but rather an imagined part of ourselves projected outwards, which plays a role in our attempts at self-mastery.[34]

Rather than looking with the eyes, we look, in effect, with the body. The 'body' here is meant not as a biological entity, but rather it is the image we have built of our physical selves as an organized unity. This social body forms through our relationships with other people. Thus all the peculiarities of our particular social world – our surroundings, how we are handled and spoken to – go into creating the social body with which we see. 'The eye', says Griselda Pollock,

> is not just our window to the world; as an erotic organ, it is very complexly involved in our fantasy life. These include fantasies of mastery and fantasies of being held by somebody's look, and fantasies about who sees what, and whether or not you see everything there is to see or that there is, in fact, a screen which makes your relationship to the world visually very partial . . .

Vision is perpetually both constructed by fantasy and desire and then blinded by it.

Mitchell's approach echoes this. 'The visual field I'm interested in has to do with the lived body, the social body, the body as gendered and as ethnographically inscribed.'

A relational model of vision also introduces the question of ethics, which is raised in different contexts by a number of the interviewees. Viola and Pollock speak of ethics in the context of the detached eye which undermines empathy with and responsibility toward others. For Enwezor the relationship of curator to artist and artwork is an ethical one in so far as curators have power to select, display, define, interpret, and – if the relationship is abused – strangle the voice of the artist, or misrepresent the work. Mitchell's insistence on the field of vision as a reciprocal one, where we are aware of both seeing and being seen, means that

The visual field is not just one of cognition or knowing, but recognition and acknowledgement. It's an ethical space and a political space . . . Visuality is plugged into the entire range of sociocultural issues and is not principally a matter of seeing things and interpreting them; that's only one small component of it.

Interconnectedness and hidden stories

In *Zeros and Ones* (1997), Sadie Plant uses the code of digital technology as a metaphor for binary divisions.

The zeros and ones of machine code seem to offer themselves as perfect symbols of the orders of Western reality, the ancient logical codes which make the difference between on and off, right and left, light and dark, form and matter, mind and body, white and black, good and evil, right and wrong, life and death . . .[35]

But although the digital code may be binary, the nature of the machine it gives rise to is one that resists hierarchal structures typical of patriarchy. Computers may have been invented to centralize, objectify and regulate, but their inherent structure leads in other directions.

Plant became interested in the way that the 'feminine' is defined as what is not masculine – the 'leftovers' from the masculine. She gathered together and examined these feminine leftovers and found they had an affinity to the structure of digital technologies – the tendency to be non-linear, dispersed, many-centred. To explore a breakdown in the distinction between centre and periphery, Plant tells the story of a woman who worked in the margins of a nineteenth-century research text about a calculating machine invented by Charles Babbage. Ada Lovelace's supporting material – indices, prefaces, footnotes – were seen as subordinate to the main text, when in fact they provided the crucial means of locating the text socially and historically. The periphery contains the vital hidden story which reveals a new way of perceiving reality. All three of Plant's books look for a hidden history inside an established, orthodox account. Ada Lovelace stands for the hidden story within the history of technology. In *The Most Radical Gesture* it is the hidden story of 1968 and postmodern theory, and in *Writing on Drugs* it is the way that sober mainstream culture has been informed by psychoactive substances. The material she uses is already in the public domain, but it had not yet been assembled into a meaningful narrative. 'It's all there', Plant says, 'it's just a matter of how you put it together.'

What is being sensed and articulated is a new kind of interconnectedness, which is about multiplicities, not unified things. The metaphors Plant uses for this are ones of decentralization and non-hierarchy. One metaphor is weaving, where patterns emerge from a matrix of overlapping threads. Another is the rhizome – the rootlike stems of some plants which form a network underground. Whereas a tree is rooted to the spot, rigid and unitary, rhizomes are underground, creeping sideways in all directions. Instead of a centre and a periphery, there are many centres moving toward and away from one another. Digital networks have this kind of structure. They are made up of threads and links that have no absolute centres or organizing hierarchies.

Sometimes art itself is referred to as 'rhizomatic' in its logic,[36] overturning the usual hierarchies of meaning, rooting out other stories. The artist Richard Wentworth photographs human interventions in cities, what he calls the 'parlance of the street': planks propping open doors, a cup stuck on a railing, the geometries in San Francisco that result from efforts to keep water out of garages. His objects combine things like a ladder and a strainer, making us read their form against the grain of their conventional use. In both branches of his work – objects and photographs – normal systems of classification are subverted. The overlooked and the everyday are transformed, by the resonances and symmetries he finds, into something eloquent and meaningful. The idea of alternative narratives is carried over into Wentworth's exhibition 'Thinking Aloud' (1999). He chose the maps, toys, drawings, photos, flags, models and artworks as part of the pattern of ideas that characterize his work as a whole. But the cluttered, flea-market style of the show encouraged viewers to find their own connections, implying that there was not one story to tell with these objects, no single route through them.

Weaving, rhizomes, matrices, webs: images of decentralization and non-hierarchy have become a way of thinking outside of binary oppositions, a way of picturing interconnectedness. 'The rhizome is reducible neither to the one nor the multiple . . . it is composed not of units but of dimensions, or rather directions in motion . . .'[37]

Enactment

If interconnectedness is being pictured through certain metaphors, there is another vocabulary emerging – one of performance, staging, enactment. Formalism attempts to reduce an artwork to an object whose meaning lies in its structure; we perceive objects. Semiotics attempts to reduce an artwork to a code of signs to be deciphered; we read texts. The idea of enactment is more dynamic than either 'perceiving objects' or 'reading texts'. Performance implies immediacy, animation, transience, lived experience. In performance, there is no clean divide between making and theorizing. Making becomes theorizing and theorizing is done through making. When we enact, we set something in motion.

In Hani Rashid's account of the activities of the US Pavilion of the Venice Architecture Biennale (2000), three 'architectures' were 'performed into space'. They were a moving body, a virtual and real spatial hybrid, and an airport environment. The performative happened on different levels. 'If you construct these projects as a kind of performance', says Rashid, 'there's the performance of the students working on the computers that inform the works; there's the performance of people inhabiting these projects and working with them; and then the works themselves continue to perform.' Bricks and mortar disappear, the vaulting gymnast's body disappears, and in their place is a dynamic flow — of data and information, of the actions of participants, of the shapes created by movement through space. Any static images or structures that are created have the status of temporary stabilizations[38] rather than endpoints.

Martin Kemp refers to contemporary artists as 'stagers of visual events'. An academic at Oxford University, he himself has become a stager of visual events in his recent involvement in large-scale curation. While organizing the Hayward Gallery's 'Spectacular Bodies' exhibition (London 2000) he discovered anatomy as even more of a 'performative science' or 'performing art' than he had expected. The act of bringing paintings, medical models and contemporary artworks together into the same space — 'in a kind of three-dimensional discourse' — generated surprises and insights which might not have come about through more conventional kinds of research.

Griselda Pollock talks about the exhibition as a form of 'encounter', which she sees as different from making works of art the object of knowledge and display. For Okwui Enwezor an exhibition is a 'dialectical space' rather than an assemblage of artistic meanings. For Richard Wentworth, curation is an opportunity to 'see what happens if you fray the edges and actually provoke more open-ended ways of looking, something that cannot be tested on paper or CAD mock-up, but can only be given form and experienced in the space itself'.[39]

Since the 1960s art practice has taken a markedly theatrical turn. Action painting, body art and performance art all use the actions of the human body in real time; installation art stages something in three-dimensional space, absorbing the consciousness of the viewer into its logic.[40] Art history, theory and criticism have tried as well to adopt a more 'performative' model. Conceiving of interpretation as performance renders it an active, open affair — 'a process rather than an act with a final goal'.[41] Instead of seeing an artwork as a self-contained object whose meaning can be uncovered by the right kind of analysis, a performative approach attends to the space between object and viewer where meanings are created by clashes, quotations and cross-references. Meaning is open, fluid, unstable, ambiguous and constantly being made and remade. Meaning comes from a dialogue between the subjectivity of the viewer and what is being confronted. As a result of the dialogue, both viewer and object are defined and gain identity. Meaning is not created or found; it 'takes place'. A conceptual shift of this kind may have something to do with the growing interest of visual historians like Kemp and Pollock in the exhibition as a form of research.

What is suggested by the language and practice of enactment is a shift from noun to verb, from considering things — whether objects or texts — to placing oneself within actions and processes. About the act of looking itself, James Elkins writes:

> There is ultimately no such thing as an observer or an object, only a foggy ground between the two. It's as if I have abandoned the place in the sentence that was occupied by the words 'the observer' and I've taken up residence in the verb 'looks', literally between the words 'object' and 'observer'.[42]

'Taking up residence in a verb' is a way of visualizing a relationship between mind and body, observer and observed — or between artwork, artist, curator, spectator — in which these entities are themselves created by an act. Similarly, Mitchell's aim in *Landscape and Power* is to change 'landscape' from a noun to a verb — to understand landscape as 'a process by which social and subjective identities are formed'.[43]

A shift of attention from things to processes ends up reshaping familiar categories. What seemed to be firm and separate concepts may now look very different, their contours blurred, their identities in doubt. New forms may materialize. For instance, by attending not to the fixed entities 'word' and 'image' but to the gap between them, to the way in which, at a certain historical moment, the difference between what is seeable and what is sayable is expressed, Mitchell finds that an unpredictable third thing often comes to light. This way of thinking enables enquiry to be both open-ended and historically specific.

What I try to resist is the notion that you can figure out ahead of time what word and image is and then just go and find the same thing everywhere. I prefer to deploy it as a dialectical trope or a figure of difference, like the figure of gender or of social difference of any kind . . . And the thing I like about doing it that way is, I don't know the answer beforehand.

Art in question

Given the rise of visual culture as a broad-based area of study, and the changing field in which art and its study takes place, is 'art' itself a category which needs to be put aside? In spite of the difficulties, there is a reluctance to dispense altogether with the concept of art. Why?

One reason is to preserve the knowledge that has grown up around the nineteenth-century concept of art. Art history as a discipline forged many powerful tools which are not simply to be overturned. In fact there is evidence of a move back toward some older forms of enquiry. For example, while film studies originated in literary theory, some film analysis is turning to art historical methods of research – painting theory, and older ideas like Ernst Gombrich's 'schema' – because these models stress the *visual* import of film as well as its narrative structure.[44] The 1990s showed a revival of interest in the work of Erwin Panofsky and the Warburgian tradition – the tradition against which, by and large, the 'New Art History' of the 1970s rebelled. The historians in this older tradition strove to attend to the small detail within the bigger picture, valuing, as one writer put it, both 'the panoramic vision of the parachutist and the microscopic attention to detail of the truffle-hunter'.[45] Less constrained by ideas of indeterminacy, the work of these historians is marked by enthusiasm for rather than mistrust of images. Perhaps it is this, along with their view of art as inseparable from, but not reducible to, its social conditions, which makes them salient again today.

Another reason for keeping art distinct from other forms of visual culture is that only then is comparison and analysis possible. 'If art history just dissolves into visual culture', says Mitchell, 'I also feel that the difference between an art museum, a natural history museum, a shopping mall becomes irrelevant. Well, I'm happy to study the relations among these things but there wouldn't be any relations if they all were just seen as one thing.' 'There has to be a distinction', says Okwui Enwezor, 'in order to be able to negotiate.'

There is a third, deeper reason for holding on to art. This has to do with what is felt to be intrinsic to art — specific characteristics art has, areas of experience it works with, or ways in which it functions. Griselda Pollock describes herself as having been 'driven back to art':

> It has been a long journey through a range of analyses of advertising, of cinema, of the less valued and less canonical aspects of the visual arts, to find a way back then to what was the heart of the canonical art historical project, with some means of speaking of it, of attending to its particularity, to what it is that it does.

Staging something in the field of art causes a certain kind of attention to be paid to it. It is the combination of historical and structural identity that means things 'of profound cultural importance can happen in the space we called art'.

W. J. T. Mitchell talks of art in terms of the sense of wonder, delight in form, delight in 'the sensuous apprehension of artefacts'. Bill Viola emphasizes the imagination, the imaging capability. '[Images] can be painted, sculpted, sung, spoken, danced, or whatever, but it is the connection and ultimately the common identity between the external image and the imagination, the imaging capability of human beings, that is at the heart of all creativity.' Martin Kemp talks about artists reshaping our perceptions by a system of invitations. For Barbara Kruger, art is about the ability to objectify experience — 'to show and tell, through a kind of elegant shorthand, how it feels to be alive'. Others allude to this kind of 'elegant shorthand'. '. . . [D]rawing and writing present the same limits', says Plant, 'and the same challenges: what can be said or done with the minimum of lines?' Art has a 'density and economy', Pollock says, in relation to the complexity of the material it is working with.

Art, then, externalizes experience using the senses and the intellect, and it does so in a condensed, economical and hence powerful and surprising way. Words like 'amazing', 'astonishing', 'powerful' and 'remarkable' slip easily into these conversations, suggesting that judgements of quality are never far away. Clearly the old definitions of quality – something inherent in an artwork – no longer hold up. There are no absolute judgements, no universal criteria to fall back on. But this does not mean making distinctions of quality is an unnecessary or invidious act. It is more important than ever to defend the judgements we make, while continuing to ask 'who decides what is good art, and on what basis?' To ask this seriously is to open up the entire range of critical questions – questions about cultural history, class and identity, questions about the way institutions work, about the nature of sign systems and the social worlds which use them, and questions about the grounds of knowledge itself.

What comes across in the interviews below is the value of posing questions through the act of bringing something into the world – whether it is buildings, books, plans, artworks or exhibitions. Bringing something into the world is a creative dialogue involving both rational, systematic investigation and a process that is groping, untidy, mysterious, of uncertain origin. It takes courage to tackle what is unknown and ambiguous. Artists, curators, writers, theorists are continually making judgements, deciding how best to make the invisible visible, how best, in a particular set of circumstances, to realize an idea in outward form. Wentworth talks about the distinctions he makes amongst his own photographs. Some he calls 'lecture slides'; others are 'bigger embodiments of something, but less nameable'. He cannot tell beforehand which kind of image it will be. Behind the reluctance to let go of the idea of art may be the belief that it refers to something big, and not wholly nameable, for which a space needs to be held open. New forms and purposes for art will undoubtedly evolve and demand fresh kinds of judgement. The search for something big, for elegance, economy and power – the need to be astonished by the things we make for one another – will perhaps endure.

Notes

1.   John Berger's *Ways of Seeing* (London: BBC Books and Penguin, 1972) heralded a new way of conceiving of, studying, and hence seeing, cultural objects and images. Berger talked about the increasing density of visual messages in society and the partisan nature of any explanation of them, including his own. With its spirit of demystifying art, studying non-art images like advertisements, and giving a central place to popular experience, *Ways of Seeing* heralded the broadening out of art history into 'visual culture' which continued over the next decades. For a summary of changes in the field since the 1970s see E. Fernie, *Art History and its Methods* (London: Phaidon, 1995); K. Moxey, *The Practice of Theory: Post-structuralism, Cultural Politics and Art History* (Chicago, IL: University of Chicago Press, 1994); and J. Harris, *The New Art History: A Critical Introduction* (London: Routledge, 2001). For an exploration of the relation of art object to languages used to talk about it, see Kemal and Gaskell, *The Language of Art History* (Cambridge: Cambridge University Press, 1991).

2.   Mitchell in interview cautions against the uncritical acceptance of 'visual culture' as a discipline – he prefers it to remain uninstitutionalized and anarchic – an 'indiscipline'. See his essay 'What is Visual Culture' in I. Lavin (ed.), *Meaning in the Visual Arts: Views from the Outside – A Centennial Commemoration of Erwin Panofsky* (Princeton, NJ: Princeton University Press, 1996).

3.   The term 'production' in this context comes from Marxist debate about the nature of the link between a society's cultural products (superstructure) and its economic organization (base). The theory that art passively 'mirrors' (or 'expresses') pre-existing economic and social relations is challenged by a view of art which actively 'produces' values, meanings, ideologies. 'The literary text is not the "expression" of social class. The text, rather, is a certain production of ideology.' T. Eagleton, *Criticism and Ideology* (London: New Left Books, 1976), p. 64.

4.   It is significant that these new terms are words, but they are also 'iconic' in Charles Peirce's sense that the relationship between the parts echoes the structural relations of what the sign refers to. 'Imagetext' is when word and image are flowing together, image/text is when there is a disjunction or rupture between them. The words, then, have a 'visual' logic. This underscores Mitchell's point about the symbiosis of visual and verbal meanings.

5.   Kate Linker, *Love for Sale: The Words and Pictures of Barbara Kruger* (New York: Harry N. Abrams, 1990), p. 13.

6.   S. Hall, 'Museums of Modern Art and the End of History' in S. Hall and S. Maharaj, *Modernity and Difference*, in IVA Annotations Series (London: Inst. International Visual Arts (in IVA), 2001), pp. 12–13.

7.   R. Krauss (1978) 'Sculpture in the Expanded Field', in R. Krauss, *The Originality of the Avant-garde and other Modernist Myths* (Cambridge, MA: MIT Press, 1985), p. 28.

8.   Bill Viola, *Reasons for Knocking at an Empty House: Writings 1973–1994*, ed. R. Violette (London: Thames & Hudson/Anthony D'Offay Gallery, 1995), p. 64.

9.   Barbara Kruger in interview with Lynne Tillman, in Kruger, *Thinking of You* (Los Angeles, CA: Museum of Contemporary Art, 1999), p. 189.

10. R. Wentworth, *Richard Wentworth's Thinking Aloud* (London: Hayward Gallery, 1998), p. 6.

11. In Chapter 5 of *Aesthetics and the Sociology of Art* (London: Macmillan, 1993), Janet Wolff discusses two other meanings of the idea of the 'specificity of art' in addition to the sense Pollock is using it here. Specificity can refer to the 'specialization' of art away from religion and other areas of social life, or to the question of what might be specific to art as a pursuit.

12. An example of the 'new formalist' approach can be found in Y. Bois, *Painting as Model* (Cambridge, MA: MIT Press, 1991).

13. Overview texts are: S. Sim, 'Structuralism and Post-Structuralism', in O. Hanfling (ed.), *Philosophical Aesthetics: An Introduction* (Oxford and Milton Keynes: Blackwell and the Open University, 1992), pp. 405–39, and M. Sarup, *An Introductory Guide to Post-structuralism and Postmodernism* (Brighton: Harvester/Wheatsheaf, 1988). It is frequently pointed out that the word-games and puns with which Derrida seeks to dismantle structured discourse only work in contrast to structured discourse. Nonsense is nonsensical only against the expectation of sense. In criticizing polarities, he sets up a polarity between absolutely fixed meaning and complete indeterminacy.

14. Meyer Schapiro analysed the pairing of profile and frontal in different representational systems, from medieval to Cubist paintings. Rather than having a fixed meaning, the frontal and profile pairing may stand for: good and evil, sacred and profane, heavenly and earthly, ruler and ruled, living and dead, or different relationships between the observer and the observed. Meaning will vary according to where a particular viewer is situated within these divisions. M. Schapiro, 'Frontal and Profile as Symbolic Forms', in *Words and Pictures: On the Literal and Symbolic in the Illustration of a Text* (The Hague: Mouton, 1973).

15. One set of oppositions, however, will not be permanently welded to another. As well as being equated with 'nature', earth and the primitive, women have also been identified with the refined and the cultured, paticularly when other terms such as class and race are introduced. In van Dyck's seventeenth-century painting *Henrietta of Lorraine*, for example, a contrast is set up between the 'civilized' white, aristocratic woman and the 'natural' and servile black boy at her side. The divisions to which masculine and feminine are attached need to be traced very carefully through their many instabilities and reversals. See D. Dabydeen, *Hogarth's Blacks: Images of Blacks in Eighteenth-Century English Art* (Manchester: Manchester University Press, 1987), p. 30.

16. See S. Gilman, *Difference and Pathology: Stereotypes of Sexuality, Race, and Madness* (Ithaca, NY: Cornell University Press, 1985).

17. O. Enwezor, 'Haptic Vision: The Films of Steve McQueen', in *Steve McQueen*, exhibition catalogue (London: Institute of Contemporary Arts, 1999).

18. S. Maharaj, 'Perfidious Fidelity', in J. Fisher (ed.), *Global Visions: Towards a New Internationalism in the Visual Arts* (London: Kala Press and Inst. IVA, 1994), p. 29.

19. See P. Messaris, *Visual Literacy: Image, Mind, Reality* (Oxford: Westview Press, 1994), for a discussion of the analytic capabilities of word and image, and a review of evidence from cross-cultural studies about learning to understand images. In *Visual Thinking* (Berkeley, CA: University of California Press, 1969), Rudolph Arnheim refers to a scale from arbitrariness to isomorphism (sharing structural features) in both verbal

and visual signs, but concludes that most words are arbitrary and most visual signs are isomorphic. In *Iconology: Image, Text, Ideology* (Chicago, IL: University of Chicago Press, 1986), Mitchell gives a summary and critique of the classic divisions.

20. It is significant that interest in 'visual literacy' since the late 1960s came from studies about the amount of time American children spend watching television. The idea was that people had to be equipped to understand ever more sophisticated images so as not be duped by them. According to Mitchell the 'television versus books' debate is an expression of a deep and recurring fear of images replacing words, of being dominated by the image. In interview he cautions, though, against over-simple notions about living in an 'age of visual media'. Television, film and computers mingle sound, image and text; the image alone would have little power if it were not linked so closely with language.

21. M. Kemp, *Visualizations: The Nature Book of Art and Science* (Oxford: Oxford University Press, 2000), p. 178.

22. W. J. T. Mitchell, 'Word and Image', in R. Nelson and R. Shiff (eds), *Critical Terms for Art History* (Chicago, IL: University of Chicago Press, 1996), pp. 47–57.

23. In Mitchell's view, verbal discourse leaks back into abstract art in two ways. One is in the increased amount of writing, talking and theory that surrounds it. Paintings are to be seen and not heard, but the banished words return with a vengeance in the talking about them that takes place. The second way verbal discourse leaks back is in the simple fact that it was always there to begin with. Abstract art is constituted in the first place, as abstract art, by language, narrative and discourse. The painting was made by brush, hand, eye and mind, pigment, canvas, but the painting as a work of art is constructed dialectically, in the domain of social discourse. Seen this way, abstract art, far from being 'purely visual' is actually 'a visual machine for the generation of language'. See W. J. T. Mitchell, *Picture Theory: Essays on Verbal and Visual Representation* (Chicago, IL: University of Chicago Press, 1994), Chapter 7.

24. M. Warner, *Richard Wentworth* (London: Thames & Hudson, 1993), p. 11.

25. See Okwui Enwezor, Chapter 3, n. 5 (p. 111), about the Igloolik/Isuma Collective film-makers.

26. B. Viola, 'World of Appearances' press material (2000).

27. For an account of the 'oculocentric' world-view – the privileging of vision over the other senses from the Greeks to the Enlightenment – see M. Jay, *Downcast Eyes: The Denigration of Vision in Twentieth-Century French Thought* (Berkeley, CA: University of California Press, 1993).

28. W. Heisenberg, *Physics and Philosophy* (New York: Harper & Row, 1958), p. 58.

29. Moholy Nagy was quoted in D. Dondis, *A Primer of Visual Literacy* (Cambridge, MA: MIT Press, 1973), p. xi.

30. Gunther Kress proposes, for instance, that (1) hand-based technologies favour ideas about human observation; (2) recording (lens-based) technologies, starting with the camera obscura, favour ideas of referentiality, and questions of truth, fact and bias; and (3) 'synthesizing' digital technologies favour ideas

of constructing signs about the world, not referring to it. See G. Kress and T. van Leeuwen, *Reading Images: The Grammar of Visual Design* (London: Routledge, 1996), p. 233.

31. H. Rashid and L. A. Couture, *Asymptote: Architecture at the Interval* (New York: Rizzoli International, 1995), p. 7.

32. R. Williams, *Television: Technology and Cultural Form* (London: Routledge & Kegan Paul, 1975). See W. J. T. Mitchell, Chapter 1, n. 8 (p. 65).

33. See R. Deutsche, 'Breaking Ground: Barbara Kruger's spatial practice', in Kruger, *Thinking of You*.

34. Margaret Olin gives an account of theories of 'the gaze' in *Critical Terms for Art History* (Chicago, IL: University of Chicago Press, 1996). See also N. Bryson, 'The Gaze in the Expanded Field', in H. Foster (ed.), *Vision and Visuality* (Seattle: Seattle Bay View Press, 1988), pp. 91–4.

35. S. Plant, *Zeros and Ones: Digital Women and the New Technoculture* (London: Fourth Estate, 1996), p. 34.

36. Gavin Jantjes calls art objects 'rhizomatic' in Jantjes (ed.), *A Fruitful Incoherence: Dialogues with Artists on Internationalism* (London: Inst. IVA, 1998), p. 13.

37. G. Deleuze and F. Guattari, quoted ibid., p. 164.

38. Stuart Hall uses the phrase 'temporary stabilizations' in relation to what exhibitions themselves do. 'Museums have to understand their collections and their practices as what I can only call "temporary stabilizations".' See Hall and Maharaj (eds), *Modernity and Difference*, p. 22.

39. Wentworth, *Thinking Aloud*, p. 8.

40. Enwezor (Chapter 3) says that installation absorbs the consciousness of the viewer into its logic. It was through the notion of the 'theatrical' that the Modernist critic Michael Fried famously sought to label emerging practices as not art. M. Fried, 'Art and Objecthood', *Artforum*, summer 1967. 'Art degenerates as it approaches the condition of theatre.' A. Jones 'Art History/Art Criticism: Performing Meaning', in A. Jones and A. Stephenson, *Performing the Body/Performing the Text* (London: Routledge, 1999).

41. Jones and Stephenson, *Performing the Body*, Introduction.

42. J. Elkins, *The Object Stares Back* (San Diego, CA, London: Harcourt Brace, Harvest edition, 1997), p. 44.

43. W. J. T. Mitchell (ed.), *Landscape and Power* (Chicago, IL: University of Chicago Press, 1992) p. 1.

44. See the Introduction to D. Bordwell and N. Carroll, *Post-theory: Reconstructing Film Studies* (Madison, WI: University of Wisconsin Press, 1996).

45. The Warburgian tradition refers to the work of scholars associated with the library of Aby Warburg in Hamburg, which moved to London in 1933. The younger members of that circle, Edgar Wind, Erwin Panofsky and Ernst Gombrich, had over the course of the century in America and Britain transformed art history into a full academic discipline. What these art historians had in common was an interest in the way that cultures 'think' through the symbolic forms of myth, language and art. It is interesting to consider why this rich tradition, which had been revolutionary in its own time, inspired such a strong reaction in the

1970s and 1980s. One factor was the concern of the New Art History to prise art away from discourses of the optical and the perceptual and locate it in the cultural and linguistic. This meant a distrust of any appeal to notions of perception. Those who appeal to the biological realities of vision to explain representation often believe there is an essential human nature which it is the business of art and other symbolic forms to express. In Panofsky's view, for example, visual signs are a language which dig deeply into the 'essential tendencies of the human mind'. This inclination to universalize what could be seen as the interests and values of a particular class of people, went against the thrust of feminist, Marxist, and post-colonial thought. The quote is from Grafton in I. Lavin (ed.), *Meaning in the Visual Arts*, p. 125.

"It *is* a long tail, certainly," said Alice, looking down with wonder at the Mouse's tail; "but why do you call it sad?" And she kept on puzzling about it while the Mouse was speaking, so that her idea of the tale was something like this :——" Fury said to

a mouse, That
he met in the
house, 'Let
us both go
to law: *I*
will prose-
cute *you*.—
Come, I'll
take no de-
nial: We
must have
the trial ;
For really
this morn-
ing I've
nothing
to do.'
Said the
mouse to
the cur,
'Such a
trial, dear
Sir, With
no jury
or judge,
would
be wast-
ing our
breath.'
'I'll be
judge,
I'll be
jury,'
said
cun-
ning
old
Fury:
'I'll
try
the
whole
cause,
and
con-
demn
you to
death'.'"

'My research has explored a double proposition about the relation between words and images. One is that they are both distinct from and similar to one another. They are different modes of meaning, representation, signalling, communication. At the same time, they cross over into one another, they support one another, they complement one another, they mimic one another, and are woven together in actual communicative practices . . . So, what I suggest is that we think of 'word and image' as the name of a kind of boundary or dividing line that shifts its location all over the field of communication and representation.'

W. J. T. Mitchell

Previous:

Image 1.1: Calligram from *Alice's*
Adventures in Wonderland,
'The Mouse's Tale.'
Mary Evans Picture Library.

KR: How did you come to be interested in the relation of verbal and visual representation?

WM: I first came to the problem of visual images and their relation to language by way of thinking about the relation between algebra and geometry – the arbitrary symbols and 'sentences' of equations, on the one hand, and the spatial diagrams that correspond to them. I was always struck by the stark difference between the algebraic sequence and the geometric array, and by the translatability between the two forms of expression. There seemed to be something magical in this ability to move back and forth between different media with such exactitude and clarity. Later, when I began to work on the illuminated books of William Blake,[1] I became interested in the relation of poetry and painting, and verbal and visual representation more generally. Of course these forms don't have the absolute translatability possible in mathematics, but that makes them all the more interesting. For one thing, the untranslatable space between the verbal and the visual begins itself to be a subject of investigation. For another, one begins to see that there are many other relations between words and images than translation or correspondence. The varieties of their interaction across the range of media (contrariety, supplementarity, adjacency, overlapping and mixture) is truly amazing, and it provides an enticement to think beyond binary oppositions and essential categories, and to consider hybrid formations and dialectical structures. Words and images stop being the names of separate compartments, and designate a field of symbolic interaction and interplay in the arts and media. The word/image problem thus became for me a way of thinking across the arts, thinking comparatively and contrastively about the media, and about visual and verbal culture more generally. It also, most importantly, became for me a way of linking formalism, the study of the way artworks, texts and symbolic forms are put together, with larger structures of political and social life.

KR: What is your take on the concept of 'visual literacy'?

WM: I think 'visual literacy' can be a useful phrase as long as you don't make the mistake of thinking that seeing is the same thing as reading, or that vision is a language, or that a picture is just a text. Clearly these things are different, and we are dealing with an interesting analogy whose limits have to be explored. People don't learn to read or write naturally; they have to be taught. But we learn to read the visual world automatically without formal instruction. So visual literacy is a metaphor for thinking of vision as a learned process – learning how to see, learning what to see, learning how to make sense of the visual environment.

KR: **We learn to see, but we're not taught to see. You're saying it's not primarily a social exchange. Is there no such thing as visual *illiteracy* then?**

WM: Actually, I do regard the visual field as grounded in social exchanges, but not mainly in pedagogical exchanges, but typically in more spontaneous and ordinary practices (e.g. an infant mimicking the facial expressions of its mother). As you said, we *learn* to see without being *taught* in the way we have to be taught letters and reading. If somebody is blind from birth and they have their sight restored, all the experimental data shows that seeing will not be automatic, and will not be easily learned. An adult trying to see for the first time after a life of blindness will have to be painstakingly taught, and the lessons will (as Oliver Sacks has shown) probably not take. Sacks's essay, 'To See and Not See',[2] confirmed a series of experiments, going back to the eighteenth century, which addressed the question of whether seeing was an automatic, built-in process, or whether you had to install the software in your brain through a series of experiences at the propitious time in human cognitive development. So, at a very basic level, you can be visually illiterate in the sense that your eyes can take in light, colour, but you won't be able to see the world, you'll just have a kind of fluctuating, meaningless environment that can be very disturbing. When you've been blind for any length of time and you have your vision restored, it takes a while to re-learn just how to see space. But this might be better described as visual aphasia, a cognitive blindness to visual (and pictorial) space. The proper analogy in the realm of language would be a wild child, possessed of all the hardware for language, but never having learned a language. We wouldn't call such a child illiterate (I would reserve this term for those who can't or don't read; in its elite formulation, it designates those who do not read books – especially the ones we happen to regard as important. Illiteracy is a term with overtones of social distinctions and hierarchies of status.)

KR: Sometimes that term visual illiteracy is used to describe people with normal sight who can't interpret images in a sophisticated way.

WM: Exactly – illiteracy is a status concept. I think it's important to understand that learning to see has many different levels to it, and not to confuse those levels. For instance, I look out the window at the buildings across the street, and I know that there are people who will know everything about what that kind of facade means, why it's that high, why the windows are that far apart. I don't know that. I'm illiterate for that part of the visual field. To have total visual literacy, to be able to read every visual sign would be, I think, beyond human possibility. There are simply too many complex visual codes, too many technical discourses of the visible in science and art.

KR: So for you, visual literacy can mean anything from the basic ability to see the world to learned knowledge of very specific kinds.

WM: No. My point is that this range of meaning stretches the metaphor of literacy out of all proportion. I would prefer to reserve the concept of visual literacy for specific forms of learned knowledge in the visual field, and call the more basic abilities something like 'visual competence'. My son is 'visually literate' with the instant intake of information from television. He immediately recognizes everything, he knows what the story is, whereas I look at it as buzzing confusion. Channel-surfing is, to me, a way of putting myself to sleep; I'm not really learning anything. So I think there are all kinds of differences and degrees and kinds of visual literacy.

KR: I would see it as historically defined, in the sense that what it means to be visually literate now is different to what it would have meant 50 years ago, or in the Renaissance.

Image 1.2: Man looking at TV

monitors. Getty Images.

wm: Absolutely. And for a hunter-gatherer, visual literacy would not involve being able to tell what a photograph is or a movie is, but it might involve being able to look at ripples on the water and interpret them. This isn't just a question of vision, it's the entire sensorium and all of the perceptual channels And there are vast differences in the kinds of visual skills that people have acquired. I think the problem with the word 'literacy' is that it immediately suggests reading, and that model is only a metaphor. Sometimes you're reading through your eyes but other times you're doing other kinds of operations which may be *like* reading but are not reading.

KR: **I would suggest that an openness to aesthetic experience,[3] sensing the emotional import of different colours for instance, might be another form of visual literacy.**

WM: That seems right to me, as long as one notes that some forms of visual literacy might involve the suspension of other forms. For instance, to sense the emotional import of colours as such might involve looking at things 'abstractly', as it were, and suspending the recognition of the objects in the world that bear those colours. One might have to stop seeing the rose in order to focus on its redness. A more drastic form of abstract seeing is proposed by Clement Greenberg, who saw the appreciation of pure painting as dependent on the elimination of literary elements – narrative, allegory and even nameable objects.[4] The peculiarity of 'visual literacy' as a term becomes clearest when it is seen, as it is by Greenberg, as antithetical to the finding of literary elements of any kind in the visual arts.

KR: **So it's very important to be specific. To ask what sorts of abilities are being brought to bear on what sorts of representations, or what part of the visual world.**

WM: Yes, I think that's the crucial thing. You mustn't allow the notion of visual literacy to swallow up everything and think there's one kind of skill that includes all of it. There are many, many different ones. They are different in degree and different in kind. There are building blocks in it, too, as well as levels. In some forms of visual literacy, you would need to be able to discriminate colours before you could talk about their meaning, just as you need to know letters before you can read words. It is a highly differentiated and structured series of skills that make up what we call seeing the world, or (better) *a* world.

KR: **Even within the same person that skill or attentiveness may vary. Sometimes you might let the visual world wash over you, uncritically, and other times you may be highly focused and analytical.**

WM: Yes. That's what I meant by seeing abstractly, seeing 'colour as such', for instance, though I don't know that it needs to be 'uncritical' (certainly Greenberg didn't think so). But there's another component to vision that I think escapes the analogy of visual literacy. So far, we've been talking about visual literacy as if it involved somebody looking at *things*. But the real key to visual culture (and I think most scholars in this field would agree on this) is the idea that *I am seen*, that I am not only the beholder but the *beheld*. I would like to suggest that part of what activates the world of visual experience is this sense of being watched, being on display. It seems to me visual literacy is not only the art of seeing things but the art of showing, and of knowing how you might present yourself. This is why we love (and hate) mirrors so much. Visual literacy, in part, is a way of understanding how we are inserted into a reciprocal field of activity, seeing and being seen – caught up, as it were, in the tractor-beam of the gaze.[5]

KR: **Are you talking about the kinds of display found in popular culture – fashion, body-piercing, various kinds of public spectacle?**

WM: Something much more fundamental than that. Evidently it's hard-wired in our brains to respond to signs in the environment that could be taken for eyes or a face. (Lacan discusses some of the evidence for this capacity as a pervasive attribute of sentient beings, all the way from the eyes of oysters to the faces of owls, which are mimicked by the *ocelli* or 'little eyes' on the wings of butterflies.) When we look at the world, like many other organisms, we tend to see faces in things. This is where imprinting comes from – your sense that there are others in the world. Your identity is partly constructed by the fact that you are seen from outside, there is another person there. Otherwise, we would just be solipsistic beings. I think it goes right down to the moment when the human subject is constituted as somebody who is seen by someone else.

KR: **This is Lacan's notion that the tin-can in the stream is looking at me.**

WM: The sardine-can in the sea, to be exact.[6]

W. J. T. Mitchell | 47

KR: **We haven't talked about being visually literate as a matter of making images or representations, rather than just receiving them.**

WM: That's a much higher level, I think. We don't expect everybody in our society to be able to make pictures, we don't demand that everyone be able to draw the way we demand that they write. So, in that sense, if literacy means a mastery of letters, we do demand writing from everyone in our education system. We don't demand drawing. Probably we should. Ruskin would certainly approve.[7]

KR: **I'm wondering if digital technology has been pushing us towards a visual literacy that may include producing representations as well as just being able to 'read' them – by giving everyone the means easily to produce images. I suppose this moves into a more general question: what relationship, if any, do you see between computer technology and visual literacy, or between technology and our contemporary take on the word–image relationship?**

WM: I think sometimes the impact of technology is overrated, but I wouldn't want to minimize it either. Personally, I find the production of digital images (in a digital camera, in a computer scanner, in a Photoshop program) incredibly difficult and tedious. I'd much rather draw or paint on paper than move a mouse around on a pad. More generally, I think we need to question the notion that technologically mediated forms of visual representation are totally changing our visual world for us. It seems to me that often exactly the opposite has happened. The technically mediated vision is struggling – often against great odds – to try to match the visual field that we already have constructed for ourselves, as it were, spontaneously or naturally.

KR: **What do you mean by 'visual field'?**

WM: I mean, for instance, the notion that objects are arrayed around us in three-dimensional space, the basic assumptions of perspective. Every time I look into a video arcade I notice that they're becoming more and more illusionist and realistic. Macintosh is perfecting graphics programs that come closer and closer to simulating old-fashioned painting and drawing. So, does that mean people's vision is changing as a result of digital imaging? Or is it the machines are getting better at accommodating themselves to what we want to see and the way we want to see it? I'm not a technical determinist, in that sense. I don't see technology as the driving force of history.

I've just been re-reading Raymond Williams' book on television, which I think is a wonderful reminder that television doesn't straightforwardly change the way we see the world.[8] The technology itself changes in response to what we want to see and how we want to see it. The world you see, say, on television, or in virtual reality, is trying to look 'real'. And what does that mean? It means to look like the world you see without the technology. The technology becomes most powerful and useful when it almost becomes invisible and transparent, and you don't see it as somehow getting in the way or changing the way you see. Now, it may be changing habits, more subtle things. But to say that, straightforwardly, it changes the way you see the world, I think is to exaggerate. We need to be more precise about what's changing and what's not changing.

KR: The art historian Martin Kemp put it this way: different ways of making images tend to exploit different capacities of the brain, but they don't change the structure of the brain and how we see. Also, as you're saying, the technologies arise when there's a cultural need for them.

Given that the relationship between word and image has been studied for centuries, how would you characterize our particular moment of looking at that relationship, if it's not to be defined by the technologies of vision?

WM: My research has explored a double proposition about the relation between words and images. One is that they are both distinct from and similar to one another. They are different modes of meaning, representation, signalling, communication. At the same time, they cross over into one another, they support one another, they complement one another, they mimic one another, and are woven together in actual communicative practices.

The second proposition is that the difference between words and images is, at the very least, a double difference: at the level of sensation it is the difference between the auditory and the visual, the spoken word and the seen image; at the level of semiotics or sign-theory it is the difference between the arbitrary sign by convention and the so-called 'natural' sign by resemblance or similarity. More generally, it seems to me that the word–image difference is a multiple one that engages many different levels of symbolic practice. In *Iconology* [1986] I laid out some of the main categories of differentiation that have prevailed in theoretical discourse about the word–image relation categories such as nature and convention (Plato), time and space (Kant and Lessing), the digital and the analogue (Anthony Wilden's structuralism), the symbolic and iconic (Peirce's semiotics), the differentiated and the dense (Nelson Goodman's aesthetics).

When you put all this together, you wind up with a dialectical relationship between word and image, one in which no single, settled binary opposition is capable of stabilizing the concept. Instead, one finds a series of partially successful attempts at explanation, each of which is densely woven into exemplary symbolic practices (is the theory being developed in the age of television or of painting and engraving?) and philosophical discourses (a metaphysics of time and space will give you Lessing's theory of poetry as a 'time art', painting as an art of space).

The problem with looking for the one bottom line which will tell you the difference between words and images is that 'words' and 'images', those two terms, are themselves highly ambiguous. When you say 'word', do you mean the spoken word or the written word? If you mean the written word, then you've moved into the realm of the visual. If you mean the spoken word, you've moved into the realm of the aural. So, right away, words themselves are divided between the visual and the aural, on a sensory axis.

KR: And words are divided on a spatial and temporal axis, as well.

WM: The spoken word is, let's say, temporal, the written word is laid out in one spatial array. We have to move through it and decode it temporally. But just asking yourself what a word is immediately deconstructs and re-inscribes the opposition between the verbal and visual. And the same thing happens if you ask what an image is. Is an image a *visual* sign or is it a sign by likeness? That's the other meaning of the word 'image' – a symbol that resembles what it stands for, an icon. So, the concept of the image is similarly divided between a sensory definition having to do with the visual and a semiotic one having to do with resemblance. Also, we know very well that if the basic criteria are resemblance and likeness, images don't only operate in the visual field, they also operate, for instance, in the acoustic field. It's quite grammatical to talk about sound images, sounds which resemble what they stand for, like a gunshot or onomatopoeia, all of the ways that language slips into mimesis as opposed to an arbitrary, conventional signal.

So, what I suggest is that we think of 'word and image' as the name of a kind of boundary or dividing line that shifts its location all over the field of communication and representation. By complicating it in this way, I'm not trying to make the difference go away. In fact, it makes it more interesting because it moves through more spheres of activity. I think the word and image problematic, for instance, operates within literary texts, in phenomena such as description, setting, space, figuration and form. 'Word and image' is not just an issue *between* literature and the visual arts, but *within* literary form itself.

KR: **I like your term 'image-text' which is akin to the Einsteinian notion of 'space-time' in the sense that you can't have one without the other. I think it's interesting to look at scales of concreteness or ambiguity or abstractness in some kind of matrix of image and word.**

WM: Yes. The big question is why it is so interesting? Why is it a problem at all? And how could we track the movements of something so slippery and seemingly unavoidable, the 'warp and woof', as it were, out of which symbolic practices are woven. One strategy I suggested was to write the image–text relation in three different ways.[9] There's the 'imagetext' as one word, which seems appropriate when

the verbal and visual are flowing into one another, so that the boundary becomes obscure, as in a rebus, a calligram, or shaped poem.

Then I suggested writing it with a hyphen, 'image-text', to talk about places where the distinction is there but image and word are knitted together, as in a comic book. In the typical comic strip, the words are there for speech and narration, the images represent bodies and actions in space. The two sign-types are 'sutured' the way the sound- and image-tracks are synchronized in a film, but they remain distinct and different in function.

Finally, I proposed a notation of 'image/text' with a slash, in which some kind of opposition or desynchronization is occurring. Formally, this can often provide a kind of humour and incongruity, as when Tony Soprano[10] is euphemistically describing his day to his therapist, and his verbal narration becomes a voice-over track accompanied by visual scenes of what actually happened. 'I had a disagreement with a colleague' is the verbal accompaniment to a scene in which Tony is beating one of his debtors senseless. In painting, one classic expression of the image/text is Magritte's *Ceci n'est pas une pipe* [1929] in which the text flatly contradicts the visual image. Another would be Poussin's *Adoration of the Golden Calf* [1634] which portrays quite directly the visible magnificence of the image in the centre of the composition, while placing the text (of the Mosaic law) in the darkness and clouds of Mount Sinai. The image/text, I suspect, often emerges as a sign of anxiety about words or images, a symptom of fear that words are covering up a reality that would be better accessed through 'direct' visual images (as in the Soprano example) or, a more pervasive anxiety I think, that images are replacing words, that visual literacy is driving out verbal literacy.

KR: Television versus books?

WM: Television versus books, the very place I started in *Picture Theory* [1994] with the National Endowment for the Humanities opening its report on the culture of the United States by saying that Americans have become a nation of spectators and not of readers. What does that mean?

KR: Interestingly enough, that was twenty years after the first Visual Literacy Conference in Rochester, New York, in 1969, which was spurred on by the fear that children were spending too much time in front of the television.[11] The fear was that television was going to be changing the way they thought and behaved.

WM: It's a very deep fear. Images are a very powerful and anxiety-provoking medium. That's why iconoclasm, iconophobia, the fear of domination by images, is not just an archaic or primitive fear.

KR: And do you think we're in an iconophobic phase at the moment?

WM: There's a lot of expression of iconophobia in contemporary culture. It's one of those soundbites that always seems to draw assent, and which therefore needs to be questioned, not just repeated. When people say, for instance, that we live in an age of visual media and visual images, I always want to resist. For one thing, all the so-called 'visual media' are actually mixed audio-visual media; for another, the supposed 'regime' of the visual image would have no power whatever without its linkage with language.

KR: **The theorists that I've talked to all have had different ideas of what the dilemma is about our understanding of word and image now. For instance, Griselda Pollock thinks the dilemma is between the mystical legacy of Romanticism with its notion of the 'purely visual', and semiotics, which can see too tight a correspondence between images and what they mean. For her, a way through at the moment is to combine semiotics and psychoanalysis. Martin Kemp thinks the old empirical art historical methods are not sufficient, but the linguistic-based ones that succeeded them have been damaging to art history and criticism. He would look more toward perceptual psychology and cognitive science.**

I wondered how you describe your position. You're coming from literary theory and criticism originally, but you draw upon philosophy and cognitive science. Can you characterize your own position in relation to the dilemma and your idea of the way forward?

WM: I'm very interested in psychoanalysis, particularly Lacanian models of what he calls the scopic and vocative, the idea that seeing and speaking, or more precisely, the seeing–touching circuit and the hearing–speaking circuit, are intertwined in experience but also distinct, and they are drives, they're not just cognitive channels. I myself don't think cognitive science is enough. Cognitive science is good at describing the fundamental elements of visual perception, but I don't think it can explain desire and anxiety and fantasy, dreaming, memory, the *affect* of the visual field. For that, I think you need something much more dynamic, drawn from phenomenology (Merleau-Ponty, for instance)[12] and psychoanalysis. The visual field I'm interested in has to do with the lived body, the social body, the body as gendered and as ethnographically inscribed, the body as a racial object.

For me, visual culture is grounded in the social dynamic of seeing and being seen. It is not just 'the social construction of the visual world' (as we often say), but 'the visual construction of the social world' as well. The visual field is not just one of cognition or knowing, but recognition and acknowledgement. It's an ethical space and a political space, not just an epistemological space projected by a spectatorial subject. So when we talk about visual literacy, we have to go further than just thinking of reading texts. We have to remember that we are reading others and others are reading us, in the visual field. If the idea of visual literacy makes any sense, it means that the texts are reading us just as much as we are reading them. Visuality is plugged into the entire range of sociocultural issues and is not principally a matter of seeing things and interpreting them; that's only one small component of it.

My work has, as you know, been largely about 'minding the gap' between word and image. The deep question is, as I said earlier, why this difference makes a difference, why it is a topic of concern at all. One possibility is that 'word and image' is a sensory/semiotic symptom of the fact that human beings are 'split subjects'. When Descartes said 'I think, therefore I am', he could equally well have said, 'I doubt, therefore I am'.[13] The terrifying motivation for Cartesian philosophy was the idea of doubting one's own existence or doubting the reality of what one might see. So, I take as constitutive the notion that human beings are not uniform, unified, singular subjects with transparent access to themselves. They have unconsciousnesses, individual and collective; they do and feel things without knowing why. It seems to me that most of human behaviour is based in complex mixtures of feelings about things – ambivalence, contradiction. Word and image is one way of focusing on this gap between the various sides of people's individuality, and the symbolic practices that make possible their collective, social existence.

KR: **Because it corresponds to, or triggers, deeper kinds of ambivalences.**

WM: Yes. 'To be, or not to be', could be supplemented by 'to show or tell', 'to see or to read'.

KR: **You talk about the word–image problematic as an 'actor on the historical stage' which absorbs the ambivalences and conflicts in a particular culture or in a particular individual.**[14]

WM: I should have said, 'a pair of actors, in dialogue, struggle'. As we know, the categories of word and image can take on gender – classically, the word seems to play the masculine role, the image, the feminine role, or vice versa. What I try to resist is the notion that you can figure out ahead of time what word and image is and then just go and find the same thing everywhere. I prefer to deploy it as a dialectical trope or a figure of difference, like the figure of gender or of social difference of any kind. And when you're armed with that figure then you can be empirical and historical about what its meaning might be in any specific situation. You don't have to assume ahead of time that it's always going to be one way or another. That's why a lot of the practical criticism and interpretation I've done works with specific cases, like the photographic essay, like the relation of sculpture and language or painting and criticism. I want to ask, at a specific moment, within an artistic institution, what is the relation between visual display and discourse, at that moment? How is that difference operating? And the thing I like about doing it that way is, I don't know the answer beforehand.

KR: **So you go in with that figure as a kind of tool to ask the questions.**

WM: Right. I think of the image/text as a wedge to prise open representations, to see how and why they are put together, and to notice what surprising things come into view when we 'mind the gap' between the visible and the articulable. So often, it seems, some fragment of a lost history or a third term (ideology, the index, the music of form) becomes evident through the cracks – between the lines of a representation in what it doesn't say and what it cannot show. There is a kind of gap between the two where an unpredictable third thing appears, something supplied by the labour of reading and seeing.

KR: A gap in what a representation doesn't say or show?

WM: Let me give you a concrete example. I'm thinking about the photo–essay issue as I say these things, and of all the variety of ways in which writing and photography have collaborated, or not, in various specific forms. In *Let Us Now Praise Famous Men*,[15] James Agee describes his work with Walker Evans as being that of a spy and a counter-spy, as if they are collaborators but they're also in tension with one another, so that the relation of text and image in *Let Us Now Praise Famous Men* is a very dynamic, animated one, in which you are not simply handed photographs with a text that tells you what's in the photographs, or photographs that straightforwardly illustrate a text. You're handed (as Agee puts it) two 'independent, co-equal and collaborative' forms. And the reader has to fill in the gap between the two, using both verbal and visual literacy. So what that illustrated text does is to activate a whole labour of the reader, in that space between word and image. In the really brilliant and successful word–image composites, I think that's what happens.

KR: Because there's enough space between them? The word and image aren't bound so tightly, or literally together.

WM: Yes. Something's deliberately left for you to do. The activity of the beholder-reader is elicited rather than being controlled or programmed. Museum signage practices, which are so mundane as to be overlooked, might be rethought in these terms. You are told that in a museum the important thing is the things hanging on the walls. And yet what do you see in people's behaviour? Where does their attention go?

KR: They go straight to the labels.

WM: They go to the label and they spend more time on the label than they do on the picture. Robert Morris says the labels are like lifelines and you go reeling yourself over to them because you're afraid you're going to drown in the image.[16]

KR: Were you going to say that museum labels could be used in a very different way?

WM: Yes. There's an uncritical tendency to overdo labelling, because (as we say) viewers need 'context'. They can't be trusted alone with the images. They don't (it's assumed) trust themselves. You walk into a museum, particularly natural history museums, I'm sorry to say, and you're overwhelmed with texts, all this signage and writing, telling you what you're seeing. And you can see that it's not working. People look at the stuff and they say: 'if I wanted to sit home and read a book, I would. I came here to be in the presence of some objects, of some things. Of course I want to know what they are, but do I need to be told all of this?' This is a very understudied area. What is really the best way, or are there many best ways, of doing the business of signage, relating word and image in the exhibition space? What if the audio tour were treated as an artwork rather than a utilitarian aid?

KR: Do you have any ideas about that? How you would prefer to see it done?

WM: Well, one thing – less is more. I think the crucial thing is to rein in the impulse to tell too much. The most purist form of curatorship says you give the name of the artist, the materials or medium, you give the date, and that's it. This is the rule that was followed at the London's Serpentine Gallery in 'The Greenhouse Effect' exhibition [2000],[17] and they did it to beautiful effect, because the naming of materials in that exhibition was so crucial. You look at a little bird skeleton one inch high, finely detailed – this marvellous little skeleton.[18] And then you look at the medium indicated on the label: fingernail clippings. And then you look back again. Now, that's activation of something between word and image, between the materiality and the name of the material. And that produces a wonderful double take, in which you ask yourself, why? How could he do it? Why would he do it? What does it mean? That's the kind of word–image relation I like: the one that activates curiosity, leads a person to fill in the gap with some kind of interpretation or speculation.

Image 1.5: Tim Hawkinson, *Bird*

(1997). Ace Gallery, Los Angeles.

KR: **There's the idea that things have to be constantly explained to people, maybe because there's a whole education or interpretation department there to do just that.**

WM: Good education departments, I think, follow the rule of restraint and parsimony. I talked at some length to Lisa Corrin, the curator of 'The Greenhouse Effect', because I was doing a seminar on the show, with students and faculty at the Royal College of Art. She's having school groups come in. It's a very child-friendly exhibit, I think. The teachers that we observed were rather good at not telling the kids too much. It's important not to say too much. If the images could all be explained by the words then you wouldn't need the images. Their distinctness, their presence, their quality of appeal could simply be dispensed with.

KR: **The silent way they work on you.**

WM: It's important to know when to be silent. And when, also, not to say something but perhaps to ask a question. The right question at the right time is often much better than a statement. I hoped to ask such a question when I was teaching a class of curatorial students at the Royal College of Art last night. I asked them to imagine under what conditions it would be necessary to make a tiny bird skull out of your fingernails, as opposed to just an option or a fun thing to do. Could you imagine a situation in which you had to do it, in which you literally had no choice?

KR: **On a desert island.**

WM: Yes. Or in a time when all birds are gone and all the fossil skeletons have vanished from the world, but you still remember them and you want some relic to embody your memories in material form. And the only material you have is your own body. So, I was imagining, for myself, a kind of Spaceship Earth idea. 'The Greenhouse Effect' is partly about the vanishing of the Earth's ecology, this premonition that is becoming more and more widely shared, that the natural world around us is in deep danger from us, and we're a big danger to ourselves. But, how do you communicate that message? One way is by information overload. Give people statistics about the number of species that are vanishing every day. They get totally depressed, defeated. Or you show them a little bird's skull made out of fingernails, and get them to think. I'll take the bird skull made of fingernails.

KR: **Are you happy to keep the category of art? Some say that the idea of art is changing in fundamental ways, that in some sense it's an outmoded notion, it's converging with popular culture. Are you happy to keep a category of art and, if so, what do you mean by it? What notion of art do you use?**

WM: I definitely want to keep the category of art. Not that it needs to keep on meaning the same thing, exactly, or that we need to make art that looks like the art of the past. I think it's a historical category, like any other. I'm also well aware that many people have argued that art in our sense only appears really in the eighteenth century and it's a modern idea, and it may have a limited shelf-life. But I think that's to take a very narrow philological view of the matter, and to confuse the history of human culture with a history of words.

I think there's been art ever since there were human beings. By that I mean the delight in form, the delight in the sensuous apprehension of artefacts of various kinds, the appreciation of sensation, of the beautiful and the sublime. And not only the beautiful and sublime. The sense of wonder is really crucial. And that's what's going on in 'The Greenhouse Effect' that's so important. It's quite different from the beautiful and sublime. The sublime is the big spectacle, the commodity offered by Imax and Cinemax. It is highly overrated. One thing I love about 'The Greenhouse Effect' is that it teaches you how to look at the tiny and the miniature, and to reawaken a sense of wonder. One of the best objects in it is a fly made out of glue, Playdo, plastic and hair. It's a perfect fly, and it's all by itself in one little white box recessed into the wall. I immediately started to think of William Blake's poem, 'Little fly thy summer's play/My thoughtless hand has brushed away.' It's an individual fly, it's not just a member of a species. There's no other fly in the world like this one. And there it is, all by itself, as an object of art. So, I'm not ready to give up on art. We've always had it. Human beings are unthinkable without forms of art. And I do think its difference from other forms of visual culture is crucial. At my university, the University of Chicago, we actually had a discussion several years about whether we should change the name of our art history department to the Department of Visual Culture.

KR: Which has happened here in many universities.

WM: Even though I'm known as 'Mr Visual Culture', and I teach courses called visual culture every year, I am against changing art history into visual culture, I'm against letting go of a notion of art as something really significant and distinct. The topic of the 'high–low' division between visual art and mass culture seems to me one of the unavoidable topics you would want to discuss in any course called visual culture, but that doesn't mean the end of any distinctive function for art. It means a re-examination and perhaps even a changed function for that distinction.[19]

I don't want prematurely to institutionalize visual literacy or visual culture or visual studies or visual rhetoric. I like the idea that these things are not located in one department or discipline; I want it to remain mobile, agile and labile. I especially don't want visual studies to become a substitute for art history. For one thing, I think that would endanger some of the traditional knowledges (connoisseurship, for instance) that are built into the discipline of art history, and that we cannot afford to lose. I also like the fact that as a scholar who professes visual studies or visual culture, I can (as I have in the last six months) go from a media conference in Cologne, to giving art history lectures at an American university, and then go to a natural history conference here in London, and feel as if I'm bringing something to them while learning something from them. And I don't need to have 'Professor of Visual Culture' after my name to do that. So, it's important to me that it remains a non-institutionalized formation, one in which you can do research, you can do collaborative work, but you wouldn't feel this need to suddenly have a required list of readings, a secretary, a letterhead, a bureaucracy.

KR: **Is that because as a concept visual culture is too broad and amorphous to try to confine it, it wouldn't be appropriate? Different from art history which has been institutionalized in that way, quite happily?**

WM: Yes in some ways it's a little too big and, as yet, undefined. And before I would want to see it institutionalized, I would need to see a much more convincing consensus about what really belongs to it and what doesn't. But it isn't just bigness or broadness. Goodness knows, art history itself is an imperial, global discipline, with ambitions that far outstrip its ability to be comprehensive. Visual culture is not any more amorphous than art history, but it's a recent and emergent formation, too easily absorbed into bureaucratic shell-games such as downsizing and the elimination of so-called 'redundant' scholars and programmes. I prefer to think of visual culture as an *indiscipline*, a place of disciplinary turbulence, where media theory, art history, literary theory, philosophy, can come together and interact and produce interesting intellectual ferment. But that can only happen if it doesn't rush into setting itself up as a bureaucratic, disciplinary entity in itself.

KR: You'd prefer something in the nature of a forum.

WM: Yes. I'm instinctively an anarchist. I like the idea that people should be pursuing investigations, research programmes, driven by what they feel they have to understand, and not to fit into a niche of a prefabricated discipline, although I'm quite happy to try to be a good art historian, to earn my union card there. If art history just dissolves into visual culture, I also feel that the difference between an art museum, a natural history museum, a shopping mall becomes irrelevant. Well, I'm happy to study the relations among these things but there wouldn't be any relations if they all were just seen as one thing.

W. J. T. Mitchell, interviewed by Karen Raney,

April 2000

Notes

1.   W. J. T. Mitchell, *Blake's Composite Art* (Princeton, NJ: Princeton University Press, 1978).

2.   'To See and Not See' is published in O. Sacks, *An Anthropologist on Mars* (London: Picador, 1995), pp. 102–44.

3.   'Aesthetic experience' is loosely used here to refer to response to the sensual qualities of a work. For the Greeks in Aristotle's time, the word 'aesthesis' referred to sensory perception as opposed to intellectual understanding. In the eighteenth century aesthetics came to be understood in relation to art and beauty, with the work of Baumgarten, Kant and Schiller. For an overview of ideas about aesthetic experience see O. Hanfling (ed.), *Philosophical Aesthetics*, part 2, 'Art and Feeling'; and A. Sheppard, *Aesthetics: An Introduction to the Philosophy of Art* (Oxford, New York: Oxford University Press, 1987). Wolff presents the sociological critique of aesthetics, and the defence of aesthetics against sociological reductionism. See J. Wolff, *Aesthetics and Society of Art*, 2nd edn (London: Macmillan, 1993).

4.   C. Greenberg (1940), 'Towards a Newer Laocoon', repr. in C. Harrison and P. Wood (eds), *Art in Theory 1900–1990: An Anthology of Changing Ideas* (Oxford and Cambridge, MA: Blackwell, 1992), pp. 554–60.

5.   The French psychoanalyst Jacques Lacan proposed two stages in the development of consciousness. The first, the 'Imaginary', is a prelinguistic phase dominated by the recognition of the self and the other as visual images. In this so-called 'mirror phase' the infant perceives herself as a visual 'whole' at a time when her bodily experience is still uncoordinated and fragmentary. Thus the sense of 'I' is based on a misrecognition – a gap between the ideal of mastery and wholeness and the reality of dependence and fragmentation. In the mirror phase the infant becomes aware of herself as being under the gaze of another person. Lacan's earliest formulation of the mirror phase was in 1936 when he was associated with the Surrealist group. He wrote a formal paper on the mirror phase in 1949, which was reprinted in a compilation of his writings, *Ecrits*, in 1966. Introductions to Lacan's work can be found in B. Benvenuto and R. Kennedy, *The Works of Jacques Lacan: An Introduction* (London: Free Association Books, 1986) and M. Bowie, *Lacan* (London: Collins/Fontana, 1991).

6.   '. . . Petit-Jean pointed out to me something floating on the surface of the waves. It was a small can, a sardine-can. It floated there in the sun, a witness to the canning industry, which we, in fact, were supposed to supply. It glittered in the sun. And Petit-Jean said to me – "You see that can? Do you see it? Well, it doesn't see you!"' The account of this incident and Lacan's analysis of it is in J. Lacan, *The Four Fundamental Concepts of Psychoanalysis*, ed. A. Miller, trans. A. Sheridan (London: Penguin, 1991), Chapter 8, 'The Line and the Light', p. 95.

7.   John Ruskin was a nineteenth-century British art critic who championed Turner and the Pre-Raphaelites and was dissatisfied with the decline in craftsmanship in the arts. When the American painter James Whistler exhibited his impressionistic 'Nocturnes' in 1877, Ruskin wrote that he was 'flinging a pot of paint in the public's face'. The painter sued him for libel and was awarded a derisory one penny in damages. Griselda Pollock refers to those who set themselves up as arbiters of quality 'in the grand Ruskinian mode', and Richard Wentworth (Chapter 8) refers to the Ruskin School of Art in Oxford, England.

8.   Kemp and Plant (Chapters 7 and 9) also raise the question of technological determinism. The phrase refers to the view that technologies, discovered by an independent scientific process, are the cause of social

change and progress. Another view is that technologies are symptoms or by-products of other kinds of change. Raymond Williams analyses these two positions and proposes a third, in which technology is not seen as separated from society, but is developed intentionally, with specific uses and purposes in mind. See R. Williams, *Television: Technology and Cultural Form*, Chapter 1, 'The Technology and the Society', pp. 9–31.

9.   See W. J. T. Mitchell, *Picture Theory: Essays on Verbal and Visual Representation* (Chicago, IL: University of Chicago Press, 1994). Chapter 3: 'Beyond Comparison: Picture, Text and Method', pp. 83–107, and p. 89, n.

10. 'The Sopranos' is a very successful US television series about Tony Soprano and his family and business associates. The show works on many different levels with complex characters, including Tony's therapist who helps him confront his increasing anxieties.

11. According to current members of the International Visual Literacy Association (based in the United States), Kodak convened the conference in 1969 but bowed out early on. The IVLA was established after the conference and has been in existence ever since, a loosely knit organization that publishes the *Journal of Visual Literacy* (Blacksburg, VA: IVLA Publications) and a collection of papers from its yearly conference.

12. To Merleau-Ponty, our intellectual functions depend on our pre-reflective perceptions and bodily experiences. The lived body is not an 'object' in the world, separate from the subject that knows. M. Merleau-Ponty, *The Phenomenology of Perception*, trans. Colin Smith (1962; London: Routledge & Kegan Paul, 1986).

13. The idea of a unitary, consistent self originates in Descartes' famous 'I think, therefore I am' and was carried forward into expression-based theories of art. Jaques Lacan's theory about ourselves as 'split subjects' offers a challenge to this concept of the unitary self: 'I think where I am not'.

14. 'Images are not just a particular kind of sign, but something like an actor on the historical stage, a presence or character endowed with legendary status, a history that parallels and participates in the stories we tell ourselves about our own evolution from creatures "made in the image" of a creator, to creatures who make themselves and their world in their own image.' In W. J. T. Mitchell, *Iconology*, p. 9.

15. James Agee and Walker Evans' *Let Us Now Praise Famous Men* (first published 1939) is considered a seminal work and a classic prototype for the genre of the photographic essay. Evans photographed tenant farmers and sharecroppers in the United States during the Depression; James Agee wrote an accompanying text. The photographs appeared first in the book, without captions, dates, names, places or numbers. Agee's text followed, linked to the photographs in ways that the reader must work to discover. The words do not explain, and the images do not illustrate. Instead they present free-standing, equal statements. Mitchell argues that the ambiguous relation between the photographs and the text is an ethical as well as a formal choice: it blocks easy access to the world that is represented. See Mitchell, *Picture Theory*, pp. 290–300.

   Okwui Enwezor refers to *Let Us Now Praise Famous Men* in relation to an interpretation of Steve McQueen's *Deadpan*. The American artist, Sherrie Levine, also mentioned in Enwezor's interview, has used Evans' photographs to raise questions about authorship and originality. See Okwui Enwezor, Chapter 3, notes 2, 3, 9 (p. 111).

16. See Mitchell's *Picture Theory*, Chapter 8, for his discussion of the work of American artist Robert Morris in relation to labels.

17. 'The Greenhouse Effect' (2000) Serpentine Gallery, London.

18. The piece referred to is Tim Hawkinson's *Bird* (1997), artists' fingernail parings and superglue (Image 1.5, p. 60), exhibited in 'The Greenhouse Effect'.

19. See Mitchell's essay 'What is Visual Culture?' in I. Lavin (ed.), *Meaning in the Visual Arts*, p. 210. 'The genius and the masterpiece will not disappear in the context of visual culture, but their status, power, and the kinds of pleasure they afford beholders will become objects of investigation rather than a mantra to be ritually recited in the presence of unquestionable monuments. My sense is that the greatness of authentic artistic achievements will not only survive juxtaposition with the productions of kitsch and mass culture, but become all the more convincing, powerful and intelligible.'

'Images have always been recognized for their transformative powers, which is a new concept for us, coming out of the literal, rational mode where texts and records are not supposed to change. It is a new idea that images don't represent fixed things. They are not static elements in a lexicon. They are living beings that are transforming and changing – in contemporary technological terms "morphing" – into all sorts of things . . . What's going on is that the basis of image-making is shifting from the visual to the conceptual. The material basis of the image is no longer founded on the behaviour of light; it is based on the behaviour of thought.'

Bill Viola

BV: In a very simple sense, visual literacy is the ability to read images. One would then have to ask 'What do you mean by read?', which is the crux of the matter. We're talking about thousands of years of literary tradition, the assigning of sounds and words to graphic symbols, which is a form of visualization. The original Sumerian/Arcadian scripts were literally pictures of things, before they figured out that the symbols could represent sounds. That was a giant leap from the concrete to the abstract. So visual literacy is a very complex term, because it is a different thing to be able to read images at this historical moment, than it would have been to read the visual image systems of ancient cultures.

KR: **What's particular about this historical moment – are you talking about the ability to decode certain kinds of political and commercial messages?**

BV: That's only part of something much larger. There is an extraordinary, momentous change that is occurring. It has been fuelled by the technological revolution, but it is not necessarily about the technological revolution. In fact, the technological revolution is subservient to it (in the sense that a car can better be seen as the necessary embodiment of the deep human desire to get somewhere quickly rather than merely the solution to a series of specific technological problems involving automated mechanical motion).

So, this necessity I'm talking about (and I'm speaking in very broad historical terms here since I see the human/technological interface as a form of evolution itself) is the current need to transform intellectual data and concepts into the palpable forms of sensory experience. Information, long associated with text and language, and the logical, analytical thought processes it evokes, is now transforming from the retrospective description or assessment of experience and perception to the present-tense forms of the experience itself. Memory, the central commodity of the new information culture, is now an active living agent and not merely a record of the past. We find that the discursive, analytical mode surrounding the object is dissipating and we are again confronting the thing itself. Only this time it is in the form of the moving visual image, which we receive in a somatic, associative, full-body way (as opposed to simply linguistically/intellectually). In other words, the representation of the world is coming to us now in the language of Art, and that's pretty extraordinary.

KR: Do you mean it is a kind of de-abstraction? You talked about the invention of alphabets as a passage away from concrete, pictorial language to something more abstract. Are you saying that in some way we are returning back to the concrete?

BV: Ostensibly, yes; but we are returning to the *image*.[1] In actual fact what is being restored, which is more interesting, is the awareness of a multilayered, multidimensional reality.

The definition of what is real in the world for us in Western culture today is based on optics. Observation and analysis. Optics was the revolution that changed everything in terms of how we interact with and make sense of the world. Paramount to this was the development of visual perspective during the Renaissance. (The word perspective – *perspectiva* – is the Latin term for optics.) This is the basic idea of a point of view and the system of positioning of objects in space relative to a viewer. This new concept was actually a re-introduction of ideas from the ancient world into the culture of early fifteenth-century Italy.[2] Images then began to conform to the way that the world appears to the eye, instead of how the world appears to the mind or the heart.

So I see this period right now as very much like the early fifteenth century in terms of the changes that are going on. Vanishing-point perspective was developed during the first decades of the 1400s, and for a long time after that artists didn't yet thoroughly understand the new optical model for making pictures. And so you see this strange perspective in some of the Flemish paintings of the time: the individual objects and people are hyper-realistic, but the rooms and the houses are skewed or compressed. The lines of the architecture don't converge. They were coming out of medieval mode of non-spatial representations into a new optical space, and they were still finding their way. That's akin to what's going on right now, but in very different terms.

The camera we use today is the direct descendant of this perspectival system. It is the embodiment of the direct, non-metaphoric view of things, the objective eye of our time and prime conveyer of consensus reality. When I started working with cameras, at first I just presumed that there was an obvious one-to-one relationship, you know, between a car going by and the video image of that car going by, and that this relationship is more concrete than the relationship between the word C-A-R on a piece of paper, and the car going by. Which it is, on one level.

When the word C-A-R evokes an image in your mind, it is very personal. The more literally and specifically that a writer describes the car, the more his or her specific image becomes defined in your mind. But it is never absolutely the same image that's in the writer's mind. A photograph is completely different. A photograph relies on light. Cameras cannot see things you can't shine light on. So if you take a photograph of that red car sitting on your street, it specifies that object. If you watch the evening news on TV, you know that somewhere in the world that person speaking to you exists. The newsreader is a real person. So are the actors we see in the movies. Now this very fact, this objective truth, is precisely what's changing right now.

KR: It is changing because of the manipulation that can be done to the image?

BV: Yes. Images are beginning to be made with the hand, not the eye. In ten or twenty years you will not be able to tell if the newsreader is a computer simulation or not. There will be a whole generation who will quite honestly not care. I don't mean to say they will think it's a person – they'll know it's not a person. It just won't be an issue for them, in the way that it's not an issue for me to see a live video image here in Frankfurt of a guy standing and talking to me on a California street. For my grandmother, that was pretty strange and disorienting.

When I started using cameras I was not thinking about this stuff, I was just drawn naturally to Eastern philosophy, Buddhism and particularly Islamic mysticism. All of these traditions were saying that what meets the eye is not real. The senses are not lying, *per se*, they are just missing the real thing which is hidden just out of view. The Buddhists call everyday experience 'the world of appearances'. This is just the layer, the facade, the reflection floating on the surface, the movie on the screen. It is not trying to cheat you, that's just the inherent nature of reality.

You know, I was painting and drawing since I was kid. Drawing is a projection of the mind on to a blank piece of paper. It's not about the eye. You can do anything you want. And then, in university, I hit video. I instantly fell in love, and dived right in. I immediately forgot about drawing and painting. I didn't feel the loss of that subjective, creative process, because I got so absorbed in this new medium. And then gradually I came to realize that these images I was taking, which seemed to be devoid of any inner expression, were in fact subjective reflections as well. They were curiously real and not real at the same time. The camera was making me aware, in a literal practical sense, that this *was* just a world of appearances.

KR: It made you aware of what the camera *couldn't* record?

BV: Exactly. That's an extremely important point, number one. And number two is that when I take these images back and look at them in some dark room, that moment when I was actually there – living, breathing, being alive, and pressing the 'record' button – is encapsulated and re-inserted into this living moment, right NOW, but meanwhile the original living moment is gone. This displacement is so powerful. So, now you are watching the car driving down in the street, but that was the car from last week and you're not there anymore, but you are here. Quick, call in the philosophers! But, in actual fact, even in the immersive environment of a big surround-sound Hollywood movie, you are always aware that all of this is just an image, and certainly not an actual car any more. Then, it's not too far from that to realize that when you are on the street looking at the car, that's all just an image too.

All of this was brought into focus by my readings and studies at the time, some of the Islamic mystics of the twelfth to the fourteenth century who were all talking about the 10,000 veils of light and darkness that exist between you and God. You are just seeing the first veil – there are 9,999 to go! Then, the Buddhists were talking about recognizing the world of illusion, so that, through practice, one can learn to read through the veil to the source of the image itself. So gradually it starts to sink in. It is incredibly empowering to know that this is just a world of images. In fact, in today's commercialized, manipulated world it is a political necessity.

KR: **But does that false world of images lead you to the reality? Or does it just make you aware of the difference? Obviously we live in the world of appearances, and you as a visual artist want to work with that world. The visible world must have strings that are attached to what's underneath it, to the invisible. Otherwise why would you want to keep looking at it? Why would you want to keep experiencing that moment of realization that 'this is only an image'?**

BV: That's a very good point. Yes, the surface and the depths are connected. The truth *is* on the front page of the newspaper, if you can read between the lines. I could have been very disappointed and disillusioned: the contemporary malaise of 'There's nothing I can do about it anyway', or 'It's all phony – nothing matters anyway' – the roots of cynicism and self-absorption. But what happened to me was that I realized that what I was really working with were the things you *can't* shine a light on. It was not about the material world any more. And that's for me the place of images in human history and in our lives now. It always has been this way, from the time of the cave paintings. The image of a bison is not the bison – it's the *spirit* of bison: the essence, inner energy, or whatever you want to call it. The picture is more real than the thing itself, not less real. The image is the intermediary, the intercessor, the form (in the traditional sense of the term) – the part of the being that is not deceived by the eye. In traditional cultures, the image has always had this special ontological status between the physical and metaphysical, between body and soul, earth and heaven.

KR: So the visual image stands for that relationship between the surface appearance and the deeper reality. That's why it is so fascinating for us?

BV: That's why it is absolutely fascinating. It has the same ontological status that an angel has. The Greek word for an angel means 'messenger' in English. It is the intermediate between the spiritual domain and the physical world. This is why images have such a special power.

Images (in the broadest sense of the term) can be visual, verbal, musical, gestural, conceptual. They can be painted, sculpted, sung, spoken, danced, or whatever, but it is the connection and ultimately the common identity between the external image and the imagination, the imaging capability of human beings, that is at the heart of all creativity. That's why art has always been considered dangerous, because artists have the ability to put something in the form of an image, to create something that never existed before.

Images have always been recognized for their transformative powers, which is a new concept for us, coming out of the literal, rational mode where texts and records are not supposed to change. It is a new idea that images don't represent fixed things. They are not static elements in a lexicon. They are living beings that are transforming and changing – in contemporary technological terms 'morphing' – into all sorts of things. That is very disturbing for the older generation, and very invigorating for the younger generation.

KR: You started off by talking about the moment we are in, and the new technologies that are leading us back to basic questions about reality and illusion. Are we being brought to those questions by what the camera can do, and what the computer can do?

BV: Yes, particularly by the computer, the key player in the undermining of the authority of the optical image. The computer started out as a kind of calculator, and has quickly transformed itself into an image machine. Designers and engineers soon realized that computers had to be visual to be useful to the society at large. Windows and the World Wide Web were born. The information on your computer screen originates as a series of numbers, lines of code, but in fact what you see are pictures. Again, the image resides above, on the surface layer.

And so what's going on is that the basis of image-making is shifting from the visual to the conceptual. The material basis of the image is no longer founded on the behaviour of light; it is based on the behaviour of thought.

KR: Is it a return to what underlies the hand-made image, in a sense? You said that a drawing is a projection of the mind.

BV: In a way, yes. That's a very good point. No one would consider what a painter could do as being objective truth. In fact the only time a painting was considered to be objective truth was when it represented things that were not of the material world, as it did in the Middle Ages. That was always its power. The things that we appreciate in people like Rembrandt are not the optical tricks. In much of seventeenth-century Dutch painting, the age of hyper-realism, we see that, in reality, those are not optical 'photo-realist' works at all. They are the symbolic, allegorical, metaphorical layers of life coming through to us in the language of high-resolution optical image-making.

KR: The thing about paintings – apart from the curiosities like *trompe-l'oeil* paintings – is that no one mistakes them for what they refer to. In fact, no one mistakes a photograph for what it refers to, but photography does favour the idea of referentiality.

BV: Yes, referentially, that's it. The camera is indexical to the world. But what is going to happen in the next ten or twenty years is that there will be this complete collapse of a distinction between whether a photographic image refers to a something that existed or whether it is entirely fictional. In fact, most likely, the notion of fiction itself will change.

KR: Is there anything about this that worries you?

BV: No, as long as the literacy of the public in these areas keeps up with the technology. This is the real social and political work of today. The transitional periods, like the one we are in now, are always the most unstable and politically dangerous.

We can already see aspects of this change our lives. I could argue that James Dean, Marilyn Monroe and Humphrey Bogart are contemporary figures. They circulate in our world with a consistency that makes them real. Young people today have access to information from all different periods and times and styles. They are not terribly concerned with the flesh-and-blood James Dean. The economic system, which has practical use for these image-beings, is driving their incessant reincarnation, but their status as fixtures or cultural icons is insuring their afterlives.

In fact, in some ways, today the afterlife is becoming OUR life. It's going to seem quite normal when young people get to be my age that these virtual characters continue to appear. James Dean was on a poster when they were kids, and then when they are 50 years old, thanks to digital technology, James Dean will be appearing in a new movie. They are not going to be duped into believing James Dean is alive, but they *are* going to feel that James Dean is real. And I think that's what is interesting, philosophically and ontologically. The disembodied continuation of a persona is going to seem natural, because in fact we do that already. Churchill is with us, and Tutankhamun is with us, and Michelangelo is with us. This is something that humans have always done. My parents are with me. They are not dead – they are living forms within me, and if there is some kind of artificial technology or device that fulfils that function in a more material way (which photography already is doing), then that's already not something outside of my own experience.

KR: It just brings it into a different level of embodiment.

BV: Or turns it into an objective cultural phenomenon, rather than some personal, private thought that I have. When teachers stand up in classrooms and teach about Winston Churchill and Roosevelt, they are vivifying these individuals who are no longer with us. That's what culture and tradition is. The striking aspect of America was not erasure, but the confusion that was caused when these continually evolving traditions were all broken and jumbled, when everyone piled into this new land from different countries with different traditions, with no national heroes yet because the ancestral bonds were broken.

It's as if someone came along and sliced all the tethers, so that these images started floating freely. That's why in a way America is so potent as a locale of this new image culture that is evolving, because the images weren't tied down or boxed off like they are here in Germany or in England. All of a sudden they were loosened from their moorings, and they started to intermingle and interact in very strange and wonderful and bizarre ways, which could not have happened in the same way in Europe.

We are in midstream in terms of the evolution of this image world, and in my lifetime I can see some indicative changes in regard to the reading of images and truth. When I was growing up and the president appeared on TV giving a press conference, they never would show an image of the crowd of press photographers with their cameras. Somewhere along the way, in the post-Marshall McLuhan age,[3] they decided that this was something you could show to the public, the tacit acknowledgement that this is a staged press conference and not just the president addressing you directly. It is just one little example of a much larger thing, the reflexivity that has crept into the media culture and this optical–visual–rational system, when deconstruction has become a household term. And of course, in the domain of politics, what that does is undermine the authority of the President, or whoever is trying to control the event. That everything is staged and manipulated is becoming common knowledge, and the powers-that-be now have to search deeper and farther for areas that can still be considered unconscious, to get their message across to viewers.

KR: Is it part of the postmodern idea of showing that history is a kind of construct? That all images, all representations are constructed and staged.

BV: Subjectivity is becoming the new objectivity. We don't have any cultural basis for that. Pull-down menus and individual customization is a required aspect of an image today. The making of documentaries, standard on most DVDs, are just as popular as the movies themselves, and co-exist together on the same disc. This all becomes very disturbing and disorienting for many people. In the postwar period, Eastern religious and philosophical systems became very popular in the West, in part because, since the Upanishads onward, these formal systems arose to deal with this very issue of the dismantling of the façade. So it is no coincidence that young people who came of age in the 1960s in America, in the TV culture, become drawn towards Zen Buddhism. It's just part of the fabric surrounding why things happen when they do.

KR: Isn't it also that certain endpoints of the Western rational system, like quantum physics, actually seem to break back into these other modes of thinking. Take the rational scientific model to its extreme and you have something that actually negates it. It negates itself.

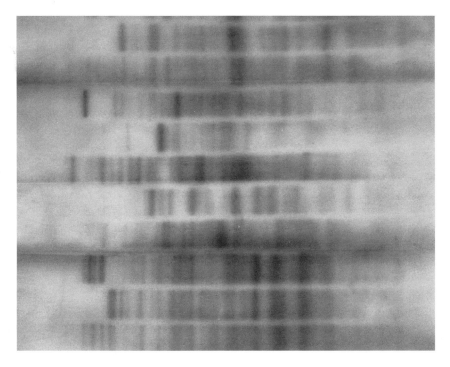

Image 2.2: First genetic fingerprint (1984). Science and Society Picture Library/Science Museum.

BV: Well, that's a good model, because quantum physics completely shattered the idea that you are separate from what you are observing, that you're the objective observer behind the glass. By the end of that same century, we can see this happening on a global, international scale. Nothing's objective. So there again, it is not coincidental that deconstruction theory evolves in the late twentieth century. It is not coincidental that one of the biggest projects right now in the history of humanity, the human genome project, the mapping of the gene sequences in our DNA, which is basically the description of a human being as a code, is happening in the age of the digital revolution, in the time when a machine that functions by processing codes has become an integral part of our daily lives. We are slowly decoding (or perhaps encoding), the infrastructure of experience.

KR: **So where does art fit into all of this?**

BV: Oh, I am an artist, that's right!

KR: **Is your artwork a way of posing the questions and turning them over and living with them?**

BV: I am not interested in an art that purports to be the answer to a question. Marcel Proust had a great line: 'A work of art which contains a theory is like an article of clothing on which the price tag has been left.' So in a way it becomes a form of illustration. There is a big difference between music theory and playing the music. Although the two are connected, there is no privileged order as to which must come first. We are currently in a period of artistic practice (with origins 150 years ago in France) that is very theory-driven and critique-oriented. Now, of course, it is very important to question all presumptions: what is a piano, what is the scale of notes, how is it played, what is the institution in which it resides, etc. One must do that throughout one's life and, in the same way, cultures need to have mechanisms in place to do that. We call it reform. But there is another, complementary, side to the critique process – also an essential part of reform – which involves the creation of a different kind of music altogether, that one feels to be more relevant and beneficial. We saw these two components lay themselves out in the late 1960s where the protests against the Vietnam War turned into a criticism of the ills of the society as a whole, and were followed by a course of action which established viable alternatives still felt today.

KR: Is that what you see yourself doing?

BV: Yes. I have never been a really negative person. I have a deep faith in the positive, creative powers of all human beings. The sixteenth-century Spanish poet and mystic St John of the Cross[4] has been an important part of my life in this regard.

Image 2.3: Bill Viola, *Room for St John of the Cross*, video/sound installation (1983). Collection: edition 1, The Museum of Contemporary Art, Los Angeles; edition 2, The El Paso Natural Gas Company Fund for California Art, (photo: Kira Perov/Squidds & Nunns).

He was persecuted by the Inquisition, taken away in the middle of the night, kept in solitary confinement and tortured, something that still goes on today in the world. Yet what drew me to him was that he didn't hate his captors after that for the rest of his life. He didn't harbour bitterness. His response to his incarceration and treatment was to write spiritual love poems. I grew up in the political era of Vietnam and social activism that regarded that response as a total cop-out. But when I started reading about him, I realized it wasn't a cop-out at all. From this incredibly hateful experience he wrote poems that are teaching stories, some of the greatest spiritual poetry in the Western tradition and absolutely enlightening works of art that continue to inspire and elevate the soul today, more than 400 years later.

KR: **What I find unusual is that you seem to be free of the attitude that says big issues can only be tackled behind a screen of irony and cynicism.**

BV: Some people don't connect with my approach today, and that's fine. You have to go for what you believe in.

KR: **Can you say something about the focus on birth and death in your work? I'm thinking of the *Nantes Triptych* [1992].**

BV: I can't be simple about a birth or a death. I think the camera showed me something very profound, that I wouldn't have seen had I been a painter or a sculptor. My wife and I had a baby and that was an incredible experience. In a previous age I probably would have gone off and painted a painting, or created a sculpture, but I happen to use a video camera, so I recorded an actual birth on videotape. So, responding to a deep personal need to deal with this incredibly powerful experience, and wanting simply to document or capture the intensity and profundity of that experience as directly as possible, without making an artistic statement about it, I found myself confronting very fundamental life issues that artists throughout history have always dealt with. And yet, what I have is this in-your-face, cinema-*verité* shot, where you stare right at the baby as it comes out! It's factual,

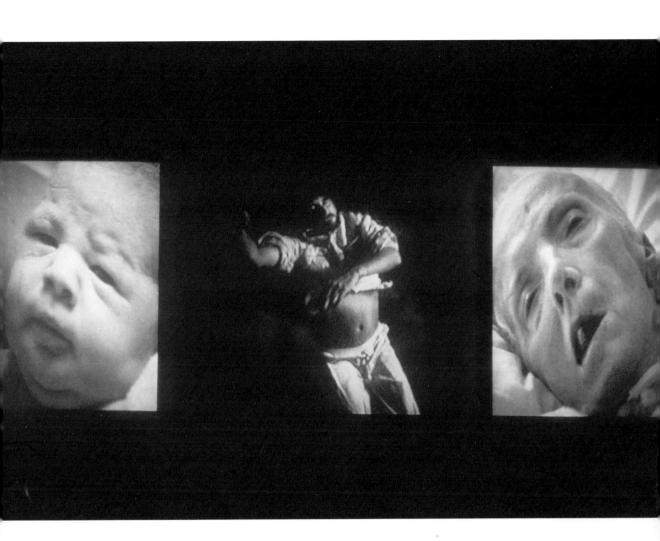

it's news — about as unsymbolic as you could get. But the immensity of the act of birth itself overpowers all of that, and you see that a birth is much more than simply a biological, literal event.

KR: But then you put that next to an image that is much more suggestive and non-literal – the middle image in the triptych.

BV: Yes, there is a guy under water floating.

Image 2.4: Bill Viola, *Nantes Triptych*, video/sound installation (1992). Collection: edition 1, Fonds national d'art contemporain, Commande publique conçue pour le Musée des Beaux-Arts de Nantes, Ministère de la Culture, Paris; edition 2, Tate Gallery, London, England (photo: Kira Perov).

KR: **If the factual recording of the birth refers back to something non-factual, the central image for me I suppose might stand for that murky non-fact, the metaphorical, everything which the photographic recording of an event cannot do.**

BV: One of the greatest dangers in our lives today is the objective eye. These news crews that go to refugee camps, and then they go to the Intercontinental Hotel and have dinner, and then they fly back to the comfort of home with their images of suffering. Rational objectivity is distancing us from the moral, emotional responsibility that we have towards other human beings. The detached eye is a dangerous instrument.

KR: **Susan Sontag says that the taking of photographs is by definition an act of non-intervention.[5] Isn't that what you are doing, though, being a detached eye, when you video someone's birth or death?**

BV: I suppose at that moment, yes, but then what I do with it in the end is something else. It's a paradox. What I want to do is to bring the inner emotional spiritual eye together with the objective observer eye. We've got this cultural situation where there is not really a place in the mass culture for art or any kind of representation that looks inwardly. It's an economic, corporate, rational system.

KR: **Art is part of the entertainment industry.**

BV: Yes, for the society at large, and you get this massive corporate structure, the entertainment industry, taking up our time with, for the most part, trivialities. In 1995 I made a video projection piece called *The Greeting*. It looks like an Italian painting from the late Renaissance. There are three ladies and one of them whispers something in the other's ear. I was thinking a lot about whispering. The sharing of a private moment, like in the Annunciation, when the Angel Gabriel comes in to tell Mary she's pregnant. That's a very special form of conversation – *sacra conversazione*.

It was a very private moment that was communicated in a special form of speech, which was not in the domain of normal conversation.

And we've lost that. The problem with computers is that they can't be vague. They don't like ambiguity. Information wants to illuminate every dark corner and hidden recess. There is no more any kind of intermediate zone for the shadowy whispered message. In our culture right now secrets are viewed strictly in the political sense or in the private lives of celebrities. The intimated truth, the hushed tones used when describing something powerful and profound, the poetic image, do not have a place in the public discourse. We have the accepted forms of public address, the ordinary conversation, the speech or lecture, the announcement or proclamation, but we don't have a language for the things we can't describe with language. The *sacra conversazione* doesn't exist.

KR: **There is still the private life that goes on behind closed doors.**

BV: But we don't know about it.

KR: **So you mean there is no place for the intimate within the public space.**

BV: There is no place for the non-literal. Consequently, there is no official position for the poet, outside of academia and literary reviews. The political innovation in the Renaissance was the elevation in status of artists to what we would call cabinet-level positions in the government. This was obviously a reflection of the perceived value and the place their work held in society.

KR: **You said something about inserting, within each of your pieces, a 'teaching moment'. Could you say something more about that?**

BV: Nature herself includes, in every one of her products, the information about how it was created. There is a built in self-reflexivity. It is one of the fundamental properties of the natural world. And this is the fuel of science, really. If you look at the flower as a kind of puzzle, the deeper you probe into it, you discover all of these things about the flower – its internal structure, its biology – that tell you why and how a flower looks the way it looks.

I was always fascinated with this, and I guess, because I've been working in a new form, I became used to the process of discovering stuff on my own. When I began, video, the medium we know today, and video art literally did not exist outside the practice of a very small group of artists. There was no book about it; it was not quantified and packaged for you in any way. You had to look outside the medium for any footprints on the path you might find useful. You were just probing something, finding the way. I finally got to a point where I was able to see that the elements of the medium I was grappling with were not just technical capabilities with specific functions, but part of a larger language. Only then was I able to use them creatively as an artist. Whereas, in conventional art forms, all those aspects have already been explored and articulated, and you are in the position of reacting to them, accepting or rejecting, or passing over the irrelevant and uninteresting.

KR: You are creating the conventions of your medium as you go?

BV: In a way, yes. I feel that this is still going on when I make work, and I don't want it to ever stop.

KR: One of the things I wanted to ask you about was the way you use notebooks in planning your work. You use words rather than images or sketches, and you wrote that you have a 'mistrust of the visual'. It interests me that you end up with work that is so visual, so non-verbal, starting from words.

BV: It's something that was intuitive for me at first. I'm more aware of it now, but I have always done it – writing in words the description of an image or a sequence of images, as opposed to making a sketch or storyboard. I think that saves me from getting caught in the image. What I'm after is not the visual aspect of images, but something under that surface, the place where the images are coming from and returning to.

These images are so sensual, and so . . . seductive. You bathe in the image. It inhabits you. There is something fundamentally problematic about analysing these sensual, physiological forms. It is fascinating to think that, as intellectual as the written history of cinema is, all these theorists and critics at some point had to sit in a dark room for two hours, in silence, and give themselves over to the sensory experience of watching a film. The cinema is inherently a bodily form. Then, when it's over, they jump into the analytical mode and the books come out. Like writing about sex, you can't do it and write about it at the same time.

KR: **So when you are developing your ideas you keep it in written form. Is that a way of keeping yourself in the thinking aspect of the work, the concept?**

BV: It keeps me centred on the real basis of the images. And this basis is not visual. What I actually write about in the notebooks is usually not the literal facts – the colour, the size of the image, the room, etc. These are the secondary aspects. What I'm writing about is the *feeling* of what it's like to experience the image. And, most essentially with my medium, writing is much better suited to dealing with the time form of the work, since it embodies the flow of time itself. What I'm getting clear to myself at this point is how this thing should feel, what the underlayers are to the experience, how the time will unfold, and not merely what it should look like. And once I get that, then I am ready to go. Then the details and the specifics can begin to get worked out. However, in the end, the work will be correct only because I have maintained the feeling for it throughout the creation process.

KR: **So the concrete visual detail comes in later on. Do you sort of leap into it at the end?**

BV: Yes. But without the underlayers, it's just an image floating in some superficial place. That's why I hate the term 'visual art'. I have a problem with art that is purely visual. Actually, I don't really think it can be. To paraphrase the great early twentieth-century art historian Ananda Coomaraswamy:[6] despite the term visual art, all works of art represent invisible things. All the art you have ever seen is in this form of a feeling image. There are the books on your shelves, OK, but you don't walk about with those books in front of your face all day long. The experience of viewing art, so central to the discourse of the art historians and critical theoreticians of today, is merely the surface level, the first input stage, to a process very profound and essential that will continue long after, and even, in special cases, for a lifetime. The image on the wall of the gallery is the plate of food that you are eating. And you can get really involved in the act of eating, the taste, the aesthetics of food. Well, I'm more interested in nutrition, in what happens after when it becomes part of your being. The invisible world is where these works live, while their bodies remain locked up in the museum. Our job is to make sure they remain free and liberated.

Bill Viola, interviewed by Karen Raney,

January 2000

Notes

1. See Hal Foster, *Return of the Real: The Avant-Garde at the End of the Century* (Cambridge, MA, and London: MIT Press, 1996).

2. For a summary of the construction of an ocularcentric world-view from ancient Greece to the Enlightenment, see Martin Jay, *Downcast Eyes: The Denigration of Vision in Twentieth Century Thought* (Berkeley, CA: University of California Press, 1993), Chapter 1: 'The Noblest of the Senses: Vision from Plato to Descartes', pp. 21–82.

   Rosalind Krauss in *The Optical Unconscious* (Cambridge, MA, and London: MIT Press, 1993) discusses the refusal of the 'optical logic' of mainstream modernism by early twentieth-century artists such as Duchamp, Ernst, Giacometti, Dali, Man Ray and Bellmer.

3. Marshall McLuhan and Bruce Powers, *The Global Village: Transformations in World Life and Media in the Twenty-first Century* (New York and Oxford: Oxford University Press, 1989).

4. Viola's installation piece *Room for St John of the Cross* (1983) (Image 2.3) is a homage to the sixteenth-century Spanish mystic who was imprisoned in a cell too small to stand up in.

5. Sontag argues that the camera makes us 'tourists' of reality. 'The camera is a kind of passport that annihilates moral boundaries and social inhibitions, freeing the photographer from any responsibility toward the people photographed. The whole point of photographing people is that you are not intervening in their lives, only visiting them.' Susan Sontag, *On Photography* (London: Penguin, 1977), pp. 41–2.

6. Ananda Coomaraswamy (1877–1947) was a Sri Lankan art historian. See A.K. Coomaraswamy, *The Door in the Sky: Coomaraswamy on Myth and Meaning*, selected and with a preface by Rama P. Coomaraswamy (Princeton, NJ, and New York: Princeton University Press, 1997).

'I work in exhibitions first and foremost to be able to declare my intellectual idea as clearly as possible to artists. I want to make it clear that I see the exhibition as a kind of laboratory setting. I do not intend to use the work of the artist for empirical performance of the theory that I am formulating. I see an exhibition as a dialectical space that needs to be animated by all of the forces of production that are involved . . . Many curators struggle with these issues constantly, at least I do: how to maintain the integrity of one's intellectual project without being seen to be strangling the voice of the artist. I think that it has to be built on a basic trust, and then we can go forward together to shape a theoretical field.'

Okwui Enwezor

OE: I was born in Nigeria where I lived up until I was eighteen, before moving to the United States in the early 1980s. Having studied political science and having worked primarily as a writer and a critic, I came to the vocation of curating, shall I say, by accident. My interest in curating came first through an attempt to interrogate the highly restricted spaces of contemporary art production. These spaces were restricted by the market on the one hand, and on the other hand by a method of art historical writing, dominated by Western academic perspectives that sought to preserve long-standing prejudices. Forms of contemporary production that were seen to have no place within the history of Western self-understanding were too often dismissed or simply ignored.

But first, I was confronted by a quandary, owing to the fact that I was neither trained as an art historian, nor did I have any institutional relationship to contemporary art. My beginning was simply intellectual curiosity and lessons absorbed through careful and constant engagement with the work of artists, their ideas, exhibitions, institutional collections. I developed a near obsession with seeing exhibitions and reading whatever I could about what was going on in New York and other places. In the beginning, I had no professional interest in art *per se*, I simply enjoyed being around art constantly, writing poetry, attending seminars.

Soon it began to be clear that there were mechanisms of power and many kinds of intentional exclusion that were shocking . The more I saw these mechanisms at work in exhibitions – whether in commercial galleries or museums – the more I was perturbed by the lack of agency by artists, especially those of African descent. This led to increasing dissatisfaction with the framework of radical art that was discriminatory, exclusionary and oftentimes downright arrogant about art and ideas it had little understanding or knowledge of. Standing from the outside looking in – at the serious issues being debated at that time about representation and identity discourse, and the idea of subjectivity as something constructed from both inside and outside – I was taken by the notion of the important historical differentiations that postmodern theory and post-structuralism presented as alternatives to the grand narratives of art.

I was interested in the insurgent rhetoric of multiculturalism, which I know today is not the correct thing to say. But I cannot be apologetic about this, because it freed me, as I am sure it freed many artists, to work radically to inscribe other articulations and experiences that art draws from into mainstream theories about art. It was a period in New York when the multicultural debate was turning towards the realization that production in the contemporary realm was not only made up of many discourses, but discourses that may not necessarily cohere as one historical tendency. The challenges of that was what led me into publishing and subsequently into curating. It also led me to work both within and outside of the established academies of contemporary art, and also to work with what I would call the informal economies of contemporary art. I dislike the term 'alternative spaces', rather I prefer to speak of 'newly empowered spaces' such as the magazine *Nka: Journal of Contemporary African Art*, which I founded in 1993. If, on the one hand, I dislike the notion of alternative spaces, I privilege the idea of parallel economies of artistic production. This means that such economies are not dependent on the unproductive tension between established and alternative paradigms which may not always respond to the dialectic of mutuality from which such distinctions are made. For me, because of the multiplicity of economies and conditions of production in contemporary art, curating has become a much more engaged and analytical work than it has ever been before. No longer is judgement to be made on the rock of taste and discernment, but on an active encounter with knowledge-based concepts that stand the very notion of a unified field of art on its head.

About my current work, I am presently the artistic director of Documenta 11 [Kassel, Germany: 2002].[1] On the one hand I am very much concerned about the present, and on the other hand I'm also concerned about certain forms of historical thought that sit outside the established categories of aesthetics in the West.

KR: I wonder if you could say something about the connection you make between iconophilia and institutional ethics?

OE: It's clear that the museum as an institution in the West represents a love of the image, of the picture, on which the objectivity of gaze confers cultural value to the image. This love for the picture comes from certain suppositions about the representation of the world. I'm interested in how that iconophilia operates outside of the institutional production of certain forms of knowledge. What happens when certain economies or ecologies of image production – that may not necessarily cohere with this regulatory body of the institution – begin to insist on the necessity of their own presence or forces new articulations and interpretations of the image and the gaze, as in for example in the context of Islam? This is not to detract from what has already been fully formulated within the Western institutional context or within the museological context. I don't want to make a categorical division between the West and non-West. I think they are tied together in very complex ways that cannot simply be reduced to oppositions between them. But I'm interested in the tension between certain kinds of images and the institutions they are displayed in.

I'll give you an example. I believe that the black image or the image of the 'other' in the museum context, is much more than simply a portrait. It's more than simply an aesthetic image. Because of the difficult relationship the institution has had with it, it can also become a political image, even though the intent of the artist may have nothing to do with that. I'm interested in this tension between the love of particular sorts of images – using notions of beauty and so on – and what these images represent within the broader imagination. This convergence of the political and the aesthetic places demands on institutions to present to the public a very clear intentionality. There can often be an over-interpretation of certain types of images, in order to speak to anxieties that are lodged in the identity of the institution, the very logic on which the institution has formed itself.

KR: **Would an example be Steve McQueen's *Deadpan* and your view that it was over-interpreted by an American critic as something to do with slavery?**[2]

OE: Absolutely. One could have talked about the falling house in *Deadpan* in relation to the clapboard housing of the itinerant farmers that Walker Evans had documented in *Let Us Now Praise Famous Men* [1941].[3] Or in connection to certain conventions of conceptualism. I think that there's always an over-determination when the black image invades the space of representation within the institution.

KR: **First you were saying there was an under-interpretation, that the image of a black man was seen only as an aesthetic object, and now you're saying the black image is over-interpreted, too much is read into it.**

OE: There's a kind of double relationship that we have to make, that is, if we are to take Gombrich's[4] notion that the encounter between the artist and her work,

Image 3.2: Steve McQueen, still from *Deadpan* (1997). Courtesy of the artist and Marian Goodman Gallery, New York.

or the viewer and the art object/image is a dialectical one that creates a space of enquiry. The function of any given image, then, must necessarily exceed the limitations of how pleasing to the eye a picture or object is. In certain cultures, the image is not something to be looked at, but something to be avoided. It is the very antithesis of beauty or pleasing to eye in the conventional aesthetic sense, because, its power is based on the degree to which such an image strikes mortal terror into the heart of the beholder. In a sense the black image may function along the lines of pleasure and aesthetics because of its eroticized nature within certain traditions of representation, but it also functions simultaneously within such a tradition as something to be avoided, denigrated, questioned, or simply dismissed as a proper subject within the canons of beauty beyond its obvious exoticism to the beholder. And in cultures of deep racial conflict, there's no gainsaying the impact it has politically, when it goes on full public display.

So on the one hand there's an undetermined part of it which works purely from its aesthetic position. On the other hand it simultaneously represents a political image, an image of repression and anxiety, which may call into question hallowed notions of equality, justice, etc. In this case, it is not an easy image to display in the traditional sense of its aesthetic existence. It is here that we may try to locate the encounter with the image of the other in the political reality of spectatorship. There's also an ethics of spectatorship in terms of how the interpretation of such a work can be done without limiting the very complex forces between the intention of the artist, the idea of the work and its status as an object within the logic of the institution. I think this really is an unspoken aspect of exhibiting certain kinds of works, which also come to disturb the iconophilia that normatively is attached to picture-gazing. This is one example of the ways in which iconophilia breaks apart the horizon of spectatorship.

KR: **The horizon of spectatorship?**

OE: Yes. In the multicultural, intercultural, global present and the historical freight that burdens representation, museums no longer can afford to have one defined audience in mind. The very authority that museums and other institutions have enjoyed for so long is today, at best provisional. I think this has political ramifications. Notions of 'multicultural discourse' or 'postmodernism' speak very clearly to this. The position from which a subject speaks is just as important as the place in which the authority of certain types of histories are carried forward. It's this confrontation that I think we have to see. We cannot simply work from the position of the colonial and bypass the postcolonial into the neocolonial. So this is what I'm trying to formulate in terms of the widening horizon of spectatorship that occurs, really, after 1945. This is something that even museums of general history have to contend with. If a Nigerian goes to the British Museum and says 'That is ours. That came from the expedition in 1897 when Benin was sacked and looted', it puts the object into a context. It's not simply a work of art. The provenance of the work has to be dealt with. We can see that happening very clearly with the looted art of the Nazis. There's a measure of ethical behaviour that institutions are called upon to exercise.

KR: **I'd like to ask you about image–word questions that you've been engaged with in different ways. You were a poet, an editor, a wordsmith, and 'by accident' you came to work with visual art and now you're very much in between the two or trying to look at how they interrelate. Do you think the state of being in between cultures has any affinity to the state of being in between word and image?**

OE: In a certain way, yes. But it's not really premised on my identity. I think it's much more premised on my experience of images, given where I've come from and given what the status of the image was, or is, in the culture that I come from. There is nothing that can be seen to be pure visuality in the context of, say, the Igbo world view. The Igbos have a saying: 'Where there is something standing, there is a shadow around it.' So there is never only the object. The object is not autonomous; neither is the image autonomous.

This interspace between the word and the image can best be understood if we look at how cinematic norms have been used, much more than any other medium, by a wide variety of cultures. For cultures that have epic traditions, India, Persia and so on, it is much easier to use this modern technological form in order to address traditional notions. This movement between modern image technology and the narrativity of tradition is very important in certain cultures, as in the culture I came from is the drive to give word to the image.

KR: **And that's what cinema does.**

OE: Absolutely. This is what I feel when I look at a wide range of cinemas. It's not possible to talk about a singular 'cinema', but of 'cinemas'. In the Nigerian video film industry today they make about 360 films a year. And I look at the very vibrant, vital, interesting Iranian film industry, or the one in India.

KR: **Are you talking about popular film or films made under some idea of Art?**

OE: The technology of cinema has opened up a space through which we can look at images — not simply from the Hollywood perspective of how cinema performs in a social context, but how these instruments have been used. I can give you examples where the production of the image has become completely necessary for how societies see themselves surviving. Take the Igloolik/Isuma Collective, a group of Inuit film-makers based in Canada, for example.[5] They use video as an instrument of storytelling in an attempt to transmit emergent notions of survival, continuity and community that links the Inuit to their historical past. Rather than carve totem-poles to transmit their history, they are now deploying technologies of reproduction to speak on questions of tradition and processes of narrating tradition. So there's always this relationship of the word and image, especially in areas where the production of the image has never been dominant, but language has been the only way to sort of 'visualize' the plenitude of what we consider the visual.

To answer your question, I *am* interested in this in between notion, but I want to relate it to the idea of being in between technology and tradition and how the possibility of narrative can be enacted. From my own perspective, I am Western – by the way that I grew up and my education. My Westernization did not come about through my journey beyond the traditional space of my culture. It was already something that was clearly inscribed, something that I had to reconcile constantly and to rework. What you call being 'in between cultures' I see more as a 'to-ing and fro-ing', a restless, ceaseless engagement with the present.

KR: **Can you say something about your interest in the real and fictional? In the catalogue for 'Mirror's Edge' (2001)[6] you wrote that the ideas of the real and the fictional are constantly figured by the conjunction between image and words, seeing and speaking. Are you talking about**

Image 3.3: Igloolik/Isuma Productions: *The Nunavut Series, 1994–95* (still from episode 8). Courtesy: Igloolik Isuma Productions and Arsenal Film, Germany. © Igloolik Isuma Productions.

the old idea of resemblance versus convention? The image supposedly being a natural thing that works by resembling the world and the word being a social sign that works by convention.

OE: I began that essay by referring back to John Berger.

KR: **'Seeing comes before words.'**[7]

OE: Seeing comes before words. Of course this is a classic psychoanalytic proposition. The 'mirror stage' is that point of recognition of the child: 'that is me'.[8] But I think it's a contradiction. The question of recognition is the possibility of speaking the image into presence. In the Bible it was: 'and there was the word'. It was not an image first, it was the word. To my mind this is not a question of resemblance versus convention. In the age of absolutes and our inundation with different kinds of images, I think it's not possible to make a sharp distinction between the real and the fictive. Especially if we think that every image possesses a very specific type of memory that is not contiguous with the ways in which it arrives and becomes a thing. Whether it's a photographic image or a filmic image, whether it's a painting or a drawing, this swing between what you call convention and resemblance is an *inter* space that constantly reworks the relationship between the real and the fictive.

KR: **All representations are social, are borrowing from convention – are fictive in that sense.**

OE: Absolutely. For me there is no line where you can say: 'this is where the real begins and this is where the fictive departs from the real'. I think there is always a co-relation. This convergence of the real and the fictive has always been, it seems to me, the very mechanism by which art is formulated. This convergence brings us to the place of the imagination. The imagination must never be seen as fictive in any sense, because it's another threshold across which ideas are brought to consciousness, to certain levels of visibility and clarity.

Image 3.4: Cindy Sherman

Untitled Film Still #4 (1997).

I think that many artists are working in a zone that tries to reconstruct the relationship between the real and the fictive. The suture that artists attempt in the dialectic between the real and fictive is apposite. It seems more like the idea of philosophical truth. Whether we're looking at the 'fictions' of Cindy Sherman's photographs, or we're looking at the quotations of Sherrie Levine – the notion of the copy and the original is always enmeshed in the field of citation.[9] There's also the fiction of the museum. The museum tries to represent the real or the truth of the history of art, but it's made up of so many conventions.

KR: **It's a hall of mirrors, in a way.**

OE: Absolutely. Of course there is this history of art. But the history of art belongs to a particular genre and a particular medium, it belongs to a specific language. The notion of pure interiority and pure exteriority are constantly working around each other. There is always a fluid relationship between the two, what I consider to be 'productive contamination'.

KR: **What did you mean when you wrote that 'artists work at the limits of, and beyond the image?'**[10] **Do you mean artists are working beyond the limits of the two-dimensional image?**

OE: The illusionistic idea of the image, yes. That is the notion.

KR: **They're working instead with objects and actual experience of space. But presumably not in the way that traditional sculpture does.**

OE: I see installation – as messy as it has been – as one artistic convention (I don't know if it's a 'medium') that has had to work within the notion of how a picture is constructed. It has a very clear spatial and pictorial logic. But now rather than standing in front of a picture you have to walk around the piece, or inside it.

And very importantly, the consciousness of the viewer has been absorbed into the logic of installation. I don't know if the artists originally intended that, but now the very presence of the viewer as an active participant in this spatial arrangement, in this relationship to the real, is essential. I think for many artists installation is an opportunity to go beyond the conventional and historical understanding of what artists are supposed to do.

KR: **Does installation create a constant uncertainty about the relationship between the artist, the work and the viewer?**

OE: Yes, but it does this because it can make use of the conventions of other disciplines. Literature, painting, sculpture, architecture – it has absorbed all those conventions and therefore it cannot simply be seen as a picture can be seen. As problematic as that may be, I think it is something that we'll have to find ways to talk about, the idea of moving beyond the usual conventions of illusionism, and beyond the usual quests of sculpture. None the less, I find it very interesting that the ways of building installations also come very close to the ways in which pictures are built. Take Dieter Roth or Thomas Hirschhorn as two examples of that.[11] Their work combines a degree of material obsolesence, as a conglomeration of things that are built to cohere as a picture has to cohere, in a sense, even though you are no longer obliged to just simply stand in front of it and let it come to you. You are now obliged to move around it, to experience its constitutive parts rather than its totality. Theirs is predicated on what Gramsci[12] has called a 'philosophy of the part' not the whole. Even though the effect of the work carries a connotation of totality.

KR: **But those parts have to be arranged in certain ways, which amounts to something like the pictorial idea of 'composition'.**

OE: Yes.

KR: **You freely use the word 'art' and the category of art. Some say that this category is an outdated one, that art has merged with popular culture. Are you happy with the category of art, and what notion of art do you use?**

OE: That's a very, very difficult question to answer. I think we have to ask ourselves how art has departed from the ways in which we regularly understand it. There is clearly a dialectical relationship between what we call art and the experience of that thing that has been named as art. The self-sufficiency of the notion of art has to be constantly questioned. By the public that visits institutions of art, but also by the makers of the objects, and also by the people who interpret them and who exhibit them. We constantly have to test our faith in the category of what we call 'art'. As annoying as it is to many people that the Tate Modern Gallery is covered with wall texts explaining to people why this is art, the naming of something as 'art' is not enough. Art's self-awareness is one thing; its self-sufficiency, as *a priori* art, is quite another matter. It is a test of faith for notional explanation that 'this is art' and 'that is not'. The faith that is invested by society in the image or object, or in being in the presence of what we call art, has to be constantly before us as professionals who work with artists, who work with objects of different categories. I cannot say to you that the notion of art has completely merged with popular culture. Of course it has in one sense. Adorno and Horkheimer's critique of the culture industry's absorption of the energy of artistic practice is quite salient, when it was first posed.[13] But I'm not sure if theirs isn't a classical response to the demand that there be a separation of the high and the low as a condition of the autonomy of the art work from corruption by bourgeois taste for the popular.

KR: But you believe that there's a need to separate the idea of art from other kinds of things, even if that separation is continually renegotiated?

OE: Yes, absolutely. There has to be a distinction in order to be able to negotiate. I think on a simple ideological level one has to begin from the presupposition that there is a separation. Whether that separation is a sharp one or the borders are very soft, is something to be negotiated. I find Walter Benjamin's idea of the aura of the work of art interesting in this discussion.[14] Mechanical reproduction, he wrote, has made it no longer possible to talk about the aura of the work of art. According to him the idea of aura belonged to premodern ways of thinking about art, the handmade object, the subjective investment of the artist, and so on. But what he then said – and this is very interesting – is that if the art object is no longer invested with this archaic notion of aura what it retains is an 'exhibition value'. I would go further to say that perhaps we not only should talk about the exhibition value of works of art, but for it to be art, it has to have a commodity value. I think this is a troubling notion. How do we make this circle from aura to exhibition value to commodity value?[15]

KR: Are there different levels of definition we can bring to bear on any account of art? Commodity value is one level of definition, but it is of a different order than, say, questions of intention. We've talked about art practice today participating in a wide range of 'research' endeavours, philosophical, anthropological, and so on. This implies to me a seriousness of purpose that maybe other kinds of cultural production don't have.

OE: I don't think that seriousness of purpose is enough. What we've come to also is the notion of quality and judgement. I don't know any artist, however terrible their work may be, who does not define what they do as serious in purpose. We've come to a point where there have been so many quarrels around what an art object is. We've gone through the death of art, we've gone through the death of the author, we've gone through the death of so many things. It's time now to go back and to say OK, there are various economies of art. I like to use this word 'economies' because it puts art into a relation of values of different sorts – exchange value, use value, exhibition value, commodity value. The various economies that exist have to be seen as a continuous process of the pluralization of the notion of art. Art is no longer something that is handed down by the Academy, which has laws about how you must see and experience it.

The notion of interdisciplinarity has become one way in which many curators have tried to bridge the gap that exists between these plural methodologies. It's not a matter of continuous absorption, something that is predetermined – when video enters into an exhibition context, suddenly it's converted into art. The question is: what makes Steven Spielberg's *Saving Private Ryan* a Hollywood film and Jeff Wall's pictures art? In fact if you look at the opening of *Saving Private Ryan* it seems very clear that Spielberg borrowed so much from the conventions of art. He

Image 3.5: Still from Steven Spielberg, *Saving Private Ryan*, (photo: David James). Courtesy Paramount Pictures.

set it up with stills. It's almost like they're all backlit images. So I think there's always this tension. Do we see Steve McQueen's or Stan Douglas's or Douglas Gordon's works as extensions of filmic language, or do we see them primarily as 'art'?[16] We have to constantly walk around the edges of these ideas of art and non-art. Is it possible for works to move back and forth between the categories?

KR: Following on from this, can I ask how you see yourself working with these questions of category, intention, value and so on in your role as curator. You used to write your own poems. Now you assemble other people's artwork. How are those two activities related? What is your relationship to the artists and the works you show? Do you see an exhibition as a 'work of art' in itself?

OE: That's a very vital question and one that many curators are confronted with today, given the shifting nature of curatorial practice.[17] Two decades ago it was not possible to talk about a 'curator of contemporary art', you were simply an 'exhibition organizer'. As exhibitions become a *medium* in which ideas of expression come into the relationship that a curator has both to the artist and to the art object, I think that we enter into a very complex zone, if not sometimes a problematic one. There is the danger that the relationship between curator and artist and art work can be misread.

I do not see a correlation between working as a poet and working as a curator; they are two separate things. I have tried to understand what a curator does beyond the notion of using other people's work to create my own expression. I would like to believe that the relationship of the curator to the art work and to the artist is a highly ethical one, albeit conflictual at times. Its ethical dimension is premised on the fragility of the relationship between the curator and the artist, especially when dealing with certain oppositional and radical practices that tend to bring to crisis the curator's place in an institutional context. It is equally a relationship of power, which I tend to see in terms of relationships between ideas and concepts of knowledge production. And where there *is* a relationship of power it has to be recognized as such, in order to mediate the obvious abuses that can come.[18]

I work in exhibitions first and foremost to be able to declare my intellectual idea as clearly as possible to artists. I want to make it clear that I see the exhibition as a kind of laboratory setting. I do not intend to use the work of the artist for empirical performance of the theory that I am formulating. I see an exhibition as a dialectical space that needs to be animated by all of the forces of production that are involved. It's difficult. I think it's very important that a curator does his or her utmost not only to understand the intentions of the work but also to be strong enough to have a proper debate with the artist. You can't simply say that everything the artist does cannot be questioned. My work as a curator is not as an administrator of the ideas of the artists. I am not a rote pedagogue for whatever the artist puts out. You have to be able to debate ideas, issues and questions with artists. It cannot only rest on a pure objective recognition of the supremacy of artistic intentionality, because it's an intellectual relationship as well.

My work is not about organizing objects or images to make them intelligible to the viewing public. It's to put forward a series of theses that lead us back to where those ideas come from. But also it's absolutely important to take into consideration the viewer. The viewer is not our guinea pig. Of course one does not make an exhibition thinking 'I will do it this way so that the viewer can be fully empowered.' But the complexities of the relationships involved in a curatorial endeavour have to be fully on display.

I don't believe that I'm making art with other people's art. I would like to go back to the notion that most artists work towards exhibiting their work. I think that what a curator brings is of absolute and vital necessary – and that is the interpretation of the relations of production of a work. How to take it beyond the conventions from which it has come from. How to place it within its proper historical framework. How to place it within its own so-called medium specificity, and how the medium in a group exhibition relates to other genres of mediums and other categories of artistic production. This is a very complex thing. It goes beyond the notion of 'arranging' or 'assembling'.

I want to see the practice of exhibition-making go beyond mere display, where the labour of the artist is interpreted and the views of the curator are put forward to cohere with the perceived intention of the artist. That would make the curator the chief propagandist of the artist. Exhibitions produce certain kinds of public sphere in which the complex relationship between curator, audience, institution, artist, art work are animated. There are so many different forces at play.

Many curators struggle with these issues constantly, at least I do; how to maintain the integrity of one's intellectual project without being seen to be strangling the voice of the artist. I think that it has to be built on a basic trust, and then we can go forward together to shape a theoretical field. Many artists are already working towards this notion of 'interdisciplinarity' (unwieldy as the term might sound). As you said, they are working in some sense as philosophers, as writers, as anthropologists, as ethnographers, and so on. What I find is a certain systematicity, a will towards the exhaustion of certain types of ideas through researching them, sometimes a mocking of all the categories of art that have been shaped. The artist is no longer a small agent in this field. The artist as curator may be trying to subvert the work of the curator. And I think that curators have also had their revenge by making meta-institutions through the work of artists within the institution. So we are beginning to see these folds and shadows that surround the practice of curatorship in very complex ways. I think we need to acquire new tools to be able to interpret what these folds and shadows mean, as we have more and more exhibitions of various kinds.

KR: **We've talked about artists working with the tools and approaches of disciplines other than their own. The other side to this is that people from other disciplines are now working to some extent as 'artists'. An example is Asymptote, Hani Rashid and Lise Anne Couture, the architects who have been included in Documenta 11. They are pushing the practice of architecture towards performance art in some of their experimental installations. I suppose what I'm saying is that the boundary is open in both directions. Artists are working outwards towards other disciplines and other disciplines are working towards what we think of as contemporary art practice. Maybe curation has to encompass that shift both ways.**

OE: If you look at an artist like Constant, whose *New Babylon*[19] is such a revolutionary attempt to rework the very conditions of what the city could be. And you have Rem Koolhaas[20] who is an exemplary thinker, an architect who has been working more and more in the artistic space in order to ask certain questions that are simply not possible within architecture. Given the fact that architects work with space and illusion, it makes sense that as the notion of artistic practice broadens, the affinities between what people like Constant and people like Koolhaas are doing become more apparent. Koolhaas is as interested in urban conditions as in the construction of space and buildings. We need to find a way to interpret this convergence and also to establish the distinction between what the artistic intention is and what looks like art and functions like art within an exhibition space.

KR: **So curating for you is a form of research?**

OE: Absolutely. One can set up exhibitions as a field of research, of various kinds of explorations between genres and disciplines rather than as an assemblage of artistic meanings alone. And that field of research could then begin to apprehend a whole range of ways of imaging the world. Asymptote works a lot with digital technology, you know, with organicist forms and perspectives, soft figures that have reshaped the ways in which we navigate the digital sphere, and the ways in which architecture has moved away from the handmade and is beginning to play with forms that were not possible without technology. These are very exciting things and now artists are working with some of the same intentions. We are witnessing new exhibition-making practices that map a more dispersed field of activity — not necessarily the merging of disciplines but their convergence and mutual rearticulation.

Staging this convergence will help us to make proper distinctions between different categories of aesthetic production. Ultimately I don't think that Koolhaas's drive is to make art. But I think that some of what he produces *functions* like art. This is one of the things that made me very interested in the work of Hani Rashid and Lise Anne Couture. Their presentation in the US Pavilion in the Venice Biennale

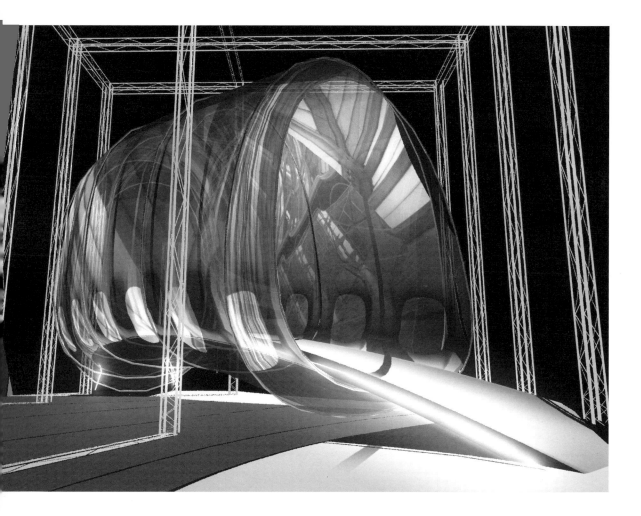

Image 3.6: Hani Rashid, *Airport*. Installation at the American Pavilion at the Venice Biennale 2000. Hani Rashid with Columbia University GSAP.

of Architecture [2000] was very interesting because it was a laboratory. It was a working sphere, a place where notions of spatial continuity and discontinuity and fragmentation could be experienced. And you could see that this was also linked very clearly with pedagogy. It also links with certain notions of interactivity for the public and so on. Suddenly you are in an environment that has certain kinds of haptic and somatic qualities that artists sometimes aim for but are not always able to produce. So again there's this to and fro that I find quite exciting.

Okwui Enwezor, interviewed by Karen Raney,

August 2001

Notes

1. Documenta is an international exhibition which has been convened at four- to five-year intervals since its start in Kassel, Germany, in 1955. It acts as a forum for current tendencies in contemporary arts as well as new concepts in curation and exhibition. An international jury selects for each Documenta an artistic director whose ideas and concerns shape the exhibition. Okwui Enwezor (Documenta 11, 2002) was Documenta's first non-European art director. His team of co-curators were: Carlos Basualdo, Ute Meta Bauer, Susanne Ghez, Sarat Maharaj, Mark Nash and Octavio Zoya. Five 'platforms' were staged on four continents between March 2001 and September 2002, extending the traditional hundred-day format of Documenta. The platforms included artists' presentations, concerts, workshops, film programmes and symposia on such themes as democracy, Creolization, African urbanization, transnational justice, and cultural translation.

2. Enwezor writes about this in 'Haptic Vision: The Films of Steve McQueen', in *Steve McQueen*, exhibition catalogue (London: Institute of Contemporary Arts, 1999).

3. Walker Evans, *Let Us Now Praise Famous Men* (a photo-series published in 1941), was considered a seminal work about tenant farmers and sharecroppers during the Depression. The American artist Sherrie Levine, referred to below, has appropriated Evans' photographs in her questioning of the concepts of authorship and originality. In another interview in this book, W. J. T. Mitchell refers to *Let Us Now Praise Famous Men* in the context of the relation between word and image.

4. Ernst Gombrich, the British art historian, wrote about the image–viewer relationship in *Art and Illusion: A Study of the Psychology of Pictorial Representation* (Oxford: Phaidon, 1977).

5. Igloolik Isuma Productions, founded in 1988, is an Inuit-owned company whose aim is to preserve the traditional stories of the Inuit as well as to articulate the realities of Inuit life before modernization. Their television series 'The Nunavut Series' (Our Land) (1994–95) was in Documenta 11. It consisted of 13 half-hour episodes of Igloolik family life filmed like an Inuit soap opera set in 1945. Also in Documenta was the film *The Fast Runner* (2001), directed by Igloolik Isuma member, Zacharias Kunuk.

6. Enwezor was curator of 'Mirror's Edge' at the Bild Museet, Umeå, Sweden; Castello di Rivoli, Turin; Vancouver Art Gallery; and Tramway, Glasgow (1999–2001). The quotation is from the introduction to the exhibition catalogue.

7. J. Berger, *Ways of Seeing*.

8. See W. J. T. Mitchell, Chapter 1, n. 5 (p. 65) about the French psychoanalyst Jaques Lacan.

9. Cindy Sherman is an American artist whose work has consisted largely of staged photographs of herself. They range from the early black-and-white 'film stills', to simulated 'old master' paintings, to a variety of fantastical and grotesque images. Sherrie Levine, also American, is concerned with questions of authorship, originality and authenticity. In the 1980s she re-photographed the work of well-known male photographers such as Walker Evans, Edward Weston and Eliot Porter. (For example: *After Walker Evans: 7* (1981), black-and-white photograph.)

10. The quotation is from the introduction to the Mirror's Edge exhibition catalogue.

11.   An installation work, *Large Table Ruin*, of the late German artist Deiter Roth (1970–98) was included in Documenta 11. Thomas Hirschhorn is a Swiss-born artist working in Paris. For Documenta 11 he created in Kassel a perishable monument to Geroge Bataille (2002). See also Hirschhorn's interview with Okwui Enwezor in S. Ghez and J. Rondeau (eds), *Thomas Hirschhorn: Jumbo Spoons and Big Cake* (Chicago, IL: The Art Institute of Chicago, 2000).

12.   The Italian Marxist philosopher and politician Antonio Gramsci is identified with the term 'cultural hegemony' which means the dominance of one group in society in shaping the interpretation of a period. The 'philosophy of the part' sets itself up against such a totalizing world view.

13.   Theodor Adorno and Max Horkheimer were prominent figures in the Frankfurt School in its exile in the United States during the Second World War. Together they published *The Dialectic of Enlightenment* (New York, 1944), trans. John Cumming (London: Allen Lane, 1973). See also A. Arato and E. Gebhardt (eds), *The Essential Frankfurt School Reader* (Oxford: Basil Blackwell, 1978).

14.   Walter Benjamin, 'The Work of Art in the Age of Mechanical Reproduction', in W. Benjamin, *Illuminations* (1936; London: Collins/Fontana, 1992), pp. 211–44.

15.   See Paul Wood, 'Commodity' in R. Nelson and R. Shiff (eds), *Critical Terms for Art History*.

16.   Stan Douglas is a Canadian artist who exhibits in the United States and Europe. His video installation *Suspira* (2002) in Documenta 11 analysed the structure of the televised image in relation to surveillance techniques. Steve McQueen is a London-born artist working in Amsterdam who makes silent films for gallery spaces. He won the Turner Prize in 1999. Douglas Gordon is a Scottish artist and film-maker, 1996 winner of the Turner Prize. (See Barbara Kruger, Chapter 4, n. 2 (p. 128) about the Turner Prize.)

17.   For an account of shifting curatorial practice, see N. Heinich and M. Pollak, 'Museum Curator to Exhibition *Auteur*', in B. Ferguson, R. Greenberg and S. Nairne (eds), *Thinking About Exhibitions* (London: Routledge, 1996), pp. 231–50.

18.   See Carol Duncan, *Civilizing Rituals* (London: Routledge, 1995).

19.   In Constant's designs for a utopian *New Babylon*, made in the 1950s and 1960s, architecture is taken to stand for social structures. His drawings and models were exhibited in Documenta 11 (2002). See also C. de Zegher and M. Wigley (eds), *The Activist Drawing: Retracing Situationist Architectures from Constant's New Babylon to Beyond* (London and Cambridge, MA: MIT Press, 2001).

20.   Reference is to the Dutch architect, Rem Koolhaas (see Hani Rashid, Chapter 6, n. 10 (p. 181)).

'I feel all my work has depended on humour and the commentary it creates. That includes the photo work, the sculpture and the installations. But I think the main motor in my work, since the beginning, has been direct address. In the pictures, and in my writing and reviews and, of course, in that last installation that I did in London, there is the method of direct address. Direct address is everywhere, people are used to using it, and being spoken to in that way. You can work with it in any form. And it has something to do with the forming of identities and stereotypes, which interests me.'

Barbara Kruger

Previous:

Image 4.1: Barbara Kruger, *Untitled*

(When I hear the word culture I take

out my cheque-book) (1985). Mary

Boone Gallery, New York.

KR: I know that your work is normally about the 'everyday' rather than the single event, but I wondered whether September 11th has tempted you to do something more specific?

BK: No, not really. It was interesting doing this installation in Zurich, which is a remake of the one that I did here in London last January. I really do like that piece very much. My belief in the brutality of how we are to one another seems to have been corroborated by the events of the 11th and since. I don't think you have to be issue-specific to comment on human behaviour.

KR: The 11th was such a visually dramatic event, maybe it would be difficult to make a piece of work that could in any way overtake that drama or speak to it. The video footage and the photographs are too powerful.

BK: I think some artists did a piece in New York using photographs, and they were criticized. But I'll tell you what troubled me was the vampiric relationship people had to another person's pain. Everyone had a camera, and when people were vomiting and crying, somebody struck a camera in their face. There's no doubt that, for many people, the video camera has become the mirror of choice, the way they document every part of their lives, to the point where they can only experience the world if it's mediated by a camera lens. I think that that's a very suspect social relation.

KR: I want to ask you about the word–image juxtapositions in your work. You've talked of the 'stunned silences of the image', and of language as an 'interruption', or an 'impertinence' to the image. Do these statements imply that the image is something that needs to be mediated or problematized in some way, and that it's language that can cut across the image and convey truth? Is this the way you see it?

BK: No, not at all. I'm very suspicious about any claims to truth. And certainly I'm suspicious about language as a claim to truth. What I think I was saying was that

there's a meaning implicit in the image itself, but it's literally mute. When an image is stilled or there's an image without a word, there's a sort of withholding, which is about coolness or muteness. The use of language over the picture, the declarativeness of that, was totally uncool, as opposed to the cool withholding of the image. So it was not a question of truth, but a flipping back and forth between different kinds of statements, cool and hot. I think that's where I was going with it.

KR: **So you see both words and the images as being precariously tied to reality, whatever that might be.**

BK: I worked at Condé Nast[1] for so many years, and ironically my job as a designer became transformed with some major changes to my work as an artist. So my

Image 4.2: Barbara Kruger, video and slide projection installation shot of *Power Pleasure, Power Disgust*. South London Gallery. (2 February–18 March 2001).

activity became a kind of substitutional one, putting words over pictures. But, it was a methodology that was dominant in the culture anyway. I've never worked in advertising, but I did work in editorial design. Everywhere you look there are pictures and words, pictures and words. That's where I developed my fluency. It was not a strategic development, it's just how it happened. I stopped going to school young, I started working at magazines. What I learned was how to put a word on a picture and get people to look at it.

KR: **When you make pieces that don't have words in them, like the more recent 'monument' sculptures, do they come about in a different way?**

BK: I think that was something that I had thought about for a long time – history and memory and heroism and how historical narratives happen around public statuary. I thought about doing a project like that years ago, but it's incredibly expensive. I went broke making that stuff. I think it's interesting that so much work happens when it does for practical reasons. When I started doing installations in the 1990s, it was because I could afford to do it then.

KR: **So it wasn't that you became compelled for some reason to work in three dimensions – it wasn't some kind of progression?**

BK: No, not really. There are constants which run through all the work. One is humour. I feel all my work has depended on humour and the commentary it creates. That includes the photo work, the sculpture and the installations. But I think the main motor in my work, since the beginning, has been direct address. In the pictures, and in my writing and reviews and, of course, in that last installation that I did in London, there is the method of direct address. Direct address is everywhere, people are used to using it, and being spoken to in that way. You can work with it in any form. And it has something to do with the forming of identities and stereotypes, which interests me. So that's been the real constant in the work.

KR: **How is direct address working in, for instance the Marilyn Monroe piece?**

BK: Well, it was less so there. But still, I think historical statuary works by confrontation. When you walk down the street and see one of those sculptures . . . there is no way that any of those could be situated in Manhattan. They were a little too confrontational.

KR: **Some of your text installations have been translated into other languages, like German and Italian and French. Were there any problems in doing that, and did the pieces work better in some languages than others?**

BK: It's so important, translation. Just the placement of a word can change the thing completely. It's important to get a really good translator who has an understanding of my work and of the vernacular of speech. I just did a lot of translations into German, for the Zurich show. My work has been translated into German quite a bit and, actually, it works very well because there's a declarativeness about German.

KR: **You tend to resist categories, yet you call yourself an artist and use the word 'art'. How do you see the category of art and artists? Do you think there's a place for some concept of art, even if it's not the nineteenth-century concept anymore, or has art rightly been absorbed into 'visual culture'?**

BK: Well, I call myself an artist because, in general, the place of an artist in America is so much more marginalized than it is in London. In America, people don't have the slightest idea what art's about. Whereas every day in London there's something in the press about visual artists. Even if it's the usual sort of scandalous, ridiculous narrative about art, the discussion is there. I don't like the competitive Turner Prize thing, but I certainly think it's great for artists to get recognition and to get some money.[2] I frequently say, 'I'm a person who works with pictures and words', but sometimes I say, 'I'm an artist who works in pictures and words', because people within an art subculture will understand that.

KR: **Do you feel yourself to be part of a community of art and artists?**

BK: I don't even know what the word 'community' means anymore. Art is a subculture, that has its proper names and its histories and methodologies. And there are a million neighbourhoods within that subculture. In film, there are people that are film-makers, and there are some film-makers who are artists. What I think I mean when I use the word 'art' is something that's done extraordinarily well, evocatively, powerfully, artfully. There are a million ways to objectify, musicalize, visualize, textualize your experience of the world. If I hear a great piece of music – pop music, dance music, rock music, whatever – if I think it's fabulous, to me those people are artists. The same with a terrific novel. Journalism is an incredibly powerful form to me. Most of it is stupid and reductivist, but when I read a terrific piece of journalism, I think that person's a real artist. I don't have a very narrow definition of art.

KR: **You once said that art was about 'the ability to objectify one's experience of the world, to show and tell, through a kind of elegant shorthand, how it feels to be alive'.[3] So much of your work seems to be about revealing the hidden struggles and nastiness of what's going on, underneath the surface of relationships and of society generally. Revealing false ideas, false oppositions. I wondered if you think there's an experience of harmony or trust that can be conveyed as well as betrayal, danger, misrepresentation?**

BK: The piece I did in London last year [South London Gallery, 2000] was really about the power of words to zig-zag between tenderness and verbal violence. There were moments of vulnerability and tenderness in that piece. And there's humour or even power or love – like the piece, *Love is Something You Fall Into*, which has this picture of somebody falling. But it's an incredible ability we have, and I think this is the territory of art, to report to one another what it feels like to take another breath. The chilling thing about reading books written 200 years ago is that it feels as if they were written yesterday.

KR: **And that means communicating with someone who's been dead for 200 years. We take it for granted, culture, but it is pretty extraordinary.**

BK: That's culture at its best, the ability to send a message out: 'This is the way it is, this is the way it has been.'

KR: **I was interested in the piece you did with architects and landscape architects in Raleigh, North Carolina.[4] Can you say something about your collaboration with people from these other professions, how that came about and what it was like to work with architects?**

BK: It's always been a big interest of mine. I know more about architecture than I do about art, in a way. I think it's hard to be an architect, because it's almost impossible to get your projects done. How many people get to build the way they want to build? And yet you look at the cityscapes of the major world capitals, and they're full of horrible buildings. There's no architecture, there's just a client and a contractor. So it's hard to be an architect but I think it's really an extraordinary practice. What was interesting in my collaboration with Laurie Hawkinson and Henry Smith-Miller and Nicholas Quennell, was there was a lot of crossover to begin with, in our interests. Laurie went to the Whitney Programme, Henry really knows sculpture, and Nicholas was a painter. So when we collaborated, it wasn't as if I was the artist, and we just stuck a 'Kruger" outside a building. We designed everything together.

Image 4.4: *Imperfect Utopia*, North Carolina Museum of Art. Amphitheater and Outdoor Cinema, Raleigh, North Carolina (completed 1997). Smith-Miller and Hawkinson Architects in collaboration with Barbara Kruger, Artist; Nicholas Quennell, Landscape Architect; Guy Nordenson, Structural Engineer. © Paul Warchol Photography.

KR: **Was there any sense of you having a slightly different approach to the architects, who might think about space in a different way, or for a different purpose? An installation in a gallery is a different creation of space than, say, a building that will be inhabited permanently.**

BK: No, we all worked together. Although I did do a lot of the writing in our textual presentations, just because I had written more. But it was not about art, it was about design. But then when I've written in general, I've never written about art. I've written about film, television, music. The closest I came to writing about art was when I did the Warhol obituary for *The Village Voice*.[5]

KR: **Why is it that you don't write about art?**

BK: I don't consider myself to be an expert on art. When I go to museums or galleries I inhabit them like anyone else. It's like anthropology, to me, on a certain level. I'm intimidated by the institutions, you know. I don't feel like an insider. In America, museums are run by a complex bureaucracy of trustees, their money and their staff whose will they buy. Some very brilliant people, who could make museums more compelling, whether they are directors, curators, education people or whoever, can't exist within the crass brutalities of this system. Museums are great places to show if you're lucky enough to; they're great theatres of spectatorship. What's interesting is how these institutions work. Art might come from the impulse to communicate. But once the art object becomes congealed, it's a vehicle for speculation and exchange. It doesn't mean it's not art anymore, but the artist might as well be dead and buried once the thing starts costing two million dollars. It's nothing to do with the thing the artist made, it's about cultural legitimacy, exchange, speculation.

KR: **You did some organizing of exhibitions in the 1980s, but not recently.[6] Is there a reason that you stopped curating, if you want to call it that?**

BK: I just sort of happened. I could do it again but I don't really see that as a project on the front burner. If I had time I might consider writing again. But I'm not a writer, I'm a person who uses words. There's a difference.

KR: **When you were writing, in what sense was it important – to think through your ideas or to have a public space for saying things?**

BK: Artists sometimes just sit around waiting to be done to, waiting for a dealer to discover you, for a museum to show you, for a critic to write about you. For some of us, my peer group, it was important, as it is for artists today, to appropriate some of that power. So we curated shows and I started writing, not about art but about stuff I felt comfortable writing about. I didn't study art, I have no degrees, I didn't have a genealogy of art history, but I knew movies and I knew TV, and I knew the music I was listening to, and I felt more comfortable writing about that. I think that's true for a lot of artists now, we feel more comfortable talking about a movie than about art.

KR: **Given your love of film, is there a reason why you haven't used the moving image more than you have in your work?**

BK: It's very hard to make movies. You have to spend so much time trying to get money. I have friends who spent years getting their movie made, it got great reviews, it showed in one place, and there was no distribution for it.

KR: **Whereas the kind of work you've done has been distributed quite widely, it's had pretty high visibility in terms of being reproduced in the art world and distributed on merchandise as well.**

BK: Well my work can exist outside of the art world. You don't have to have a graduate degree in conceptual art to understand my work. I'm not saying that the kind of work where you have to 'crash the codes' is bad. I have tremendous respect for conceptual work. But my choice is to make something a bit more understandable to a broader audience. There are a lot of different ways of addressing people and I think it's interesting to exercise as many of them as possible. Addressing people in a slightly more narrow, subculturally defined way is important, which is why galleries and museums are great. Doing a billboard on the street is fine, and making a movie is terrific. I wouldn't be dogmatic about it and say you have to have a broad audience. Besides, I'd be deluded if I thought that as a visual artist you can access the kind of audience that you can with a TV show or a movie.

KR: **Your work has spanned, say, a 30-year period where computers have made some big changes in terms of information exchange and communication. Does this technology have any bearing on your work?**

BK: Well, certainly in making images it does. I'm not interested in the Internet functioning like a gallery, by any means. I don't have a website. I think that if you're going to do work involving the Net it should have to do with the fluidity of the Net and not just be a gallery of images.

KR: **Are you interested in using the Internet as a medium in that sense?**

BK: At some point, maybe. I'm interested in any kind of work, you know, I'm interested in painting, I'm interested in web-based stuff. I don't think there's one correct way of making work. You just do it and see what works.

KR: **Does computer technology have any more subtle consequences to power relationships, or any of the ideas that you've explored in your work?**

BK: Yes of course, in terms of communication, it is absolutely central to the way we live today. It's still very geographically bound and class-bound, to an incredible degree, that people don't always acknowledge. But it's absolutely central in terms of the distribution of information, in terms of being a reference, a research tool.

KR: Would you ever want to paint? Do anything with the old hand technologies?

BK: I love ceramics, and I love weaving. I wove for a while, when I was young. I think it might be fun to try that again. Anything's possible.

KR: Any idea of what direction you're going in next?

BK: I'm working on new ideas and new work, but we'll see what happens. It's been such a distracting time for everyone.

KR: Do you have a particular way of collecting ideas? Do you use notebooks, sketchbooks, collections of photographs?

BK: Not sketchbooks. Sometimes I write ideas down in notebooks, but nothing formalized, I don't sign them. Hopefully no one will ever see them. I like shredders. I hate the notion of art ephemera. What I am is a newspaper junkie. I read newspapers and I watch TV and I go online and I collect stuff. I saw a show in Zurich of Thomas Hirschhon's work. I thought it was interesting that he's chosen a way to

Image 4.5: Thomas Hirschhorn, *Wirtschaftslandschaft Davos*, (2002). Kunsthaus, Zürich, 28 August– 2 December. Courtesy: Galerie Susanna Kulli, St Gallen.

indulge his collecting thing, his need to gather information. I think that a lot of artists do that, now more than ever.

KR: Now more than ever, because of the way we live? Bombarded by 'information' from different sources that we have to make sense of?

BK: Our relationship to images has certainly changed from the time when the only way that we could record something was through painting. The world has changed in interesting ways. And in the end we're all a reflection of the culture that constructs and contains us. There is a broader range of stories being told, with different kinds of images and words and art forms, and I think there's also a greater understanding of the many forces at work which produce lived experience.

Barbara Kruger, interviewed by Karen Raney,
October 2001

Notes

1.   Kruger worked at Condé Nast Publications from 1966–71 as designer of *Mademoiselle* magazine.

2.   The Turner Prize is a yearly prize established in 1984 by the Tate Gallery, London. Its aims are to bring contemporary art to a wider public, to promote discussion of new developments in visual art and to encourage the directions being taken by emerging artists. The conditions of the prize have changed over the years. Currently (2002) £20,000 is awarded to the nominated artist under 50 years of age who in the view of the jury has contributed most to British art in the preceding year. The work of shortlisted artists is exhibited at the Tate Britain for some months before announcement of the winner. The television station Channel 4 has sponsored the Turner Prize since 1991 and broadcasts the prize-giving ceremony. Since the start of the prize, there have been debates about the criteria, age-limit, nature of the jury, the kind of decisions made, and about whether such a prize courts controversy and novelty for its own sake or fosters a 'horse-race' mentality inappropriate to the arts. In any case, the Turner Prize and its airing on television has made the work of selected artists visible to a wider audience.

3.   In interview with Lynne Tillman, in Barbara Kruger, *Thinking of You* (Los Angeles, CA: Museum of Contemporary Art, 1999).

4.   *Imperfect Utopia* (1987–96), Barbara Kruger in collaboration with Smith-Miller and Hawkinson Architects and landscape architect Nicholas Quennell, Raleigh North Carolina.

5.   For a list of Kruger's writings, see *Thinking of You*, catalogue for Barbara Kruger retrospective (New York: Museum of Contemporary Art, 1999).

6.   Exhibitions curated by Barbara Kruger include: Creative Perspectives in American Photography (1981), Hallwalls/CEPA Gallery, Buffalo, New York; Pictures and Promises: A Display of Advertising, Slogans and Interventions (1981), The Kitchen, New York; Artists' Use of Language: A Display of Books, Periodicals and Posters (1982), Franklin Furnace Archive, New York; Picturing Greatness (1987), The Museum of Modern Art, New York.

'It's important not to forget that the visual arts have been fundamentally graphic. They traditionally involved mark making. I'm very interested in images of people making paintings, for here we have a new form of documentation that privileges the act of art making, of the painter's body in action over time. The product of that activity is a visual field, not just necessarily a visual object. But in terms of painting or whatever, you are creating a field that calls to the visual fantasy of the viewer, but also speaks to the visual fantasy of the embodied maker.'

Griselda Pollock

GP: I am the Professor of Social and Critical Histories of Art, at the University of Leeds, which is a wonderfully elaborate title I invented for myself. I'm also the Director of the Centre for Cultural Analysis, Theory and History at the University of Leeds. I studied history at Oxford, and then I went into art history at the University of London. I became increasingly interested in areas marginal to orthodox art history, such as the developments in film and cultural studies. I have been through the whole process of questioning if I am now involved in *visual* representation or *visual* culture? Is art history now redundant, to be replaced by a new paradigm? Or are there other concomitant developments and reshaping of theories, methods and fields of study? What are the relations between the different orders of culture? I suppose part of what made me not so much leave art history as a disciplinary space as find myself a dissident within it, having a difficult relationship with the standard forms of art historical practice, resulted from my being involved with contemporary art. Because of my work as a feminist cultural theorist and analyst, I have been forced to break the moulds that art history has established for art to be studied historically in order to engage with living artistic cultures.

In the early 1990s I devised a suite of new MA programmes in feminist studies in the visual arts at the University of Leeds that now include Feminist Theory and Practice in the Visual Arts and Gender and Difference in the Histories of Art, as well as the inclusive Feminism and the Visual Arts. It is this space that best represents my interests at the moment. That space lies between general cultural theory, that alerts us to what art might be about, and the historical framework in which making art and its reception function – a sort of prehistory, therefore, of the present. On this MA, we use the practice of very close reading – using theory and history – as a means of deciphering what I call artistic inscriptions. I run a module that is titled 'Inscriptions of the Feminine'. This module studies work by contemporary women artists. So, in referring to inscription, I am using a writing metaphor for what I suggest that art brings into visibility across a boundary from places where certain processes and insights are not available to us. Art is a way in which they do become available. Thus art is presented as a productive practice, creative not in the old bourgeois sense of the creative genius. Rather, following Julia

Kristeva and Bracha Lichtenberg Ettinger, I see artistic practices as producing meanings and shifting sense in ways not yet imagined or known by culture in advance of this poeisis. This is of vital importance in thinking about inscriptions in, of and from the feminine since the feminine as the still yet not known remains outside of the dominant cultural/symbolic order at the moment, although artistic practices may have already visited and reported on that potential in ways not yet 'read' by a phallocentric culture that lacks the codes to decipher these inscriptions.[1]

KR: Do you ever use the phrase 'visual literacy?'

GP: I suppose I've used it in two senses. The first occurs in teaching histories of art to both art history and fine art students. In our department, we have been reviewing ways of ensuring that our students have a certain level of either historical or contemporary 'visual literacy'. That's to say, they must have what we might now name a kind of database in their mind which they can access in order to do the kind of creative or analytical work they want to do. We need to help them to become familiar with and understand a whole range of cultural practices, which we as their teachers already know, so that, for instance, students can read a silent movie and appreciate its rhetorics and poetics – a skill that might possibly assist them in developing a more complex studio practice. Some areas of visual culture have become less available to younger people, and they can't make art if they're making art in a vacuum where they don't have the fullest range of visual references/ resources of expression. It's a matter of having a deep knowledge of the ways in which visualities have been used in cultural traditions, so that we can be sophisticated, flexible and inventive with them.

But there's another sense in which I use 'visual literacy'. I'm interested in it because I have a dyslexic daughter. One of the tests she was obliged to undertake to determine her dyslexia examined her capacity for retention of numbers and her memory for images. I was intrigued, given that dyslexia is inherited, and it's assumed it's inherited from me, to see that she had terrific visual recall. If they gave her sets of images, she could both read them, remember them and she could make interesting comparisons. If I go round an art gallery with her, she can instantly remember what a Berthe Morisot looks like compared to a Claude Monet, which you'd think is what, in art history, you'd be teaching students to do as a transmitted knowledge. It's the capacity to recognize what are, in fact, quite minute distinctions between painting methods and formal decisions and effects. Perhaps we can recognize in this a distinctive kind of visual interest, or interest in the ways things can be visually transmitted or represented. For many people, they cannot see what artists and art historians are actually talking about when they discuss a painting, for instance. What they would see would merely be the general category such as modern art, or Impressionism rather than the significant differences within that overall tendency. Certain people, therefore, may have brains that are wired more favourably to grasp the world through modes of visualization and visual information.

KR: You're saying there are two kinds of visual literacy. One is something that can be taught, to do with exposure and familiarity and having thought through the connection of an object with the circumstances of its making. Now you're talking about something that's maybe more to do with an in-built perceptual skill or sensitivity?

GP: Yes. A relationship might develop between the two, because one would presume that the people who tend to be artists, or are interested in the visual arts, are the people for whom these specific sign systems we call art or cinema are both intelligible *and* interesting. I was really trying to make a distinction between a simple act of intelligibility, which enables you to decode or distinguish, and this other kind of visual literacy, which is about a sense of the cultural uses of the potentials of visual sign systems.

KR: Do you have any reservations about using a 'linguistic' term like 'literacy' when referring to visual things?

GP: Well there has been a struggle over the last 25 years, between a sense of the visual as the ineffable 'other' of language and the argument that visual representation is equally, if differently, semiotic (i.e. structured to produce meaning and affect). Therefore, you have John Berger's curious statement, that 'seeing comes before words', indicating some sense of a pure or primary visual contact with the world which is corrupted then by the imposition of language.[2]

Then I see the next stage as a complete swing to the other side of the argument, which was to try and protect us against the mysticism that is implicit in the supposed ineffability of the visual. Through this you arrive at the notion – which came through semiotics – of imagining the visual to correspond entirely with language. This leads to the dominance of a linguistic metaphor. There are some very interesting works of art and writing that came out of the attempt to read images, both historical and contemporary, using that very, very strict semiological model. Everything could be a matter of codes and decoding and various strata and functions. There is a moment in Roland Barthes' early work in the 1960s[3] which epitomizes this ultimately impossible task. What remains, however, from the attempt is a double sense of both the codedness of visual sign systems, and that which, as it were, nebulizes the codes, which are no longer ineffably beyond words, but are the transformative affects and potentials at the margins of symbolic unities we call meanings.

For my own work, Julia Kristeva[4] has been a very key thinker in questioning the adequacy of the linguistic metaphor for dealing with things that are pre- or non-linguistic according to a theoretical viewpoint that conjugates semiotics with psychoanalysis, the latter serving as the analysis of how we come to become language-users. Kristeva's contribution lies in analysing the conditions of language psychoanalytically, so that while we become speaking beings that process is always lined, haunted even, by what language comes to order and upon which it is built, without ever completely mastering it or covering it over. This other of language is not non-linguistic in an absolute sense, but refers dialectically to the process, drives and materialities of the psychosomatic 'becoming' of the subject. Kristeva, therefore, challenges the absolute hegemony of the linguistic metaphor. She makes two moves. One is to say that the linguistic metaphor has tended to think of language only at its most rigorously abstracting and directed pole, like a legal document, saying only what it wants to say. But within language, moving towards the poles of literature and poetry, there is a way that the linguistic has a filtered relationship with what is pre-linguistic. That gives rise to an edge or margin of language where there is a movement between these two terrains that Kristeva names as the symbolic and semiotic. The latter functions constantly to renew language, renovating the will to fixity typical of the symbolic pole. Once you start attending to poetic language, which is what Kristeva calls the 'semiotic' – as opposed to little 's' 'symbolic' which is very communicative, purposeful speech or writing – you begin to see that the linguistic metaphor is itself troubled by rhythm, by sound, by certain things that obviously show the impact of the non-linguistic and open up representation to desire, fantasy, affect, the drives. In the realm of the visual arts, we might identify the semiotic with colour and with the pulsations that arise from colour and the mark.

Kristeva suggests that no field of human practice is without some kind of order, something that moves toward the pole of unity, that enables us then to think it, to respond to it, to understand it. But it's equally shaped in potentialities that are more, shall we say, to do with processes, and indeed, processes of very fundamental psychic formation, the processes of corporeality and fantasies relating to it.

I, therefore, do not like using the concept of visual literacy too tightly. I think you can use it in a very general sense, as a metaphor for registering a certain understanding of the significance of the visual, but we must not submit it to the linguistic model exclusively. There are certain visual signs whose purpose is to be as uncluttered in their communication with the receiver as possible, to use space and colour in certain relations within a field, in order to convey a specified message. And there are kinds of signs whose purpose is precisely to push that field where we make sense of the world, to the borderline with that which resources it: an opening, provoking, inventive practice that enables the ordering of gender, language, identity and so forth to be shifted and renegotiated. Julia Kristeva theorized this in relation to avant-garde writing, but she also identified some aspects of the semiotic shift in the work of Giotto, notably his use of blue, and in the iconography of the mother's face in Bellini.[5] She has written also on Jackson Pollock and on contemporary installation art.

In the present circumstance, 'visual literacy' touches on this interesting debate around whether or not we can save the visual from the mystical legacies of Romanticism, by passing it through too tight a semiotic field, or do we, by putting semiotics together with psychoanalysis, get a whole new possibility for talking about visuality: beyond the visual, in the realm of the fantasy of the gaze.

KR: **So you can preserve what's specific about the visual mode, but avoid mystification, by combining semiotics with psychoanalysis.**

GP: Not prescriptively. I don't think that I'm saying this is the only way. For my work, at the moment, such a conjunction is an extremely interesting and productive space. I'm interested in, for instance, the ways in which Kristeva writes about the function of colour. What relationship might you have to colour, which is, on the one hand, a physical property that you can talk about, rods or cones or whatever it is, and, on the other hand, you can talk about it in terms not just of physiology but of a psychology of perception. Apparently blue is perceived around the margins of your eyes, and because the child's retina develops very slowly, blue is one of the first colours that the child perceives. So that then moves from the psychology of perception into a psychoanalysis of the erotics of seeing colour. Why then is the virgin's robe blue, and how do people use blue? What does blue do to the shapes you paint blue? In fact, it de-materializes them, it goes against the drive of painting to represent something, to materialize it for you, to materialize a vision into a visual field.

At the other end of the spectrum, there's another aspect of psychoanalysis. I was involved in an exhibition in 1996 that was first shown in Boston and Washington before coming to the Whitechapel Gallery in London. Curated by Catherine de Zegher, it was titled: Inside the Visible. The show looked at a whole range of works by 30 women artists, who have not found their place within the normal histories of art. The thesis of the project was that these are very interesting works because

Image 5.2: Bracha Lichtenberg

Ettinger, detail from *Matrixial*

Borderline (1990–91).

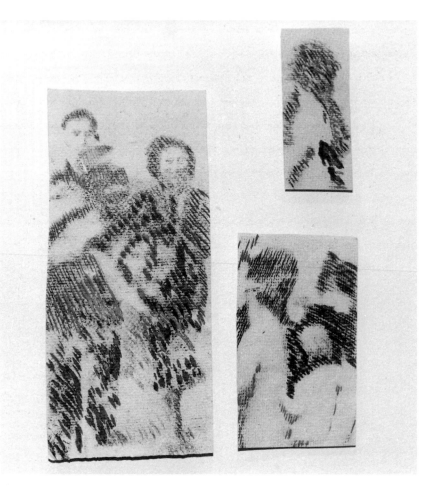

Image 5.2: Bracha Lichtenberg Ettinger, detail from *Matrixial Borderline* (1990–91).

they allow – the phrase is 'they fold into the visible' – meanings which are, for a variety of reasons, psychologically or, I suppose, psychoanalytically, conceived to be 'beyond the visible'.

KR: What sort of meanings are 'beyond the visible?'

GP: These are not mystical, but concern the dimensions of experience of marginality, protest, dissidence, cultural, sexual, gender, class difference. If you take the John Berger proposition, 'seeing comes before words', that suggests that vision provides a direct and almost complete access to the world. Whereas psychoanalysis argues that vision, just as much as the use of the voice and the mouth is simultaneously organically based and libidinally invested with fantasy. The eye can in fantasy become an erotic organ, as can the relays of seeing and being seen become a kind of intensely fantasized zone, invested with erotic 'interest'. To learn to speak and use language depends upon investing in the mouth and the muscles of the mouth with the pleasures of that oral zone. So there's a way in which the psychic field of fantasy and desire and the physical ground work together.

The eye is not just our window to the world; as an erotic organ, it is very complexly involved in our fantasy life. These include fantasies of mastery and fantasies of being held by somebody's look, and fantasies about who sees what, and whether or not you see everything there is to see or that there is, in fact, a screen which makes your relationship to the world visually very partial. Such theorizations of looking and being seen interrupt the idea of vision's directness, completeness or neutrality. Psychoanalysis theorizes seeing as 'the gaze', which, instead of being an image of perfect perception, which is the pre-enlightenment view of it, is transformed. Vision is perpetually both constructed by fantasy and desire and then blinded by it.

The other legacy of psychoanalysis is that there are things which almost cannot by definition enter into any level of our psychically constructed perceptions/ recognition/imaginings, yet are the very cause of what we are. Lacan argued that the subject is in a constantly deferred relationship to the Real of the body, the world, which has to pass through the peculiar conduits to enter into intelligibility or affect for the subject.[6] There is a constant relationship between what we do see, what comes into the field of the gaze, what the gaze is, and what must, by definition, be outside of that, but none the less haunts us, like a spectre, because it's an ancient trace of archaic processes and encounters that have no means of entering into signification. So, for instance, being in the womb is clearly not something of which we would have any visual memory. But you might be able to make paintings which, in a sense, translate that archaic sensory experience of contact, being carried into an affect that can be perceived via a visual encounter with a painting of a visual field that otherwise evokes those memories than through direct representation. It's completely impossible at the level of cognition; there's no way it's intelligible.

There's no memory of it. There's no image for it; but it could, as it were, be invited across the threshold from where it lies, as a kind of archaic trace registering on our very ancient sensory systems, by means of colour generating other kinds of associative psychic–cognitive responses. It can then be invited into a level where we can perceive it or recognize it or be affected by it, through something that would happen on the screen of the visible. You could create, in the experience of painting, a visual scene which, through uncanniness, folds into the visible world, that which is non-visible, and never was in the order of the seen.

So, to go back to your original question – do I like the term visual literacy? I'll accept it as a metaphor that deals with certain things. But I do not want to subjugate the visual to the linguistic, nor to say that we need something specific for the visual, but to say that both language and visual representation come to find themselves in a different relationship once they are passed through the prism of semiotics or psychoanalysis.

KR: **They find themselves in a different relationship – do you mean as they both evolve over time? Or do you mean that the kind of visual work that's being done now has a different relationship to language than it had before?**

GP: There has to be a history. We could probably suggest that there's been a particular regime of vision in the West since the seventeenth century. Michel Foucault looked at the development of what he calls the 'classical' system of representation. This regime changed at the beginning of the nineteenth century to the society of 'surveillance', which produces a whole new set of technologies of vision that we internalize as an interior gaze.[7]

Our visuality[8] has been radically altered by political, social, economic and technological histories. We may have to try to teach people nowadays how to read a silent film, or even be able to tolerate watching a black-and-white film, to recognize its visual rhetoric and beauty, to appreciate what formal choices have been made to shoot it this way, with this kind of density of film, this blackness and whiteness, this lighting and all the rest of it. Viewers today in the era of postmodern spectacle and computer games are so used now to very fast cutting, very mobile camera work, high-realist colour. They can't look for long enough; they can't bear a long take.

KR: **I want to raise the question of digital technologies, and different ways of making a visual image. Do you see digital technologies as having any profound effect on the ways we have of looking and making?**

GP: One of the things that strikes me immediately is that it's a process of accelerated disembodiment. It's important not to forget that the visual arts have been fundamentally graphic. They traditionally involved mark-making. I'm very interested in images of people making paintings, for here we have a new form of documentation that privileges the act of art-making, of the painter's body in action over time. The product of that activity is a visual field, not just necessarily a visual object. But in terms of painting or whatever, you are creating a field that calls to the visual fantasy of the viewer, but also speaks to the visual fantasy of the embodied maker.

In the case of Abstract Expression, the painters were trying to make that producing self-evident, and the practice was about the body that laboured to produce art. Photographs of these artists at work emphasize that the paintings they produced were the traces of labour – which are very intimately connected with the movements of the body in the real and fantasmatic space of that activity. There's one image that I have of Lee Krasner, where she's painting on a table. There's a sequence where at a certain point she'd stopped, and she's just seeing with her hands. The hand gestures are crucial. You can see her trying to measure her painting through her hands. And I think, how often do I see people do that? They're looking at their paintings, and their hands are part of the elaborate process of 'seeing the space', marking the movement of vision in space and body. It's almost as though the work is not disembodied visuality, but a place.

I think that digitally produced art is really interesting. It's too recent to have anything really profound to say about it. But watching kids with the mouse and the keyboard I am fascinated and horrified at the same time by the way that they are so glued to this visual box. I watch my son playing the games. It's such an extreme suspension of any sense of his body. He'll sit there for hours, and the only thing going on is the visual scanning and the slight hand movement of the clicking mouse. I think that's quite new and different. It breaks the link between visuality, tactility and the body that has been so fundamental to what we have called art. I think there are going to be implications. It does change the status of the visual but the technology is an extension of aspects of our world that have been there since industrialization: like the difference between the handloom weaver and the factory hand overseeing huge weaving machines.

In all the arguments around the Gulf War, it was rightly stressed that by being the first totally spectacular war it became a kind of virtual war that undermined our empathy with its real, bodily horrors that previously photographic record had functioned to make vivid and real. The mimicking of computer simulation could manage to erase from our screens that the war did have a body count and an enormously tragic dimension, through our susceptibility to a completely artificially constructed visual world, whose intelligibility, again, was highly sophisticated and not obvious. You saw it, not even as it happened, but through the simulation that registered the event somewhere else. I don't know, I think that massive dislocation is one of the issues that's coming up in cultural criticism.

KR: **Can I ask you about the term 'visual culture?' I'm interested in the question of distinctions and where people make, or decline to make them, particularly now when art practice has come to encompass so many different kinds of activities. One reservation about a very broad term like visual culture is that it might erode important distinctions between things. Do you organize activities or products within 'visual culture' in any particular way?**

GP: I think the term 'visual culture' arrived in order to erode not distinctions but hierarchies, and to try to make us pay attention to the multiplicity of visual systems that are in operation in culture, rather than to think of the visual as only the privileged site of art, for instance. And so there was a moment, particularly in the 1980s, when if you went to art history conferences, people were very interested in seeing, for instance, a discourse of sexuality that would thread itself across a whole range of visual and verbal representations and practices. Lynda Nead's book on the nude exemplifies this very well.[9] She both looks at manuals for drawing the nude as well as pornography and fine art paintings, films and all the rest of it. She is trying to track the dissemination of related concerns across a range of different sites, which in any one cultural moment will have critical relationships. This model is fundamentally derived from the work of Michel Foucault whose discourse analysis has been creatively influential in liberating art history from the straitjacket of elitist connoisseurship and aesthetics.[10]

So I think in that sense it was a very productive move. If that then becomes, under the rubric of political correctness, a kind of automatic assumption that it's as justifiable to study street signs or comics as it is to study art, then we're into a battle of values, into which I do not particularly want to descend. I much prefer to be in a Foucauldian position, to say: you must research the entire range of visual representations in a culture. But I'm not in favour of saying programmatically we must study x, y and z, because the nature of the distinctions that one would want to draw are not valuative but structural.

I think one of the models that I'm using, this semiotic–symbolic distinction that Kristeva draws, is probably applicable to any of the different regimes. I do, however, want to argue that the specificity of how the visual is articulated in this practice as opposed to that practice matters. Not for the purpose of saying, this one is better or more perpetually valuable or greater or more intrinsically civilized, a reflection of humanistic values, etc., but because we cannot work out what is going on in any visual representation unless we can identify what is specific to each practice.

KR: How would you start to get at that specificity? Would it be how something looks, how it's put together, the conceptual structure, the motivation or intention behind it? Are you still happy with the category of 'art'?

GP: Yes. I think I've been driven back to 'art'. Or rather, I have been able to understand what is specific to an artistic practice, as a result of working through this critical, deconstructive and anti-hierarchical process associated with discourse analysis, semiotics and psychoanalysis. The word 'practice' is very important as a clear signal that I am interested in the artistic/aesthetic in a radically different way from that which informed the art historical establishment against which I rebelled in the 1970s.

I now view what has happened in my own particular professional trajectory like this. I was someone who was deeply dissatisfied with how art was being represented and delivered to us in the 1960s and 1970s. Art history was inadequate to explain art. There were much more interesting ways to account for concurrent regimes of visual representation. So, for instance, I found myself much more interested, not in cinema compared to painting, but in how people were analysing cinema in the 1970s. They were able to talk about vision and visuality and the gaze, and the psychodynamics of visual pleasure, and how things are constructed through time and editing and spatiality. This discourse provided access to the specificity of the practice of cinema that was much more interesting than simply imposing on cinema the art historical models of great directors, great films, national cinemas and genres of film-making.

It has been a long journey through a range of analyses of advertising, of cinema, of the less valued and less canonical aspects of the visual arts, to find a way back then to what was the heart of the canonical art historical project, with some means of speaking of it, of attending to its particularity, to what it is that it does. There are things that happen within that space called 'art' because of the combination of a historical and a structural identity. What happened in the seventeenth century happened because of a whole series of inventions, lenses, journeys of adventure, colonial mercantilism, whatever, that characterizes ways of seeing in the seventeenth century as opposed to now. But also there are structural properties which you could probably as easily discern, maybe crucially discern, in art from various periods, that are not so completely tied to a historical moment yet always come clothed in the specificity of history that we can then analyse structurally, as we did with cinema.

KR: And those structural properties would be . . .?

GP: In the case of painting, for instance, colour and space. I think that's one of the things that have been identified and reformulated in a psychosemiotic approach of the last 20 or 30 years by people who are really trying to work out how to understand semiotic practices but not with old-fashioned formalism.[11] There is a critical difference between formalism and structuralism. We are using a structural understanding, which is what semiotics developed from. What is specific to a regime of representation, a system of signification, what makes it possible for these signs to produce meaning? We are not just interpreters, asking what meanings are produced. We address what makes it possible to produce any meaning at all, to have an effect, to create an affect. There is a relationship between some aspect of systematicity, and something of what it actually is resourced by, which is outside of the system. The practice of artistic creation: three words that are oddly conjoined – is both a movement towards the production of meaning and an inscription of a play beyond communicable meaning, that is evocative at other levels than the communicative.

So what does it touch on? What is it that the visual arts allows us to know about or feel about, within the social or within the personal, that is organized by a particular sort of system of visuality? That systematicity is a structural systematicity, but it will be subject to historical particularities. And in that sense, I now feel, for historical reasons, that there are things that can happen in the so-called visual arts which are of profound cultural importance. Far from being marginalized by the other technologies, like the more commercial technologies, or new technologies, or cinema, or any of the other sign systems which are so massive in our culture, the visual arts are important precisely because they are structurally, in a sense, the product of an individual embodied subject working within his or her moment.

KR: And the 'embodiment' of the individual is crucial?

GP: I think it's the singularity of the activity, not individuality which is the old 'cult of the great individual', but singularity, which is a kind of ethical singularity as well as a way in which that singularity is a particular configuration of the larger forces which work upon any one of us. So, in a sense, it's not to say here's the individual, and then there's culture, returning to the old myth of the artist as somehow outside of the culture who just presents his or her individuality. But the singularity of the particular articulation can deliver to us in this unique statement something which is productive of understanding, which provokes into the field of our knowledge something which hasn't been there before but is motivated by the pressures on this particular person in what I call their generation and geography, their historical and geopolitical particularity. And so there is a way in which, against the massification of information society and the false individualism of commodity culture – where we're all stimulated to want, but to want to be part of the same thing by buying into a culture of identity – artistic practice resumes an ethical/political/strategic role that it was necessary 30 years ago to challenge in favour of something that was then marginalized and disclaimed. This is a dialectic at best, and an irony at worst.

So it's not that I think art is great, or I've now decided that there's aesthetic value in advertising. I think we've learned that every sign system is immensely complex and interesting, and there are great moments and somewhat more prosaic moments in any of them.

I prefer the idea of art not being expressive but provocative. What does the art work allow to enter into our field of understanding via the emblematic act? A lot of people criticized the photographer Sally Mann[12] when she started doing the photographs of her daughters. One defence I heard, which was very compelling, ran as follows: Independent of whether we personally think she should or she shouldn't 'explore', expose, represent her children (regardless of the question: Are they or are they not pornographic?), the point is that, in their existence, these photographs provoke our culture to think about the borderline of sexuality and childhood, public images, authorship and cultural usage or abusage.

KR: **They pose certain questions, without necessarily answering them.**

GP: Questions that were not raised to this level of 'visibility' before. So it's not a matter of whether Sally Mann says 'I'm a great mother and I love them, and my kids didn't mind it', and all the rest of it. It's independent of that Romantic concept of the artist and her authenticating motivation. Rather the work in its singularity, as somebody's particular project, provokes us into a recognition of a problem, of an issue, around which we will then make decisions and from which certain other kinds of work will or will not come. And it marks in that space called the fine arts an issue that is a real one: the sexual abuse and pornographic exploitation of children.

Orlan[13] is a performance artist who is doing major surgical reconstructions of her physical identity. She is bringing across the frontiers of professional knowledge what's going on in reconstructive and cosmetic surgery, and staging it in the field

Image 5.3: Orlan, *Refiguration-Self-Hybridation No. 2*, Cibachrome, 100 x 150cm (1998). Technical aid from Pierre Zovilé.

of art. Staging it in the field of art causes a certain kind of attention to be paid to something which is, as it were, both happening and not known, or known privately, or has no standing as a problematic. Women do it or they don't. But by carnivalizing it, by turning it through the particular rhetoric and processes which we call art, Orlan puts bodily manipulation on a different stage. It both stages it differently and then demands a different kind of knowledge or conditional response to it. The artistic act works to make a practice the object of a critical cultural debate.

KR: **How conscious of the critical context of their work does someone have to be in order to produce something provocative? Sally Mann may feel a need to do that work for her own reasons, but this doesn't mean she's necessarily engaged with the debates about pornography and fine art. Earlier, you seemed to be implying that quite a high level of understanding of the debates, and the history of images, was necessary in order for people to then be able inventively to make their own images. I was wondering how you see the relationship between making (in that singular, provocative way) and critical understanding.**

GP: I think there's a very dialectical relationship. I can see a situation in the last ten or fifteen years, where art schools that were interested in critical theory have made it difficult for students to make art, because they have required such a degree of critical self-consciousness, that it is very difficult to be in the place where the art comes from. I think there is a balance to be struck.

The other thing I would stress, in terms of the concept of poetics of the visual arts, is a sense of creativity. I think one can go back to that concept now, which was in the past so romantically overloaded that it sank into mystical mud. But I would now use the term 'creativity' with an entirely different set of possibilities. We've cleared some space, reclaimed the productivity of art from connoisseurial mystification. Art has a rhetoric; it does need to be worked on in order for it to have the density and economy that an art work has *vis-à-vis* the complexity of material with which it's working.

So in answer to that question, I think you do have to have highly educated and astute artists, very much resourced in the potentialities of the medium and all related practices. Artists also need to have some critical relationship to their moment, to understand it. But that is not the same as having people who are predictably keyed into what is the off-the-peg idea of the moment. Art produces something that has not been produced before, which is creative in the sense that it is an inventive shifting of meanings in the collective space called culture, that comes out of something that is singular, located, motivated in a particular history. By using the concept of generations and geographies[14] rather than the usual string of race, class, gender and sexuality, I am attempting to situate the artist as producer in historical and political time and space, at the intersection of many histories.

KR: Can you say more about 'the place that art comes from'?

GP: Even in conceptual art, in the most deeply analytical and theoretical projects, we find a poetics. One looks at some of Mary Kelly's work.[15] Even at the highest point of its engagement with this tension between the fantasy of the mother and the discourses of medicine or science, there is a strong poetics in the sequencing, in the shapes of things on the walls, in the size and height of objects. I talked to Kelly about the way she makes formal decisions. She talked about playing for months with certain kind of metal-processing, until she got exactly the finish for the *Interim* piece, to do with the metal greeting cards which had formally to evoke the whole world of kitschy romantic stuff, without it being directly signalled by imitation. So she insisted on the immense importance for her of extremely formal decisions and poetic play with materials without which the work is not realized as an artistic practice.

And that's what I'm interested in. That's what I meant by 'the place that art comes from'. It's about judgements and things that are to do with the working of an 'aesthetic intelligence'. That is a term I'm prepared to use, a form of intelligence that can know what to do when making, which is different from some kind of notion of inspiration welling up and muses, and all the rest of it. Mary Kelly said when she got that sheen right, she just jumped up and down for joy, because that was 'it' –

Image 5.4: Mary Kelly, *Interim, Part II* (detail, *Conju*), silkscreen on galvanized steel, 5 of 20 units, 40×16×29cm each (1989). Collection, Vancouver Art Gallery.

a realization in form and finish of an effect necessary to a meaning that only came to exist when that exact effect was found. The metallic sheen is in excess of the project; the practice actually creates what the project yearns to find and in doing so, transforms the project so that there is more, at a different level, in the final art work.

And I think for most artists, it is the 'that's it' that matters. We art historians would then spend hours, years, saying, 'Oh, that's interesting, what is that "it", and which are the different elements of the "it"?' But not to a point where you can somehow reconstruct precisely the journey to the 'it'; otherwise why would there be art? Why would there be that form of human activity, if it didn't have a specificity in terms of what it could create in these processes and relationships?

KR: **Can you say something about judging art – as good or bad, successful or unsuccessful?**

GP: Those are two different things. Successful is the approximation between what you manage to do and what you hoped for. Good or bad brings us into the world of Brian Sewell.[16] I tend to think all of art is remarkable, and that which is not remarkable is usually interesting as well. As an art historian, I know from the work of women that so much is seen to be banal because we don't yet have the grounds for its intelligibility. And much of what I do when I lecture is try to create those enlarged contexts. I give these incredibly long lectures, and I never usually quite get to the end, because it takes so long to put in place what needs to be put in place for the thing itself to buzz. Sometimes it's for me to get to the place where it buzzes for me. Sometimes you need to try to get other people to the place where the buzz I got can be got, but where people can actually see and feel that this is just astonishing stuff.

KR: **So certain works are astonishing.**

GP: What's astonishing for me is probably massively overdetermined. What I'm hoping to do is to share what I'd call the covenant that I have with this particular work, to share it with other people. OK, there are things that aren't satisfactorily realized, or the whole project is trite, you know, and I don't value it very much. There are certain areas I'm just not interested in or I can't understand what all the fuss is about. But at the moment, certain people in the art world constitute the hierarchy of what is interesting and what isn't, what's good and what's bad. They're all trying, in a grand Ruskinian mode,[17] to legislate for us, morally, aesthetically, what's right and wrong.

KR: **You speak from your role as teacher and as writer, historian, theorist. You've also been involved in organizing exhibitions. Could you say something about your role as curator? How much does curation differ from the other things you do – perhaps in its collaborative nature, or in**

the kind of responses it elicits, or in the way it forces you to think and work with image and text?

GP: In fact, I have never been a curator of any major show. I have wanted to do exhibitions but there is a major demarcation dispute between art historians and curators. Exhibitions involve a lot of money and for the most part my ideas or selections have not found their sponsors in either the major museum world or in smaller events.

I did an intervention last year at the Clark Art Institute, in Williamstown, Massachusetts, which is relevant to this discussion. They own a number of paintings by a nineteenth-century Belgian artist, Alfred Stevens, who was important as a figure in the complex art world of Paris in the 1860s, although the decisions he made were not those that later proved important for the avant-garde. The paintings are part of the collection which includes many important Impressionists, but the Alfred Stevens are illegible in that context except as minor sidelines that embarrassingly witness 'taste' and its changeability. I offered to do a feminist reading of these works. The idea was to take each tiny painting and hang it on its own wall so that people would actually pay attention to the world each painting creates. Beside the painting was the standard information a visitor needs to begin to engage with the painting. Then I created what was called the art historian's laboratory on a side wall. This involved creating a large screen on which we placed a range of comparative pictures and a series of one-page notes, each dealing with another aspect of the visual or historical culture out of which this painting came and into which it intervened.

KR: **Was the idea to show the complexity of the act of 'reading' a painting, or to show how art historians work, or to give alternative interpretations to the usual ones?**

GP: I wanted to reveal how much work we need to do to allow any painting whose cultural frames we no longer inhabit to become a working entity. The curators and educators were horrified about the amount of text I proposed. The purpose was not to revalidate Stevens as a great painter unjustly forgotten, but to reopen his

part of the visual field of the 1860s in Paris, when many possibilities were explored in that unsettled moment of discontent and new experimentation that the phrase 'painter of modern life' inspired. I wanted to make visible to the visitor to the museum, how I 'read' the painting, using a range of other visual references, comparisons, differences, and tracked the consistencies, habits, desires of the artist within a cultural field that involved chemistry and costume, theatre and poetry, art history and marketing.

Image 5.5: Installation shot from 'Interventions: Griselda Pollock looks at Alfred Stevens', at the Sterling and Francine Clark Institute, Williamstown, MA (21 October 2001–8 April 2001).

The second project which I am working on at the moment is called *Towards the Virtual Feminist Museum*. It is not about a cyberspace or digital museum. It is politically virtual since it acknowledges the lack of financial resources for any practice of exhibition that does not conform to the marketable. I want to create the cultural linkages and encounters that are necessary to re-establish or even establish for the first time other ways of conjugating art practices and artists, especially by figures marginalized by dominant art histories, i.e. women. I need to curate imaginary exhibitions that will create the spaces of intelligibility so that what has been excluded or rendered uninteresting by the canon can become vivid and important.

KR: Is it important to use the exhibition format rather than, say, an article or a lecture?

GP: I have begun to use the exhibition as model of encounter and creative connectivity, making exhibitions via video formats that then themselves create the spaces of encounter and relational difference that I would like to produce in a real exhibition – but could not do even there. The constraints of size and lighting, media and conservation might well demand separations and not allow the kinds of movements between images and practices that I would like to foster. So the virtual feminist museum points up real political and ideological constraints on what is allowed to be circulated in privileged sites as visual culture. It also allows me, as a result of that exclusion, to create a new kind of imaginary museum, using video technology rather than digital imaging, to make the exhibition itself a creative intervention that can trace my thinking with art, as well as across its texts. I am inventing a space not merely of display but of critical intelligibility and argument.

I have made several videos of this order and am now working on another. All my lectures deploy this structure of the virtual feminist museum as a model for an exploration based on the idea of visual encounter. This is in contrast to the usual art history lecture in which art is reduced to illustrative material.

KR: **Do you see organizing an exhibition as a piece of research? Or does it put you almost in the role of an artist?**

GP: What I'm doing blurs the line between curation and academic research. The exhibition as 'encounter' is what interests me. I think it is a form of research *and* a form of art. Or rather there is an aesthetic consciousness at work in trying to find forms of presentation and contextualization that are sympathetic to the art works I am dealing with. That is radically different from academic work or curation that imposes a frame upon works and makes them the objects of knowledge and display.

The question is: How do we change the way we know and work with the visual arts? I am experimenting with a borderspace between traditionally separate zones: a borderspace that makes working with art more covenantal and creative.

Griselda Pollock, excerpts from interviews by Karen Raney,
1996–2001

Notes

1.   'Phallocentrism' is a term meaning the privileging of the phallus as the main marker of sexuality. The concept is central to the feminist critique of patriarchy. The French psychoanalyst Luce Irigary analysed the phallocentrism of Freud's theory, in *Speculum of the Other Woman* (1974; Ithaca, NY: Cornell University Press, 1985). Bracha Lichtenberg-Ettinger is an artist and theorist whose work has informed Pollock's analysis. See B. Lichtenberg-Ettinger, *The Matrixial Gaze* (Leeds: Feminist Arts and Histories Network, 1995).

2.   J. Berger, *Ways of Seeing*. Okwui Enwezor also refers to this quote from *Ways of Seeing*, which was a seminal work for the New Art Histories.

3.   R. Barthes, *Myth Today* (1956), repr. in Susan Sontag (ed.), *A Roland Barthes Reader* (London: Vintage, 1993).

4.   Julia Kristeva is a psychoanalyst and literary and cultural theorist. In her theory, the 'semiotic' is the raw material of meaning, based on the pre-verbal, chaotic drives and impulses of the very young child in its relation to the body of the mother. These drives are later harnessed and organized for social ends through the 'symbolic' – the rational world of language, laws and the father. Both semiotic and symbolic are necessary for psychic functioning and for the ordering of social institutions. The symbolic could not exist without the energy of the semiotic; the semiotic is only available through its representation by the symbolic. However, at moments of cultural upheaval, and in avant-garde art, the semiotic 'breaks through' to refresh and transform the social order. For a selection of Kristeva's writing, see Toril Moi (ed.), *The Kristeva Reader* (Oxford: Basil Blackwell, 1985).

5.   Kristeva wrote about the paintings of Giotto and Bellini in light of the above distinction. She argues that these works are disturbing because they show the semiotic disruption of the Symbolic (conventional representation systems). See Kristeva, 'Giotto's Joy' and 'Motherhood according to Giovanni Bellini', *Desire in Language* (Oxford: Basil Blackwell, 1980), Chapters 8 and 9.

6.   Along with the Imaginary and the Symbolic, the Real is the third element in Lacan's theory of psychic life. Though the account of the Real changed as Lacan's thinking developed, in general it refers to the idea that the world is only available to us in a mediated form, through visual, sensory or linguistic representation. The relationship between what is visible in an artwork and its (invisible) subject is similarly indirect. Any sign system, such as painting or writing, will struggle to create equivalents for, allude indirectly to, or conjure up its subject – hence Pollock's description of the invisible being 'folded into' the visible. See also W. J. T. Mitchell, Chapter 1, n. 5 (p. 65).

7.   In *Discipline and Punish: The Birth of the Prison* (London: Allen Lane, 1977), Michel Foucault wrote about the replacement of one form of social control with another. In the feudal, monarchical system, a few individuals were punished by example in order to display and uphold the sanctity of the law. The modern system which replaced this is one of constant, impersonal surveillance and regulation. In institutions such as barracks, prisons, hospitals and schools, each person internalizes the threat of being watched to the point where they police their own behaviour.

8.   The term 'visuality' refers to vision as something which is mediated by the beliefs, attitudes, practices, categories in place in a given culture at a given historical moment. Pollock is using 'visuality' here to refer to habits and skills of looking at representations, which have changed along with changes in image-making.

9.   L. Nead, *The Female Nude: Art, Obscenity and Sexuality* (London: Routledge, 1992).

10. Discourse analysis examines the phenomena – texts, images, theories, laws, the structure of institutions and so on – through which meaning is produced. Foucault studied the discourses of science in *The Archaeology of Knowledge* (London: Tavistock, 1972); medicine in *The Birth of the Clinic*, trans. Alan Sheridan (London: Tavistock, 1973); discipline in *Discipline and Punish*, and sexuality in *The History of Sexuality*, trans. R. Hurley (London: Penguin, 1985), Vols 1 and 2; Vol. 3 (New York: Pantheon, 1986). Pollock has examined the discourses of biography and narrative through which the artistic subject is produced in 'Artists, Mythologies and Media – Genius, Madness and Art History', *Screen*, 21,3 (1980): 57–96. In art practice (*Interim*, 1985) Mary Kelly explored the production of 'the feminine' through the discourses of medicine, fashion and romantic fiction.

11. 'Old-fashioned formalism' refers to the approach of proponents of early twentieth-century modernism such as Clive Bell and Roger Fry, and Clement Greenberg who carried formalist ideas forward into the 1950s. In 'The Aesthetic Hypothesis' (1914) Bell wrote: 'To appreciate a work of art we need bring with us nothing but a sense of form and colour and a knowledge of three-dimensional space' (repr. in C. Harrison and P. Wood (eds), *Art in Theory, 1900–1990* [Oxford and Cambridge, MA: Blackwell, 1992], p. 115). Formalism reified the formal qualities of an artwork – colour, shape, texture, composition, materials – and believed that meaning was conveyed to an educated viewer directly through these qualities. The 'new formalism' of the 1990s sought to look closely at the materiality and structure of works without losing sight of critical historical and social perspectives.

12. Sally Mann is an American photographer who has photographed her own children, clothed and naked.

13. Orlan is a French artist who has voluntarily undergone surgery to change her appearance. The operations have been staged as performances, with the artist a conscious participant. As well as the operations, her work consists of highly staged photographs of herself prior to, during and after the surgery, as well as digitally produced images of herself transformed in different ways. See Michelle Hirschhorn, 'Orlan: Artist in the Post-Human Age of Mechanical Reincarnation: Body as Ready (to be Re-) Made' in G. Pollock (ed.), *Generations and Geographies in the Visual Arts: Feminist Readings* (London: Routledge, 1996), pp. 110–34.

14. This concept is explored further in the introduction to Pollock, *Generations and Geographies*.

15. Mary Kelly is an American-born artist known for her feminist works *Post-Partum Document* (1973–78) and *Interim* (1985).

16. Brian Sewell is a British art critic known for his strong views against contemporary art.

17. See W. J. T. Mitchell, Chapter 1, n. 7 (p. 65) on Ruskin.

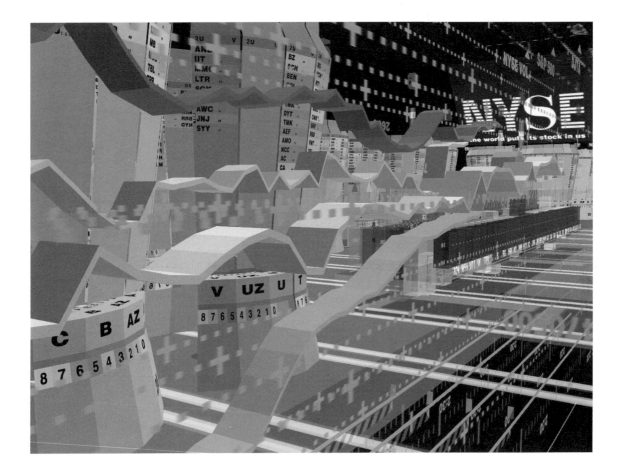

'Because of the work I'm doing, I'm a big believer in the physicality of the virtual. I try and understand what that means. Space is concretized in a certain way. I guess a definition of architecture is 'the place we believe we inhabit', where we are conscious of dwelling. So in physical space we translate that into walls, the manmade, the artifactual, shelter, plasticity and so on. We are beginning to develop languages and cognitive ways of dealing with virtual space in a similar way. We're beginning to comprehend what it means to inhabit a virtual reality.'

Hani Rashid

Previous:

Image 6.1: *New York Stock Exchange, 3DTF Virtual Reality Environment* (1997/2000) New York, New York. Architects: Hani Rashid with Lise Anne Couture, Philippe Barman, Sabine Muller, Jan Loeken, David Serero, Tobias Wallisser, Gemma Koppen, Suzanne Song, Takeshi Okada, Carlos Ballestri Remo Burkhard, Florian Baier, Florian Pfeifer. Programmers: SIAC, Brooklyn, New York RT-Set, Tel Aviv, Israel. Images courtesy of the New York Stock Exchange.

HR: I'm interested not in visual literacy but in 'spatial literacy'. By this I mean an education in various experiments with spatiality. That runs into things like conceptual art and installation art, and it can also overlap with painting and sculpture and performance art. In anything dealing with a 'spatial condition' there is a kind of a literacy that I'm interested in.

KR: **Do you mean being able to interpret space?**

HR: Yes, and out of that hopefully comes some kind of understanding, not necessarily of how to create space, but how to understand spatiality as a concern. That's a shift I've made in my teaching in architecture. I have always been interested in experimenting with notions of spatiality, what constitutes a spatial condition, what are the phenomena around spatial conditions. But when I began teaching I was preoccupied with describing space through analogistic means, usually by encouraging my students to describe space as something recognizable and thereby translating it to another spatial description or operation. Today I am more interested in spatial entities that have no precedent or analogy in the world, but are formed from new mechanisms for reading and comprehending space such as through the tools of digitization and augmentation.

KR: **Spatiality – as opposed to simply 'space', or location. Does spatiality have a specific definition?**

HR: The way I've interpreted it is it's a term that encompasses the entirety of a spatial condition, which can include events, it can include geometry, it can include information, it can include the temporal. The spatial concern is made up of all of these different facets. It's not just one or the other but an unpredictable combination of them. Historically we've tended to look at space in terms of each of these particularities. We talk about space as geometry, we talk about it as perspectival. I like the word spatiality because it encompasses all of these phenomena in one entity. It's an interesting way also of deciphering and defining what various people are doing in cultural enterprises like the visual arts, for example. You have installation artists today who don't fit into any one definition of a sculptor or a painter or a photographer or a film-maker; they're dealing with the very things that architects are interested in, and they sometimes transcend architecture because they bring a lot of these other entities into play – things which architecture historically has been concerned with but seems to have left by the roadside.

KR: You mean the combination of all modalities – time and space, visuals, sounds, text.

HR: We used to call it metaphysics, and in many ways that became a negative way of understanding architecture because it was interpreted as being too much about the intangible. We started looking for much more definitive mathematical methodologies. But you can't separate those things out of our daily inhabitation of space. So I'm interested in how we bring those things back into the discourse, how we re-evaluate what makes up an architectural space, or what I call a spatiality.

KR: Before starting a project you try to map the urban environment, by taking what you call snapshots of what it's like and what happens there.

HR: Urban environments are, I think, particularly interesting because they bring so many things into a concentrated form, into a plasticity that you can deal with. And there's a kind of resistance there because of the large number of factors that play into an urban spatial condition – more so than, say, in a landscape. Every condition has its spatial considerations, but the urban brings so many of them into a strange confluence or collision.

KR: So when you're designing for an urban environment you try to blend your design with the spatial condition as you have come to understand it.

HR: It's a double motive, I guess. On the one hand it's an attempt to read that spatial condition. The urban tends to give us a lot of potential readings. Then we try to make an artifact, an object, a field or whatever it might be, that re-instigates itself

Mercedes-Benz Museum

Image 6.2: *Mercedes-Benz Museum*
of the Automobile, Stuttgart,
Germany (2001). Architects: Hani
Rashid and Lise Anne Couture,
Ruth Berktold, Jose Salinas, Birgit
Schoenbrodt, John Cleater, Noboru
Ota, Hannah Yampolsky, Jonas
Brasse, Andreas Derkum, Cathrin
Loose, Markus Randler. Engineers:
Ove Arup, New York.

into that situation and becomes part of that situation, and ultimately dissolves into it. In architectural history, what separates me and some of my generation from preceding generations, is that our architecture is meant to dissolve into the urban fabric and become part of those collisions. As opposed to the older idea of creating a fetishized object, or making a heroic or noble attempt to remedy something, which is the utopian approach to urbanism.

KR: Is that why you do this extensive reading first, so you can create something which is so like its surroundings that it is almost invisible?

HR: Well, it's partially a reaction. I was educated in the late 1970s, early 1980s, went to graduate school in the mid 1980s. The postmodern ethic at that time was about being sensitive to the urban condition – or at least supposedly sensitive – and this sensitivity came as a result of understanding certain geometric patterns, certain aspects of ornaments, of grafting. There used to be a lot of talk about 'grafting' buildings into the city. You would pick up on the cornice lines that were there, or else you would import wholesale some aesthetic, Italian Renaissance or whatever, onto that space and that would somehow be OK, that would be a noble act on the part of the architect. I found this completely hypocritical and ridiculous. It was architects yet again inserting themselves and their ego into the urban fabric.

So our interest came out of trying to work in so many different contexts and figure out what in fact constitutes a sensitivity to those contexts. In the early years we found ourselves working on international competitions. We were working one week in Los Angeles, a few weeks later in Alexandria, Egypt, then we did a project in Seoul, Korea, and all the time we were asking ourselves: what is it that we're doing in these places? If we're not going to resort to a kind of pat regionalism, is

Image **6.3**: *Alexandria Library* (1989). Architects: Hani Rashid and Lise Anne Couture, John Cleater, David Currie, Scott Devere, Philip Teft, Diane Kramer, Ursula Kurz, Mark Wamble, Beth Weinstein.

there another way to approach urbanization? That's what got us involved in the notion of globalization and the global village, an extension of Marshall McLuhan's argument.[1] That's how I think we found ourselves side winding into technology, virtual reality, datascapes. We realized that it's not so much the formal and aesthetic concerns that are important, but these other considerations that make up what I'm calling a spatial condition.

KR: When you use a phrase like 'writing space' in relation to architecture, does that have a meaning beyond the idea of assessing and then working with the spatial condition of a place? Why use the word 'writing'?

HR: Well, in my graduate training at Cranbrook Academy,[2] Danny Libeskind was teaching us and he was obsessed with James Joyce and a number of other literary and philosophical luminaries that very much became part of our education. I think in that time I began to be intrigued by the fluidity, the agile ability to spatialize through writing. It became in a way a kind of anti-aesthetic. The idea that you could 'write' architecture became really compelling to me. In our experiments we started to look at different ways of writing architecture, within a field which is normally about making and fabricating and moulding.

KR: When you say 'write architecture', are you talking about the planning or the design process, where writing might help shape your ideas, or do you mean more directly, the idea say of writing with light?

HR: I mean writing not in the sense of actually writing words but more as a phenomenal event, more as a method of making. *Writing Space*, for example, that project in Germany in 1997, was literally an attempt to go into a gallery and to create architecture out of an act analogous to writing with pen and paper. In other words, when we construct thoughts and structures and sentences and stories with words, is there an analogous action in architecture? Is there a way to formulate a spatial condition through some kind of methodology that's akin to writing? That was an early experiment. It ended up being about digitizing paper, the folding of

paper into a kind of digital stuff, and then sending that into the space with video projection to kind of scroll, or notate, into the space something that we thought was inherent in the event of mutilating paper.

Image 6.4: *Writing Space,*
International Paper Biennale 1996,
Hösch Museum, Duren, Germany.
Architects: Hani Rashid and Lise
Anne Couture, Oliver Mack,
Henning Meyer, Oliver Neumann,
Takeshi Okada.

KR: How does this differ from a performance artist doing the same thing?

HR: It's not radically different. That's what I think we've realized in our work – the kinship which architecture shares with other creative disciplines like performance art, or photography in the case of *Optigraph*. In the *Optigraph* work we did an experiment in a dark room with rudimentary technologies, photographic topologies. The difference, and it's a subtle difference, is that ultimately our goal is not so much to create a spectacle, but rather to create an inhabitable environment. That's a fine line, but our ultimate goal is to fall on the side of the notion that somebody can inhabit this space that we write, not just watch it, and not just inhabit it momentarily. Inhabitation with a sense of permanence.

KR: Did the *Writing Space* experiment lead to anything which became an inhabitable space?

HR: Yes, they all do. We've got such a multifaceted practice that it's allowed us to do a lot of these experiments, to delve into these kind of worlds. We use the privilege, let's say, or the opportunity to make something quickly, not to have to deal with building codes and budgets and clients and economies and all the other things that make up the building side of architecture. Just to take the parameters that make up the conceptual side of architecture and push those to the limit, see where we can take them. So our installation works and our experimental pieces which have somehow found their way into the world of art (which is strange to us because we don't think of ourselves as artists, but we're in Documenta 11 [2002])[3] are the result of taking the opportunity to make these worlds into experiments. Then we design buildings and urban plans and interiors; we just did a furniture line, for example. I think in a not very self-conscious way what comes out of the experimental work finds its way into these projects.

The key is that we've opened up our parameters and our definition of what constitutes these kind of spatialities. When it comes time to tackle a real problem, something as functionally driven as furniture, for example, the experiments come into play somewhere in the process. But we're purposely not dogmatic or didactic about it. We try not to say, 'Okay, we did this in *Writing Space*. Let's make sure we do this in a house for somebody.' But it's interesting, because every time I put a lecture together I'm surprised by the affiliations I find between the projects, that I didn't realize were there. This is part of our methodology of not being too strict with the theory behind the projects, because I think ultimately that would kill them. That's my feeling at least, but maybe that is a vestige of the artist in me.

There has to be an open-ended search?

HR: Well, it's a belief that these conceptual things ultimately are compelling, and if they are compelling enough they will survive and find their way into the work. We just did a museum project in New York for a competition that we're in the running for, and it's remarkably similar to *Writing Space*. Many aspects of *Writing Space* have found their way into this museum project four years later. It was pointed out to me by the woman putting together our book in our office. The affiliations range from formal, let's say, to phenomenological. In formal terms, in *Writing Space* we had folded and crimped and mannered the space in terms of the virtual – the virtual unravelling of this paper – and in the museum project we did some similar kind of moves. But on the phenomenological side, *Writing Space* was all about the dissolution of the material, and our building is trying to do the same thing. The whole side is made up of pixellated panels in glass that try to dematerialize the facade. I think it's because we've seen it, we know it's possible and then it becomes part of our vocabulary, which is what's so compelling about continuously pushing ourselves to create the conceptual works.

KR: **When I interviewed the video artist Bill Viola, he talked about using notebooks and writing rather than sketchbooks as a way of developing his work. Apparently when he's working on a piece, he does very little preparatory work in a visual medium. He describes it as not wanting to be seduced too much by the visuals until the ideas are right. If he's got the conceptual structure solidly set up, then the visual 'leap' at the end will be right. Is this at all the way it works for you?**

HR: Yes, it's a similar procedure. It's funny you mention that because I was thinking about it the other day. You know there's this great myth in architecture about the architect and the sketchbook. Architects go to places, they sketch things, they have these Corbusian notions of travel and the notebook. I tried that when I was in school because I felt it was something you're supposed to do, but it isn't the world that we live in today. I carry around a digital video camera which I don't use as a

video camera. I use it to capture still frames. It's a weird thing. I should just shoot photographs probably, but I shoot six or eight frames, as a kind of visual notebook. That's become my sketchbook which I conceptualize projects in.

What I'm doing is trying to capture the abstract and fleeting spatial conditions that are around us. It's a bit like the work of Stan Brakhage. He is a purely conceptual film-maker, I guess, whom I am very intrigued and influenced by. One of his famous films is *Mothlight*, where he put the wings of a moth directly onto film, to create a series of effects of the shadow of a moth and its wings as pure motion.[4] I don't know if it's not to be seduced so much as it is to try to look at something from a point of view which is, by my definition, authentic. Maybe for Viola it's more authentic to structure a project than to visualize a project, which makes a lot of sense to me.

KR: Do you not use hand-drawing at all in your work?

HR: I used to say I didn't use it ever, but it's not true of course. Sooner or later we have to draw to communicate things to each other. Cranbrook Academy was a very craft-oriented curriculum, very much anti-technology: it was all about spending months on a drawing, creating everything with your hands and making models and so on. That was the training I came from, but when I started to get interested in computers, I went through a period when I said I'm not going to draw any more. I remember saying that in a conference once and, you know, it had architects up in

Image 6.5: Still from Stan Brakhage film, *Mothlight* (1963). Courtesy of the BFI Still Department.

arms, because of the supposed power of the sketch. Still, I'm not completely convinced about drawing by hand. I will draw to communicate to others, to do what in fact sketching was originally meant to be and always has been for the architect – a form of language and sharing of ideas between them. But the notion of the masterful sketch of the architect of a preliminary idea, and so on – I just don't buy it. My preliminary sketch, if there's anything masterful about it whatsoever, is maybe a six-second film-clip or a sound recording of something, the capturing of a moment which is in fact inspiration for the project.

KR: So again it's acknowledging the multi-modality of modern life. The idea that a sound could carry with it enough to actually generate a building.

HR: Absolutely.

KR: That is fascinating. You did say that making architecture is ultimately a poetic act.

HR: Did I?

KR: In *Architecture at the Interval*.[5] Do you believe that?

HR: I believed that then. I probably still believe that, yes, with the emphasis on the word 'act' as opposed to the word 'poetic'. The question for me always is: at what level do we define something as being architectural, or being of architecture? And that needs the word spatiality, because ultimately it's very hard to discuss. I mean, the apartment building you can see out that window is architecture, someone thinks it's architecture, someone spent time drawing that and modelling it, and yet it is not architecture in actuality, it's mere building.

KR: **Maybe that building came from a sound.**

HR [laughing]: I doubt it.

KR: **You're assuming that it didn't.**

HR: But see, that's the point. I think for the most part you can tell where buildings come from; it's really hard to know where architecture comes from. When you walk into a piece of architecture, or when you have an architectural experience, what is that? When does it happen? Sure, it happens when you walk into a beautiful baptistry on an Italian hillside. I think it happens underside of the Brooklyn Bridge. It happens in the canyons of Wall Street in New York. A Japanese magazine once asked me what my favourite architecture in New York is and I said 'six in the morning on a Sunday on a bike in Wall Street.' That's the ultimate architectural space. They said, 'Well, is there a building?' I said, 'No.' Again, it's this whole set of circumstances that create the thing we call architecture.

But the origin of that is ineffable, I guess, and that's why it can come from a sound, or from a piece of time or a notion, and maybe historically the sketch falls into this category. In the drawings of Mendehlson, Finsterlin, Taut or Corbusier, you have these beautiful gestural moves that were perhaps in their time a way to understand speed or motion or flight. But we have other ways to make those gestures now. So yes, I think that might be a definition of architecture – that the origin is unknown, or at the very least, uncertain.

KR: **When you say 'architecture' you're talking about a total experience rather than an object or a location.**

HR: The experience manifests into something physical, something plastic. Ronchamp[6] is architecture by everyone's standards but the point is nobody really knows why. People have their theories, but ultimately it's that poetic act that is an ineffable thing, that is of some uncertain origin. It sits in that very interesting oscillation between the irrational and the rational, between uncertainty and something we know.

KR: **Between the concrete and the abstract?**

HR: Very much so.

KR: **So a virtual space would not be architectural in that sense, because you said it has to be concrete, physical?**

HR: Because of the work I'm doing, I'm a big believer in the physicality of the virtual. I try to understand what that means. Space is concretized in a certain way. I guess a definition of architecture is 'the place we believe we inhabit', where we are conscious of dwelling. So in physical space we translate that into walls, the man-made, the artifactual, shelter, plasticity and so on. We are beginning to develop languages and cognitive ways of dealing with virtual space in a similar way. We're beginning to comprehend what it means to inhabit a virtual reality. I'm convinced we're only at the beginning of that. I watched our clients in the New York Stock Exchange project develop a whole set of mechanisms towards – and languages to deal with – what it means to inhabit the virtual stock exchange, in parallel with the real one. It's very real to them, the data is real, the numbers are real. It has a spatial map now that's equally real, to the point where they're privileging that over the physical space, which is really interesting. In their advertising, in their branding, in the way that they see their world, they're actually using the virtual environment as if it were what we would call a physical building.

KR: **So on into the future, is that your real interest – developing and understanding virtual space? Or are you wanting to explore it in tandem with more conventional physical spaces?**

HR: I'm really interested in hybrid spaces, hybrid reality.

KR: Like the Stock Exchange project?

HR: Well the Stock Exchange is a first attempt, a kind of embryonic move. We still have a physical space that's tied to the virtual by virtue of its data feeds and its displays. And we have a virtual space that's tied to the physical by virtue of its data inputs and financially generated topologies. But ultimately the goal would be to create a completely hybrid space where one is not relying on the other, but they both simultaneously exist. So that's the trajectory and I think it's kind of an asymptotic trajectory, it will never fully happen. If it did fully happen there would be nowhere else to go. But the trajectory towards it is really compelling.

We've also developed a museum for the Guggenheim which is for all intents and purposes a museum, albeit one made of pixels and polygons.[7] Once it starts being filled up with work and has people who visit it and people who work with it as a medium and as a spatiality, it becomes a very real place that exists in pixels as a museum venue on the Internet. And it may find itself one day as a physical museum as well, locating the virtual in the real. It may very well be the case one day that a great deal of art that was created inside the Internet, as part of the virtual realm, all made in pixels, at some point might need to achieve a physical status of sorts.

KR: In order to continue, or in order to evolve?

HR: I don't know. I think it's just part of the human condition. We need ultimately to meet and to talk. We could do this interview by email and by telephone and by teleconference, but you flew here, I flew here and we meet and we share ideas in a physical space. Then we go back into our virtual existences or our virtual relationship in terms of what we're both doing. That need to bring things into the physical will probably always be there.

KR: Because we've got bodies, we're not just brains, there has to be that physical touchstone.

HR: Yes. Although it's getting more and more interestingly elusive.

KR: **A lot of what you've written about digital technologies and the virtual world, and even the way cities are structured by surveillance and voyeurism, strikes me as rhapsodic in tone. I wondered whether there's any aspect of all this that you find . . .**

HR: Negative?

KR: **Yes, or even sinister, in the Foucauldian sense – technology used for social control.[8] And apart from that, isn't there a potentially disturbing side to the disembodiment or dislocation associated with new technologies? You seem to be working very very positively with those ideas, with the implications of technology, and wanting to replicate them in what you do.**

HR: You're not the first to tell me that. It's an interesting reflection on myself when I think about it. Maybe I need a psychoanalyst! It may very well be that because of a deep-seated fear I have of these things, my reaction is to swing the other way. In technology you have the notion of a Luddite,[9] who says that we have to retreat completely and not embrace these things because of all their negative possibilities. I've said, well let's take the other approach. What if we were to embrace it with a positive kind of interest?

Because architects are trained in a humanist tradition, we're constantly trying to work within that territory. So if we bring technology into our realm, really try to understand it and work with it, perhaps we can make something interesting and good out of it. If you pick up any architecture magazine you'll see right away that the main pages are advertising things like surveillance cameras, sensors that can detect breakdown in materials or movement of a building, windows that are there for solar panels, all these kind of functionless parameters around the technology being used in a building. And I've said, well, what if we were to take the technology and ascribe it to the human condition? What would happen if, rather than your windows turning dark and light by virtue of solar energy, they changed according to your temperament and your attitude in a space? What if you want to invigorate a space with a kind of spatial flux, let's say – these are things that we're interested in. The space literally throbs or literally oscillates according to your demands on it. So you can get into this area of the poetic, the metaphysical, the humanist. In many ways I think it's my way of taking the bull by the horns and taking up the challenge of these things, rather than shying away from them. It's imperative, and I think historically important, to recognize that architects have done this throughout the history of architecture.

KR: How have they?

HR: The Futurists embraced speed and movement. Marinetti and the architects around the Futurist movement looked at speed as something inevitably coming down the chute. I have always been intrigued by the famous story or image of Marinetti screaming with glee about driving 30 miles an hour in Picabia's Bugatti. That kind of embrace, through the minds and hands of the artist–architect, can be positively funnelled and used as a means of grappling with progress. It may be a naïve belief, and I accept that criticism, but I really feel it's something that we have to deal with. I think we're doing more of a disservice by not embracing these sorts of changes and shifts, be they technological or otherwise.

Take the 1920s and speed. Those who shied away from the inevitable changes that took place in the early part of the twentieth century – the onslaught of speed and technology and communication and all the things that came later – really were left behind, still steeped in a nineteenth-century romanticism about the ornament and the picturesque, which in the end was a world that became increasingly closed and dark. I think it is our responsibility to understand the potentially positive aspects, as well as to be attentive to the potentially negative possibilities.

KR: I suppose if you opt out you're leaving that territory to the more dehumanizing uses for technology.

HR: I'm talking about seemingly benign things like building sensors and electronic glass and computerized H-VAC systems. Those are things in the end are very benign, though some would say they're in actuality dehumanizing because they're not about the human condition at all, but rather about mechanization and automation: they're about the machine. Inevitably they could lead to something sinister. My question is, can all of those things be moved towards the human condition? Can we talk about what it is to be watched in some inspired and forward thinking way? It may be we can't, and then again it may be we can. We're doing a project now which is a showroom where we're using surveillance cameras everywhere. They're being used to celebrate the notion of people watching each other in a public space. If all goes well I think people will be fascinated. It's fascinating to see people watch each other in a space and be consciously under surveillance.

KR: **It's quite a radical thing that you're doing, in the sense of the notion of resistance, of subverting the negative or displacing it in part with something else.**

HR: Again, I think history has shown that when we come out of any of these potentially sinister things, we find a way to create something positive. It's our natural modality as human beings. The atomic bomb – horrendous as it was and continues to be – is the very same technology that generates heat and energy, and the same technology, through nuclear fission, will probably keep us all alive in the future. But science has to deal with that deep and disconcerting dilemma all the time, and perhaps because science doesn't come out of a humanist concern *per se*, necessarily, it tends to be very quantitative, that's where the potential is for the demonization of technology. It's interesting that Hollywood always picks up on things that are emerging and yet to be fully understood, such as datascapes and information environments. I'm fascinated by the fact that *The Matrix* [1999], for example, treats the world of data as an inevitable evil. It sells box office tickets and people inevitably believe that all these things are sinister and will somehow do us all in because the premises are there in vivid simulation and technicolor. But that's not necessarily the truth. These evils have as much potential for good as they do for bad, so you just have to figure out how to use them. And as an architect or spatialist I need to develop as compelling and vivid arguments for their deployment as Hollywood does on the other side.

When I first heard about the Internet I was fascinated, and ran a series of projects on it at Columbia University in 1994. Now I'm involved in a number of professionally related works at Asymptote. It's all because of an early interest and above all, curiosity. I remember films came out like *The Net* [1995], you know, and people were talking about what this is going to do to our world. And look at us today. We're moving into that stuff headlong – for better or worse.

KR: **There's a kind of inevitability in it.**

HR: Yes, and on whose shoulders does it rest to create interesting, compelling things out of these inevitable situations? The nay-sayers, in the Foucauldian sense, who are very powerful and discursive at a philosophical level, are equally important. I'm not in any way demeriting that approach, it's just that it really needs the other side. This reminds me a little bit of my own dilemma in graduate school, because the architects that preceded me, like Mr Koolhaus and Mr Libeskind[10] and a number of others, were hellbent on levelling architecture.

KR: **Levelling architecture – how do you mean? Democratizing it?**

HR: No, there were statements like 'Architecture is dead.'

KR: **Ah yes. Painting is dead. History is dead.**

HR: All those great clichés, which are attempts to sort of clear the field. Now, ironically, this group of architects are all quasi corporate. It's interesting. But I think my own generational dilemma was: 'They've done such a good job of that, what am I going to do?' I remember thinking this at twenty-five. OK, if the field has been cleared, the next radical procedure is to build on that field. So that's what I'm trying to do.

KR: **Can you say something about your event at the last Venice Architecture Biennale [2000]? You set up what you called a 'laboratory' for research into spatiality, that involved students as well as established architects. What was the idea behind this, and what came of it?**

HR: It was a fascinating opportunity. I can't think of a better way to have approached it than what we were prompted to do with Max Hollein's curatorial guidance – to get hold of state of the art technologies, bring them into a sort of laboratory, and showcase them to the world through the Biennale. And then also to showcase many of these theories about spatial-mapping, spatial-making, and architecture – how to envision an architecture that we're moving headlong into. My interrogation with the

Image 6.6: *Digitizing a Gymnast.* Installation at the American Pavilion at the Venice Biennale (2000). Hani Rashid with Columbia University GSAP.

students was based on three things. One was the dissolution of the body through technology. We did that by digitizing a gymnast, creating this structure that was a physical mapping of a gymnast's movement through the space of the American pavilion.

KR: You had a representation of the movement without the body.

HR: Right, the body had kind of disappeared, and all we were left with were the vertices of the movement and the structure that it created and the animations of those actions. Another project was about the physical merging of virtual and real space. We created a wire-frame structure that was meant to be perceived originally as a kind of virtual space on a very large screen, but then ultimately one would realize it's real, you could walk around inside this actual construction. It was tied to the Internet, so there was a data feed. That really was very much looking towards the hybridization of virtual and real space.

The third piece we built there was an interrogation of urbanisms. A new kind of urbanism that's emerging, that we should probably think about and start to discuss more seriously, is the airport. Our airports are becoming urban centres, not just peripheral pseudo-urbanisms. That project was kind of a hybrid of a fuselage and a gangway and all the tubular geometries or tubular architectures that you move around in in the space of an airport. And then all the data was driven into that, so it was a kind of datascape of an airport, what I dubiously was calling 'airport urbanism'. The idea was to perform these three architectures into the space.

KR: Perform them into the space?

HR: At least that's what I told the students that we have to do. Instead of building buildings or building models, we try to create something which in fact goes back to your question about performance art, or our close proximity to other forms of art. If you construct these projects as a kind of performance, there's the performance of the students working on the computers that inform the works; there's the performance of people inhabiting these projects and working with them; and then the works themselves continue to perform. But again with the caveat that they all ultimately are inhabitable and not just passive or even active observation mechanisms.

That was the move, and it was met with a lot of interest. We got a very, very positive feedback in the European press, we got a very negative feedback in the American press. I think it was telling as to the way that cultures embrace the potential for things to come out of experimentation, especially in architecture which has tended to be a very staid art form. The American pavilion before us housed things like the Disney buildings or the works of Philip Johnson, which met with better American response because they were commodities, pragmatic at some level, comprehensible, because we'd seen it before. Ours was truly a Dada pavilion.[11]

KR: **It was something in process, something that hadn't already been made. That's difficult to market.**

HR: But I'm convinced that down the line it will be much better understood.

KR: **Was it important that there were students involved in it?**

HR: Very.

KR: **And why is that?**

HR: Ultimately it was the research of the students. I might have instigated it but ultimately what you were looking at was student research, and students, if funnelled correctly, point to the future. The students today embrace Internet protocols and virtual reality and computer forms of research.

The nay-sayers say, 'Oh no, students don't use pencils any more, what are we doing? We're training these people to be special effects experts.' I hear it all the time. Well there's another approach to this. I just graduated my first class that have never touched a pencil. I asked my students, 'Have any of you ever drawn without a computer?' And they all said no. It was the first year that that had happened, and I didn't educate them for the four years prior to my meeting them in their graduating year. My premise always was that that's inevitable. I remember in 1995 saying that that's going to happen. Now it's happening, and our question is – what do we do with that facility, with that approach, and how is it going to create our new world? What will our worlds look like and become with these kind of procedures? It's imperative that we embrace these new tools, work with them, conceptualize them and then find ways in which to educate with them.

It doesn't make any sense for me now to take a student to Rome and have them draw the Tempietto. It makes a lot more sense for me to have a student fabricate some kind of a flash-based programme about the Tempietto, let's say, or a strange immediate piece of media. Just because (a) it interests them more, and (b) it's a way of trying to unravel what these tools are, how we use them, and how we ultimately translate those things into new spatialities.

KR: Is your teaching important to your practice?

HR: It has been extremely important. I started teaching when I was twenty-seven and up until when I was about thirty-five it was a passionate obsession of mine to teach. It still is, but I now have a real practice with all kinds of real problems, so unfortunately I don't have as much time as I used to. But, yes, it's the place where the laboratory is alive and well in the right school, and Columbia University, particularly in those years, was, thanks to Bernard Tschumi, a really vital place for experimentation. He allowed me to do things that probably most deans would have fired me for, or not allowed me to do, or not wanted me to do. Especially when it came to accreditation time when everyone was wanting to see how well we were teaching students to put stairs in buildings.

Hani Rashid, interviewed by Karen Raney,

May 2001

Notes

1. Marshall McLuhan and Bruce Powers, *The Global Village: Transformations in World Life and Media in the 21st Century* (New York and Oxford: Oxford University Press, 1989).

2. Hani Rashid received an MA in architecture from the Cranbrook Academy of Art, Michigan, USA.

3. Documenta is an international exhibition of contemporary art (see Okwui Enwezor, Chapter 3, n. 1 (p. 111)).

4. For a discussion of Brakhage and *Mothlight*, see P. Adams Sitney, *Visionary Film: The American Avant-garde*, 2nd edn (Oxford: Oxford University Press, 1979).

5. H. Rashid and L. A. Couture, *Asymptote: Architecture at the Interval* (New York: Rizzoli International, 1995).

6. Le Corbusier's Notre Dame de Haut (1950–54) is a pilgrimage chapel on a hilltop near Ronchamp, France, built with curving, biomorphic forms.

7. The Solomon R. Guggenheim Museum commissioned the firm Asymptote (Hani Rashid and Lise Anne Couture) to design the Guggenheim Virtual Museum, to house their digital and Internet-related art collections. The project exists solely on the Internet as a 'digitally' accessible museum that uses architecture and other spatial paradigms as its basis for design and experience.

8. M. Foucault, *Discipline and Punish*.

9. The Luddites were English artisans who rebelled against industrialization by destroying machinery (c. 1811–16). The term now is used to describe anyone afraid of, or opposed to, new technologies.

10. Rem Koolhaas is a Dutch architect who collaborates with the Canadian graphic designer Bruce Mau. See R. Koolhaas, *Mutations* (Bordeaux: Arc en reve centre d'architecture, 2001), and R. Koolhaas and B. Mau, *S, M, L, XL* (Office for Metropolitan Architecture, Cologne: Taschen, 1997).

   Daniel Libeskind is an architect known particularly for his designs for museums such as the Jewish Museum in Berlin, the Imperial War Museum in Manchester, and the spiral addition to the Victoria and Albert Museum, London.

11. Dada was an anarchistic, nihilistic movement. It was launched in Europe by writers and artists who had congregated in Zurich during the First World War, and in New York through the work of Marcel Duchamp and Francis Picabia. Dada is a nonsense word which stood for the mocking of all established values, including the value of art: 'The true Dadaist is against Dada.'

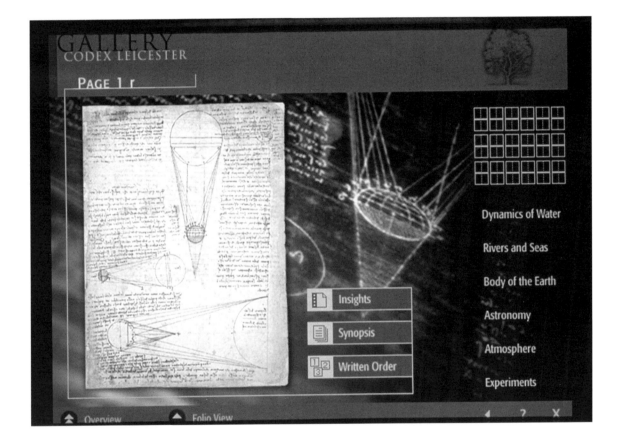

'This process of opening traditional [art historical] categories is very closely related to what is happening in the visual arts today. The nineteenth-century definition of fine art that we had is a very short and transitory phase in fact; most civilizations deal with a much more fluid category of visual communication. I think new technologies – video, film, TV, installation, and the new computer technologies – are resulting in an assault upon the traditional boundaries . . . If you look at what you'd see in a pop video now, you're dealing with a density of imagery, often a surreal, strange, inverted imagery, incredibly rapid intercutting of images that at one time would have been regarded as very extraordinary. Now that is accepted almost as a norm.'

Martin Kemp

MK: The most relevant part of my background, which probably accounts at least for some of the prejudices I have, is that I went to Cambridge and studied natural sciences, particularly zoology and botany. My background in natural sciences does still remain with me, not that I think that art history is a science, or writing about the arts is a science, but it's given me a sense of the status of different sorts of evidence, of how hypotheses operate, of how to respect different kinds of argument.

KR: **After science you went into art history.**

MK: I did the part two of the tripos at Cambridge, then I studied Renaissance art history at the Courtauld Institute with John Shearman. At that time, it didn't seem to me then that there was any obvious connection between the worlds of art and science at all. My sense was that I had moved out of one world into another. It was only subsequently that the strands have come back together in a major way. Now I see a much deeper liaison between bodies of scientific and technological visualization and how the visual arts proceed.

KR: **I'm interested to know what caused the change in your thinking, and could you say more about that liaison.**

MK: It isn't recent in terms of my own practice, inasmuch as some of the earliest research I did was on Leonardo da Vinci. But I assumed that the relationship between bodies of scientific knowledge and artistic knowledge, if you wish to call them that, came together in definable episodes, and particularly within the work of individuals who were using material from both these fields. What then developed was an interest in the visual cultures of art and science where there wasn't that obvious connection, where somebody wasn't deliberately practising in the two areas.

KR: **Do you mean you started seeing affinities between the kinds of visualization that the arts and sciences use in a particular period?**

MK: What I began to get a sense of was that there were both superficial and deeper relationships between the material. The superficial things are to do with what I would call the *look* of objects. You could say, well that obviously is a sixteenth-century bronze or that obviously is a nineteenth-century book. You can do that not just on the grounds of content but on the grounds of style. So an interest in streamlined forms might cut across all areas of design and popular culture and high culture.

But what that was manifesting was deeper structures of the way in which things are visualized, the kind of mental pictures which lay behind the creation of the objects. That deeper aspect of visualization began to be of interest, the constant dialogue between the styles of objects and the processes of mental modelling.

KR: **Could you give me an example?**

MK: An example would be, say, from a Renaissance book of anatomical illustrations, which has a certain way of portraying things to signal that it is the real thing that you are looking at. There are strategies in the illustrative techniques to make the thing look as if it is a surrogate for the real thing, using perspective, using tricks of naturalistic illustration, even showing the tools for dissection. They are attempting to give these things what I have called 'the mark of truth'. And, of course, the techniques which are used to indicate the reality of what is being portrayed – I'm using reality not in terms of naïve realism, but in terms of their claims of reality – the techniques are those which are pioneered by Brunelleschi, by Masaccio, by successive generations of artists.[1]

KR: **So this 'new history of the visual' you're interested in forging – is it trying to link the surface style with the deep conceptual structure in any given period?**

MK: In some ways it's almost a form of old-fashioned style history. At one time art history was very much concerned with style history, but within the domain predominantly of high art. Now I think that had a certain power and that that power has become lost. We've lost a sense as to how we can handle the look of things.

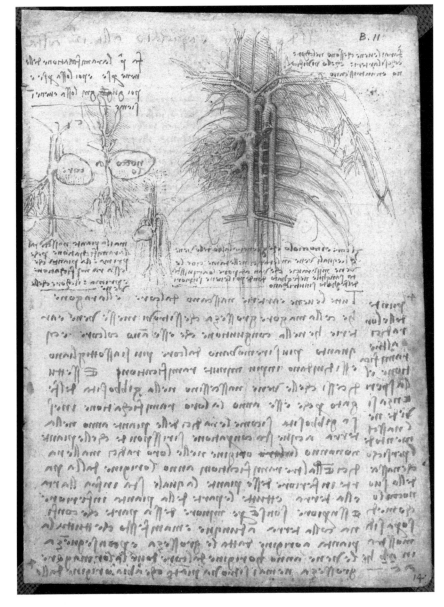

Image 7.2: Leonardo da Vinci, *The main arteries and veins of the thorax and studies of the heart and blood vessels compared with a plant sprouting from a seed* (c. 1501). The Royal Collection. © 2002, Her Majesty Queen Elizabeth II.

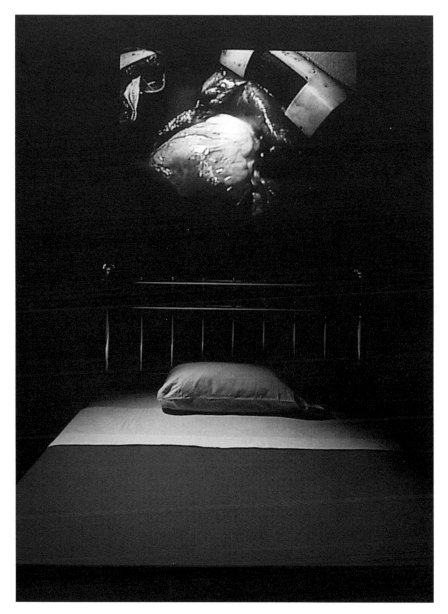

Image 7.3: Bill Viola, *Science of the Heart*, video/sound installation (1983). Collection: edition 1, Collection of the Frankel Family; edition 2, Milwaukee Art Museum; Gift of the Contemporary Art Society (photo: Kira Perov).

Style history isn't an end, it's a tool for asking questions about why things have a particular visual texture in a period, why unexpected conjunctions of style occur.

KR: You said that studying science and art history has given you a sense of the status of different kinds of evidence, and how to respect different kinds of evidence with regard to the hypothesis you're looking at. Could you say more about this in the light of the link between art and science that you want to talk about?

MK: That's an interesting and difficult question because if you're looking at the history of science, you're dealing with notions which are subject to some kind of independent testing. I don't believe that all knowledge is relative. I believe that the law of gravitation, for example, can be discovered as a consistent explanation. It's an expression, as we now know, of much bigger things in the physical world, but that within its own parameters it works, and you can get it right or wrong. So in that sense the history of science is an interesting and unusual kind of history, because it's not simply dealing with the history of human institutions in terms of power, the interaction of scientists, laboratory culture, or whatever. There is in the history of science a body of material which is testable, not for some absolute, eternal truth but for efficacy as repeatable experiments (in the broadest sense of that term) which provide sound predictions. This gives the history a rather different feel from other histories.[2]

Whereas, we are not inclined to say that you can test Michelangelo and say that that is somehow more true than Giotto, or more true than Picasso. That's not a primary test you operate. But in terms of how you construct the historical model, that is, how you model a discovery, say, of the Galilean laws of motion, and how you reconstruct the way that Poussin painted his pictures, the processes of historical argument and modelling are not essentially different. The ways in which you use and take evidence are not essentially different. All the time I'm concerned with how far, if you set up a hypothesis, there is some body of historical evidence which can bear upon it. It's easy to set up historical hypotheses which you can't prove are right or wrong.

KR: So what would be a hypothesis in relation to Poussin?

MK: A hypothesis in relation to Poussin would be that he was looking for a certain order in nature and in his systems of representation, articulated both in relation to the history of art and also in relation to greater ideals of what is the proper order in society, intellectually and morally. And that, I think, is potentially testable in relation to what he says about what he's doing, in relation to what contemporaries say he's doing – then in relation to contemporary bodies of artistic expression in written, visual and, in Poussin's case, musical media. We can gradually move out into more tenuously connected areas of cultural inference. But I think we should be clear what we're doing at each stage.

KR: Arthur Danto makes a distinction between what he calls 'surface' and 'deep' interpretations.[3] He says that the surface interpretation is the artist's account of what he or she is doing and that in relation to that interpretation, what the artist says is authoritative. What he calls a 'deep interpretation' comes from any other body of theory brought to bear on someone's work, say, psychoanalytic theories, political theories, whatever. The artist himself or herself might propose a deep interpretation of their own work. But they are not privileged in relation to the deep interpretations, as they are in relation to the surface interpretations. Is this similar to the different kinds of explanations and evidence you are talking about?

MK: I like that in some respects, but I don't accept it if the terms 'surface' and 'deep' carry values attached to them. I look for the interaction of all these layers of interpretation, without thinking that one is necessarily deeper in some qualitative sense. The role of artists' writings is something that has to be looked at very critically. We cannot take what Poussin says about painting without saying what vehicles he is doing it in – what is he using – is it a letter, is it a theoretical treatise? If it's a theoretical treatise, what are the possible parameters for a treatise that could be written at that time? Who was it written for, what job was it doing, how does it fit within institutions of art? So one of my concerns with the status of evidence is not just to recognize layers or levels, but to recognize different types of communication that do different jobs. Don't, say, take a Michelangelo poem and assume that it's art theory, as we might assume that Leonardo's *Treatise on Painting* is art theory.

KR: What bodies of theory would you want to bring to bear on visual things?

MK: I think there is no adequate body of theory we can bring to bear at the moment and that's one of the things which I'm interested in forging. The old notions of an empirical study of the visual, which spoke for itself, clearly don't hold up. Semiotic theory, structuralism, post-structuralism, Foucault, Derrida, deconstruction, and so on, have done a useful job in demonstrating that earlier approaches needed to be prised open. But I think that for all the good that the scrutiny of traditional methods has done, the adoption of these linguistically based strategies has actually been detrimental to art history and criticism. Terms like 'reading images' and 'visual literacy', which were used as reasonable kinds of analogues, now play so much into a certain kind of theory – which simply sees the visual as subsidiary to a series of linguistic categories, objects as subsidiary to words, and the whole act of seeing as entirely articulated through verbal categories – that I am no longer prepared to use those terms because they stand no chance of getting towards the irreducibly visual nature of visual things. If there wasn't something distinctive about visual communication people wouldn't need to do it.

I would look much more to areas like psychology of perception, cognitive science, and to look at images which lie outside the normal range of visual history, because you can tackle those much more freshly. You don't come encumbered with this enormous burden of existing interpretation.

KR: I'm thinking about the reasons for the rise of linguistic terms for dealing with art. Feminist theory arguing that visual images are better

seen as a kind of cultural 'writing', than as something mainly to do with perception and optics. A criticism of a perceptual psychology approach to art would be that it downplays the social and implies that looking at things takes place in the privacy of one's sensorium, rather than as a social act.[4] How would you answer that?

MK: There are a number of things to say. One is that I am not proposing the perceptual model of art as *the* model of art. By talking about something that is irreducibly visual, I am not thinking of art as a perceptual model of the seen world in an illusionistic sense, though within the Western tradition, and later within other traditions, that is a very powerful part of it. What I'm talking about is that the visual image works in relation to the whole range of cognitive, imaginative and social processes in a different way from the written word.

The relationship of the visual image to the written word – and this is the second point – is incredibly fluid. On occasions it can clearly be used virtually as a form of grammar and there will be occasions where that is a very appropriate model, although I think if the visual thing is doing a visual job, it is never a complete model. There are other times where the interplay, say, between a literary subject and the visual work is very symbiotic and is necessary, without the picture at the end of the day simply being a kind of text. And there are other cases where it is almost impossible to get a handle on it in terms of words.

Now I don't myself see the visual–verbal question as a feminist or non-feminist issue, and I don't see it as necessarily being vulnerable from any sociological standpoint. Because you can say, for instance, that one picture of a tree has more complex resemblances to a tree than another one, it doesn't mean to say that one is 'better' than the other, and it doesn't mean to say that the one with more points of resemblance is somehow inevitable. You only will get those many points of resemblance when certain demands are made upon images. I think where I differ in emphasis from Gombrich, who is my mentor in such matters, is that he tends to see this almost as a gravitational force, or is generally seen as saying this.[5] He doesn't really mean it in that inevitable, deterministic way, but that's how it tends to be read. Now I can see it as non-arbitrary, as does Gombrich, but entirely conditioned by functions of visual images and the demands made upon them. So you can say at certain points the perceptual model is itself in a very complex interaction with the social demands upon art, whether they're gender-based, whether they're power-based or whether they're thought of in a more orthodox way in relation to patronage. So I think the two issues need to be disentangled. The relationship of Western naturalism to the perceptual model needs to be looked at in its own right and it needs to be scrutinized in relation to the social and intellectual imperatives. But simply to package them together and say that the visual model surrenders before sociological, feminist, semiotic or the varieties of postmodern analyses is mistaken.

KR: **So if art history has broadened out into a 'history of the visual' or perhaps 'visual culture', let me ask you this: is there any reason to keep the category of art? Or can it be put aside now?**

MK: No, I think it's very important, and there is a history of art which is about the history of the concept of 'art'. Our concept of 'art' has been generated over a period of time, from the Renaissance onwards, but in terms of the autonomy of art as an activity in relation to aesthetics, it really is a late eighteenth-century idea originating with Baumgarten.[6] The definition of aesthetics as a kind of science, a philosophical system on its own account, evolved gradually through Romanticism and into Modernism, in conjunction with the institutions of 'art' and the Modernist notion of the 'artist'. It's a history that needs scrutinizing, so I'm not saying that 'art' is not a valid category. Indeed it provides a framework within which people look at things. But it's historical, it's very specific to a certain period of time, and I think it's undergoing a radical redefinition. The way the institutions of art are working at the moment is increasingly elastic, with a concept that still has to call the works 'art' but which is no longer really helpful as a defining category.

KR: **What distinctions would you want to keep between visual products?**

MK: You can define objects in different ways. My argument about the visual object is that it is incredibly fluid. That almost immediately it's been made it can be seen and can take its place in multiple taxonomies. A plate, for instance, made at the time of the Festival of Britain, can obviously be regarded as a utilitarian object; it can be regarded equally as speaking of a certain ideal of design. It can also be read in terms of certain economics of production and of concepts of 'British' design in broader political fields. It can be put in a history of the evolution and design of plates. It could be put in a history of eating styles. It could be put within the context of a history of design, and so on. The object itself assumes a different look according to what taxonomy you use. I think that is why the visual has a particular and remarkable fluidity, and why I'm interested in talking now about a history of the visual which doesn't get trapped by the definition of fine or applied arts, or scientific instruments, or whatever.

I accept that these are useful categories and they designate something real. But if we don't start by saying that there is a single or primary relevant taxonomical category, visually interesting things start happening.

I think as a historian that this process of opening traditional categories is very closely related to what is happening in the visual arts today. The nineteenth-century definition of fine art that we had is a very short and transitory phase in fact; most civilizations deal with a much more fluid category of visual communication. I think new technologies — video, film, TV, installation, and the new computer technologies — are resulting in an assault upon the traditional boundaries.

KR: **Can you say more about that? How do you see new ways of making images in relation to the changes in art practice and the definition of art?**

MK: I think there's something remarkable happening. I'm resisting straight causal explanations and I'd rather say it's a conjunction of a series of factors which we're probably too close to tease out adequately in a historical sense. If you look at what you'd see in a pop video now, you're dealing with a density of imagery, often a surreal, strange, inverted imagery, incredibly rapid intercutting of images that at one time would have been regarded as very extraordinary. Now that is accepted almost as a norm.

KR: **You've written that the kind of manual skill used in Renaissance and Baroque prints presupposed an audience that was skilled in viewing in a certain way. Maybe today different sorts of viewing skills are emerging along with different sorts of images.**

MK: I think that is undoubtedly true, and I think there is a generational aspect in this as well. The generation of children who've been brought up with computer games, with pop videos, with the ability to zap across 40 television channels, exhibit different visual habits. The ability to tolerate and use a plethora of rapid, often inarticulate and inchoate images, is very different from what an older generation would be able to do readily. I suppose this could be called a new 'skill' in viewing, but it might better be described as a 'habit'.

KR: **What's your view of the 'non-linearity' and 'interactivity' that's talked about in relation to digital media?**

MK: I think, myself, the non-linearity is overplayed. There's a lot of non-linearity in the design, say, of a CD-ROM, which I've helped devise on the codex by Leonardo da Vinci,[7] which is owned by Bill Gates, but the kind of deeper mental habits by which people join up information in different contexts might not be quite so different after all. I think the mental processes which go on have always been rather untidy and non-linear. They're articulated in a linear way during a later stage, in the course of verbalization and exposition, and the vehicles for linear exposition have varied enormously across cultures.

KR: **Maybe there's a distinction between what the medium itself permits you to do or not do – interact with it or move around in certain pathways – and how you internally process it.**

MK: Yes. I think there is an argument for saying that the new media are working with things that the brain has always done, but they're playing to a particular kind of potential skill, much as we might say a perspective picture in the Renaissance did not invent the skill to see three dimensions. We didn't go around bumping into chairs before Brunelleschi's time. Perspectival space wasn't an articulated thing: one didn't think 'I'm seeing this table and chair in perspective.' A kind of picture was then invented to tweak some of our mental proclivities. It was only invented to tweak those proclivities when it became valid for a whole series of reasons to make a picture which seemed to have illusory space in it. It was a culture-based thing. It was not inevitable. If I could make a historical analogy, what I could say now is that the new media are tweaking different proclivities in an analogous way, proclivities we've always had, but they're being newly articulated in a particular kind of a way. So I would see certain processes of conception and visualization as highlighted and extended, but I wouldn't see them as radically new at the deepest cognitive level.

KR: **What about the relationship between the producer and the receiver of images? One of the things about digital technology is that a representation is provisional, it's there to be changed. This seems to me to change the idea of what the product is. Is the art form the software program, is it what comes out of the printer, is it any state of the image after a viewer's interaction with it?**

MK: There are things produced, like CD-ROMs, which have a certain level of interactivity. But at the moment it doesn't seem that the conceptual shift is made where the spectator expects to have more than a small role in the shaping of the thing. I think most people are set in the idea that an artist produces something which they look at. In theory I suppose the interactive program could realize Joseph Beuys' utopian ideal that every person is their own artist.[8] But the conception of the producer and the spectator still seems to be pretty conservative, and it may be that's where we're stuck.

Potentially, if the program is sufficiently fluid and inviting, it could take the spectator through procedures which the artist envisages as being open, but wouldn't determine the results. That would be very attractive in some ways, but it does require this conceptual shift and it would require the artist to make a field for the spectator to work in. To be very generous in a way.

KR: Giving over power of representation. Traditionally you've got that control over what you're representing.

MK: Absolutely. And I think one of the notions of the artist, which is very difficult to get away from, is someone who reshapes our perceptions, not by dictatorial acts but by a system of invitation. But if that invitation isn't cast within certain very clear parameters then they are surrendering power, and surrendering their ability to do that. So it's a subversive and dangerous business.

KR: I wonder if a computer is not just another medium but that it alters the very idea of 'medium'. Let me ask you this: what is a medium?

MK: My reaction to the question 'What is a medium?' is that there are different styles of taxonomy that you can apply to it. One is the obvious one, which is material-related. That is to say, you talk about paintings, subsection tempera painting, or oil painting, or acrylic painting. You talk about sculpture, subsection bronze and so on.

Intersecting with that, and probably inseparable from it, is what I would call the conceptual and institutional definition of media, which would involve such things as art colleges having departments of fine art. The fine arts are defined partly in terms of media. So you've got materials which provide the obvious classification, but in a given society the media are defined by aesthetic, institutional and social factors. How the taxonomy of materials relates to that is actually, I think, a rather complicated business.

KR: How do you view the contemporary approach where artists move from one medium to another to explore a set of ideas or propositions?

MK: There are various things to say about that. First of all, painting and sculpture are not going to go away, they're still going to be recognizable as part of the practice. But many artists today I would describe as 'stagers of visual events'. This is very much in the context of the visual arts becoming one of the media, in a way, like television, like film, like theatre. It's much more analogous to that.

Where it becomes problematic in my view is if somebody is simply cannibalizing a whole series of different ways of doing things and is not very good at doing them, then I think you end up with something which lacks skill, wonder and quality. And I still believe in quality in that sense. I don't mean in terms of some abstract aesthetic quality, but just doing something extremely well, at a professional level. If you make videos then you should know exactly the parameters of the medium, and a video shouldn't look amateurish because you're an incompetent video-maker. It should look amateurish because you can do it professionally and you're deliberately doing that to achieve an effect. Very often there is no overt control over the medium, so it can be made to do something amazing. I think that's where the problem comes, not in whether we can't describe it in terms of some kind of taxonomy.

KR: I suppose it's a question of working within a tradition, however you want to define it, working with its powers and limitations.

MK: We have to accept that visual art practice now is linked into art criticism, colour supplements, television, the cult of the artist, the cult of the extreme, the bizarre, the surprising. An artist as a 'stager of visual events' works quite decently as a concept, because it acknowledges the media framework within which this activity takes place.

KR: Is it that new media and traditions are emerging and we're not sufficiently familiar with them to be able to judge them?

MK: As soon as you make a video or you saw a cow in half,[9] you are operating with the parameters of something which has certain inherent qualities to it. It may be we don't have a way of describing that yet.

One of the great virtues of the traditional media, with something like a sonnet, with something like a piece of blues, with a black-and-white drawing, is that in spite of its apparent limitations it's a container within which you can do things. And since people know the container, they can get a sense as to whether a given work is pushing the boundaries, whether it's operating narrowly within them, the kind of shape it makes in relation to the frame which it's working with. And that's why I think painting, the novel, the symphony might mutate, but they won't go away.

One of the difficulties of going in for a medium which hasn't got that tradition, is that that frame, which is an immensely creative thing to have to work within and against, isn't there. I think that's where one of the discomforts comes. If you're dealing with video then there *is* a frame, it's just that we don't quite know what it is at the moment.

KR: It's still developing. Maybe what's not there yet is a sense of shared, acknowledged, or somehow agreed-upon limitations.

MK: Yes. I think this probably happened in the early period of abstraction, which still, after all, gives some people difficulties. The nature of the container which gives shape to the activity and to people's judgements on it simply isn't recognized. It's an interesting question.

KR: Artists are working in so many different ways now, with many different 'containers'.

MK: I've written about James Hugonin,[10] who does these absolutely immaculate pictures. That's an extraordinary kind of monastic business. Each painting takes ages, and it's done with an enormous meticulousness and a level of manual and visual skill and control which is just awesome. But I wouldn't lay that down as a requirement for all artists. I've also written about Richard Wentworth, who sticks light bulbs together.

If you look at some of the impossible objects which Wentworth makes, like his buckets which are fused together, they're just beautifully, amazingly done. They look like obvious objects, but you start looking at them and they are very extraordinary visual things. Even when he puts a whole lot of sweet-wrappers in a dictionary, it's done quickly rather like a sketch in a sense, it probably doesn't take all that long slotting those things in. But somehow or other you feel that there's ages of contemplation about words, meanings, the relationship of a dictionary to labels on the sweet-wrappers. You feel there's a 'bottom' there which

Image 7.4: Richard Wentworth, *Tract (from Boost to Wham)*, (1993), book with paper and plastics, dimensions 8×10×24cm. Courtesy of Lisson Gallery London and the artist.

provides a kind of visual skill. I think an object, even a quickly and a relatively casually made object which hasn't required enormous overt manual dexterity or discipline, can none the less speak of the kind of quality of having got there by a long route, as it were.

KR: And the long route will be embedded in, recognizable in, what is made.

MK: Yes. And probably embedded in the totality of the artist's work. I think you can't necessarily isolate each one. One characteristic now of lots of artists' works is that they have to be viewed in the context of the whole of their works. This is one of the factors in being an 'artist' and having catalogues of works, and retrospectives and all these things, rather than making altarpieces that sit in a church. Lots of works now are made on the assumption that you do know the internal commentary and the artist's own statements about his or her work. That's a shift in which the industry in publicizing and writing about art has somewhat altered the practice. A work now can be a commentary on a greater whole which the viewer is implicitly meant to have some knowledge of. An altarpiece certainly isn't like that. So all these things shift, you can't go back to 'innocent' days.

KR: Recently you've become involved in organizing exhibitions. What led you to want to do this?

MK: For me, the practice of art history, or visual history, which I now think of myself as being in, has always been one of juxtapositions. The way that images relate to each other is absolutely at the heart of what I do. And the act of exhibiting, putting things together, is a wonderful way of giving the objects a particular eloquence. Not that there's a single message to get out of them, but it's a way of making them speak.

KR: Is organizing an exhibition a form of research for you?

MK: Organizing an exhibition has two elements of research, one of which is the orthodox one. That is to say, the business of finding material, finding out about it, asking all the normal questions – what is this and how can we understand it?

The other element of research is slightly more nebulous and more intuitive. That is going perhaps across periods, or whichever taxonomies you're working with, and getting a sense of which things might belong together that aren't often seen together. Doing an exhibition of Raphael drawings is great, but my buzz comes from putting a Raphael drawing next to something it wouldn't normally be seen with. It's that element of visual surprise in relation to the way you can group something. It may be chronological, it may be geographical, it may be by type of thing. I'd be perfectly prepared to put a Raphael drawing in an exhibition beside an image from twentieth-century science, if it seems to be resonant in some way.[11]

KR: **Is the starting point of an exhibition this act of putting images beside one another? Does the conceptual structure come from the visual intuitions that you've made, and the surprises that you find?**

MK: Exhibitions come up through a whole series of routes. However the concept comes about, whether it's a commission, whether it's our idea, the fundamental move is rather like organizing a lecture. Before I write the lecture, or even start seriously to think about it, I get all the visual material and move it around to see what it looks like.

KR: **Do you ever see yourself as taking on something of the role of an artist or a film-maker? In the sense that you're assembling images or objects and creating a framework for looking at them.**

MK: I would say, if you wanted an analogy, it is more that of a film director, or maybe a director of a stage play, where you've got some content and you have to decide how to present it and organize it. And you're doing that with a team.

KR: **Is the collaborative nature of curation what distinguishes it from the other kinds of research that you do?**

MK: I've always been interested in collaborative ventures, and to someone who retains at least some distant memory of science, I like the sense that research is not a purely individual activity. The old idea of humanities research, which still is very prevalent in Oxford, is the lone scholar whose life's work is in publishing this personal quest, this personal obsession. I've always enjoyed working with other people for two reasons. One is that you share the excitement. In collaboration there's a human element which I enjoy.

The other point is that if you're working across disciplines, then it is an enormous help if you can bring in people with different skills and different perspectives. Again, the model is somewhat a science one. If you're working, say, in molecular biology, you might well have biophysicists, you would have people who are coming at it through natural sciences, you may have people who come in with a more mathematical background. That sort of team of people with different perspectives is often how the best science research gets done, and I'm not sure why humanities research should be essentially different from that.

KR: **An exhibition brings into the public sphere the complex relationship between the people who are setting it up, the artists, the objects and art works that are shown, the viewing public and the institution that it's in. How do you see your relationship to the works of art and the artists? For instance, 'Spectacular Bodies' at the Hayward Gallery (London, 2000) showed the work of eight contemporary artists.**

MK: Well, we [Marina Wallace and myself] have a particular way of working with artists in the context of exhibitions, which is not to be drawn up, necessarily, as exemplary, but it's how we like to do it. We work with what I call 'researching artists' – artists who are interested in sustained investigation in relation to what they produce. It's not necessarily academic research, though it may impinge upon that. But it's people who are interested in relating to bands of imagery, historical and contemporary, and who do a lot of cannibalizing of images, drawing upon a wide range of visual culture. All artists do this to some extent but some do it more consciously and in a more sustained and organized way than others.

The idea is to engage the artists with the kinds of visual environments they want to work with. So, in 'Spectacular Bodies' we got some of the artists into collections of historical material; we got them in contact with scientists, anatomists and so on. They were an active part of the curating of the show. We got grants for four of the artists to go round collections – for instance to the Padua Anatomy Theatre. So there is this continual dialogue.[12] Now, some of the people writing up that exhibition, said we had simply 'dropped' the artists into the exhibition. If this was the perception, it was our fault. But in fact five of the artists had been involved in the curation, the research, even the selection of objects.

KR: And in deciding where their work would go within the exhibition?

MK: That was all discussed with Paul Williams, the designer. The artists staked out territories, as it were, in relation to the kind of work they were doing. We walked round with the artist Katharine Dowson, for instance, and together we came up with the idea of activating the very neutral staircase at the back. One of the problems of the Hayward Gallery is that people go into these concrete stairwells and suddenly they're in an inert area and they simply slog upstairs to get to the rest of the exhibition. So we thought, well, let's activate that space.

KR: You turned the staircase into the spine of the building.

MK: Absolutely. You proceeded from body to head. And Beth B wanted this enclosed, low-ceilinged area for her work on hysteria – to get that kind of claustrophobia. Some of the placing was more conventional. We had an existing Bill Viola piece, which we simply found space for, and for Tony Oursler's pieces it was a fairly straightforward matter of 'we'll put this one here and that one there'. But that isn't the ideal situation to my mind. The ideal situation is that the artist is involved in the whole intellectual exercise, the plastic exercise of manipulating the space and the spectator's movement through it.

KR: **Does that mean there has to be a consensus on what the exhibition is trying to do?**

MK: No, inasmuch as one of the roles, I think, of contemporary artists, is to provide a particular sort of visual commentary, an angle of looking at things. One of the things I was concerned with in the exhibition, from a historian's point of view, was not to push a historical thesis, whether it's a feminist, a deconstructionist thesis, or a thesis about body and culture. Whereas an artist like Beth B, who is a strong feminist artist can come in and she can do it in a much more complex, multilayered, way. A good artist doesn't produce a single-line polemic. I love the way that you can get this suggestive, complex layering, having the huge Charcot picture of Blanche Whittman, with Beth's rather complex commentary on the question of how insane women are viewed, the question of pre-Freudian female psychology.[13] I thought this was more interesting than us ladling on points about Charcot and hysteria. A historian could study that in a multilayered way by writing a book, but this wasn't a book, it was an exhibition.

KR: **Are there cases where things can seem to have a visual resonance and yet they derive from completely different motivations and periods? Is there a danger of making visual connections which don't stand up to deeper scrutiny, or which smooth out important distinctions?**

MK: Absolutely. One of the dangers in any historical enterprise is producing what I would call a 'pseudo-insight'. That's to say you can produce something, maybe a text in relation to an image, maybe two images in relation to each other, which seems to produce a very creative act of looking but, in fact, has nothing to do with what is inherently there and how those images were ever thought or made to work. Pseudo-insights can be exciting. If you let an artist loose in a museum, you might find that they put two things beside each other and it produces an extraordinary effect. But, for me, as a historian, I would always ask, 'is there some foundation to this?' So the intuition is an informed intuition, it's not a completely open field, you can't just put things together arbitrarily. I think that's where I would differ from an artist, who hasn't got that responsibility. I hope I would work with a constraint which is a responsibility to the integrity of the material in its historical context.

KR: Did the response to the exhibition change the way you saw the endeavour? It's a more public response than what you'd get from writing a book or publishing a piece of research. I assume that there's a wider audience.

MK: I love exhibitions which engage audiences beyond the conventional art audience. I think the least interesting reactions to the exhibition came from the art critics, because they had ideas about exhibitions of the body, and although it got very lively reviews, a lot of it was pretty predictable. The most interesting reactions came partly through the education programme. We had people like Jonathan Miller and Steve Gould and Tony Damasio – neurologists, physiologists, doctors, historians, cultural figures more broadly. That is the area of reaction which I most enjoy. It's partly based on the conviction that art is too important to be left to the art world. Speaking as an historian, the visual imagery which we classify as art was once communicating across a much wider range of people than just those who claim to be interested in art.

KR: What about for yourself, what did you find out from putting on the exhibition? What surprised you?

MK: There were relatively focused technical discoveries, where something you borrow turns out to have some surprises. For instance, two of the wax standing figures that came from the Science Museum proved to be in exactly the same pose as an Ercole Lelli figure in Bologna.

But I think the overall sense I got was that anatomy was even more a performative science than I'd anticipated. One knew intellectually that public dissection was an act of theatre, an act of ritual, a drama. But once you'd got all these things together you realized that the drama had very little to do with what we now think of as medicine in the technical sense. It was about the whole intellectual, psychological, social setting of medicine. So, my sense of anatomy as a performing art became enormously enhanced. And seeing all these things – paintings, objects or whatever – all in a kind of three-dimensional discourse, was just extraordinary.

KR: **Without enacting it yourself through the exhibition, that wouldn't have become apparent to you.**

MK: No. For instance, having the Houdon *écorché* from Paris standing high above the room with the Hunter anatomies,[14] and getting some of the small-scale bronze *écorchés* together, seeing them almost as a kind of collective tableau of parading the body. You see how all those muscle-men lift up their arms and move their legs and flex their muscles. It's a kind of wonderful parade. You get a real sense of a theatrical drive collectively behind them, a kind of collective competition going on between these amazing gesticulating *écorchés*.

KR: **You talked about choosing artists who had done sustained research, in psychology, biology, medicine. Does this suggest that the boundaries between art research and scientific research are somewhat permeable at the moment? And is the boundary permeable in the other direction?**

MK: It can be permeable the other way. I think it's less customary and we're only beginning to learn how to get it under way. The exhibition, called 'Head On', which is opening the new Wellcome Temporary Exhibitions Gallery in the Science Museum, is about the human brain. Marina Wallace, who is the main guest curator of that show, has paired together artists who have an interest in issues of how the brain functions with psychologists, with neurologists, with physiologists and so on. I think a number of the scientists agreed to take part thinking that, basically, they'd be

telling the artist what was what. But the more responsive ones, like Colin Blakemore, have found it incredibly interesting working with an artist, who has certain ways of looking and seeing and thinking about visual material.

One of the artists involved is Claude Heath, who does these blindfold drawings. They're remarkable and I think extraordinarily beautiful. He does drawings by touch. He will take a cast of a head, for instance, and feel it, and he will have a location on the paper, and then he will draw in relation to what he feels, as his hand moves over the surface of this head. For a perceptual psychologist interested in representation, who may have been thinking about the issue of touch in relation to sight, which is a great historic question – whether seeing was just seeing or whether it was linked in with tactile and motor sensations as well – that can undoubtedly produce ideas, insights or questions. Many scientists, to practise their science at a high level, have to look at things incredibly hard. It's a very focused act of looking,

Image 7.6: Installation shot from 'Spectacular Bodies: The Art and Science of the Human Body from Leonardo to Now', Hayward Gallery, London, 19 October 2000–14 January 2001, (photo © Martin Kemp).

Image 7.5: Claude Heath, *Head Drawing*, (1995), ink on paper, 75 × 50cms. Bought by the Henry Moore Institute 1998 (photo: Steve Marwood).

filtering out all the noise and just concentrating on one thing. And to have an artist come and look at it as hard as you look, but to see different things, is very stimulating. Many scientists don't realize how hard artists look at things. I think that remorselessness of directed scrutiny coming through a totally different keyhole, as it were, from the keyhole they're using, is terrifically interesting.

KR: Bill Viola said that his work was about 'things that you can't shine a light on'. In the *Nantes Triptych*, for instance, he used the most literal, factual medium of a camera to get at what is not literal about birth and death. In his view the basis of image-making is shifting from the structure of light to the structure of thought. Any thoughts about this?

MK: I think artists and critics always like to get the sense that they're moving into a new territory. As a historian, I tend to see continuities. For Leonardo, one of the great aspirations for the artist was to portray the soul, which was obviously not visualizable. It's something which I think is a fundamental human instinct, to look at each other's faces and draw conclusions. It's why portraiture works at all. You think you can see something behind the mask. And, in a way, art is profoundly physiognomic, even when it's not dealing with faces, because it plays to this sense that we can read through a surface. The way that is done is obviously different in different media and different times, but I think the great power of the visual arts has always been this paradox: it's an irredeemably physical, visual thing, literally about surfaces, And yet it can be about deeper, unseen things behind that surface.

Bill Viola certainly has a tremendous sense of how he relates to the art of the past, in relation, obviously, to Bosch, in the case of the work he did in 'Encounters' at the National Gallery (2000). The video piece he staged, I thought, was spine-tinglingly brilliant, just awesome, with those very slow-moving expressions. Leonardo knew he was limited to a single expression. He did it incredibly well, but how he would have loved to get these fluid expressions which sort of melt one into another! There are new ways of combining time-based media and static media – there's a lot going on now that simply was impossible in the past. But the human instinct for what the visual image can do in relation to this unseen, apparently transcendent dimension, I think is constant.

KR: **Can you say something about your curating company, what sort of projects you're doing, and how you see that as a way forward, if you do.**

MK: What Marina Wallace and I have done – she was my co-curator on 'Spectacular Bodies' – is that we've set up a company called Wallace–Kemp Artakt. We've set it up as a company to do projects we want to do with greater mobility than through official organizations. That's to say, we can take on a commission for a show and employ really good people without always applying for grants through university administrations and trying to get offices for staff in university buildings, and all that kind of thing. We can respond much more instantly and put together teams to do projects whenever we want to do so. It has become almost accidentally big, in that galleries and museums, particularly in the science area, become interested in the delivery of a total package for an exhibition, which includes publications and design, as well as the curation. Even in the short time we've been in existence, about a year, that service is already under tremendous demand. We have three or four big projects on the go. One is a huge Leonardo project for 2005, in which we are mounting simultaneous events and exhibitions in London, Paris, Florence and Milan. We're moving people around and making electronic linkages, and this will include most of the Leonardo paintings.

KR: Do you mean at any one site you can have access electronically to all the other exhibitions?

MK: To the other exhibitions and to the central resources. You can have access via the Web. You'll have a coordinated programme of electronic and hard copy publication. And there will be some things you would recognize as relatively orthodox exhibitions, but they'll be set in this total context.

Another big project we have on the go, which is a really concrete one, is that we were asked, following 'Spectacular Bodies', by an Austrian group of geneticists, to look at the abbey in Czechoslovakia, where Mendel did all his pea experiments, and initially to create an exhibition, again involving contemporary artists, with a view in the long term to setting up the world's first ever museum of genetics. If all goes well, this would be, I think, the first time that an external company has ever done a complete public museum, which is as much a surprise to me as it is to anybody else.

KR: Very timely, in terms of the human genome project.

MK: These art–science territories, which seemed pretty arcane in the late 1960s when I first started researching them, have now become terrific growth areas.

KR: Are you seeing curation as an essential part of your work?

MK: I see it as a way of achieving different kinds of things than I can achieve in an academic context, but also some of the same things at much greater pace and with much greater flexibility. We set our own agendas. If we're commissioned to do an exhibition, we're obviously accountable to the people who commission it. But we haven't got this academic bureaucracy peering over our shoulder the whole time and dragging us back. And, ultimately, the reckoning is between the people who commission the exhibition, ourselves and the public, and I find that a much better system of accountability than the so-called accountability which is visited upon us within academic institutions. I'd much rather live and die professionally in that public arena than in relation to the kind of pedantry which comes through the academic review processes.

KR: **And the company allows you to research in a different way, or in different areas than you can in academia? You can be more adventurous. And you don't have to classify what you do as one thing or another?**

MK: Absolutely. There is no way of doing what I'm doing through conventional funding sources or conventional academic structures. Before this interview we were visiting the Plant Sciences Department in Oxford, looking at an early herbarium which has some of the earliest preserved plant hybrids. Mendel came to his discoveries partly through plant hybridization. It's where his initial evidence came from. Now, if I, as an art historian, said to the Arts and Humanities Research Board visual arts panel, 'I want to go off to a herbarium to research plant hybridization in the eighteenth century,' the answer would be, in effect, 'This is barmy.' So, oddly enough, the constraint of the commercial company gives an extraordinary degree of freedom, because the only people to whom we're accountable are ourselves and the people who want us to do the exhibition.

Martin Kemp, excerpts from four interviews by Karen Raney,
1996–2001

Notes

1.   The Italian sculptor and architect Filippo Brunelleschi (1377–1446) is credited with devising the method of creating pictorial space through fixed-point, linear perspective. If a picture is seen as a window inserted between an observer and a scene, all parallel lines at right angles to the 'window' will appear to converge on one point – the vanishing point – at the level of the viewer's eyes. Visible objects can be situated within the net of these lines. Brunelleschi's system was codified in his friend Leon Battista Alberti's treatise, *Della pittura* (On Painting), in 1435. Linear perspective was quickly taken up and elaborated on by painters such as Masaccio (1401–28). See M. Kemp, *The Science of Art: Optical Themes in Western Art from Brunelleschi to Seurat* (New Haven, CT, and London: Yale University Press, 1990).

2.   For a critique of scientific enquiry which calls for science to question its own grounds of knowledge, see J.-F. Lyotard, *The Postmodern Condition: A Report on Knowledge* (Manchester: Manchester University Press, 1984).

3.   A. Danto, *The Philosophical Disenfranchisement of Art* (New York: Columbia University Press, 1986) pp. 47–67.

4.   For a criticism of 'perceptualism' see introduction to N. Bryson, M. Holly and K. Moxey (eds), *Visual Theory* (Oxford: Polity Press and Basil Blackwell, 1991). The criticism is that the focus on perceptual capacities lowers the discussion about representation to a trivial level at which the reading of images can be seen as a 'universal' phenomenon.

5.   See E. Gombrich, *Art and Illusion: A Study in the Psychology of Pictorial Representation* (Oxford: Phaidon, 1959). W. J. T. Mitchell, in *Iconology*, analyses the ambiguities in Gombrich's account of the 'resemblance' theory of images (pp. 75–94).

6.   In 1735 Alexander Gottleib Baumgarten gave the name 'aesthetics' to his 'science of perception'. Aesthetics referred to knowledge coming from the senses as well as to the science of the beautiful.

7.   In 1994 Microsoft's Bill Gates bought Leonardo da Vinci's notebook known as the *Codex Leicester* from the Armand Hammer Museum. With Martin Kemp's help, Gates' private art-licensing company Corbis produced a CD-ROM from the notebook. The CD provides different ways of viewing both drawings and text. With a 'codescope' – a sliding window you can move over the page like a magnifying glass – the text underneath turns to English or Italian, depending on your settings. Clicking a 'mirror' button reverses Leonardo's mirror-writing, leaving everything else on the page untouched.

8.   Joseph Beuys (1921–86) was the influential German avant-garde artist – painter, sculptor, teacher, performance artist, theorist and activist – aligned with the Fluxus movement. Beuys used non-traditional materials and everyday objects. In one legendary performance he decorated his head with honey and gold leaf and talked about art to a dead hare as he walked around a gallery. Beuys sought to integrate spirituality and political ideals with art.

9.   Kemp refers to the British artist Damien Hirst's *Mother and Child, Divided* (1995). The preserved bodies of a cow and a calf have been sliced in half and presented in glass cases in such a way that the viewer walks between the two halves.

10. M. Kemp, *James Hugonin* (Cambridge: Kettle's Yard and University of Cambridge, 1996).

11. For discussion of the move toward thematically organized exhibitions, see D. Meijers, 'The Museum and the Ahistorical Exhibition' in B. Ferguson, R. Greenberg and S. Nairne (eds), *Thinking about Exhibitions* (London: Routledge, 1996), pp. 7–20. Also D. Freedberg, *The Play of the Unmentionable: An Installation by Joseph Kosuth at the Brooklyn Museum* (London: Thames and Hudson, 1992).

12. The contemporary artists whose work was included in 'Spectacular Bodies' were: John Isaacs, Katharine Dowson, Marc Quinn, Beth B, Christine Borland, Gerhard Lang, Tony Oursler and Bill Viola. See the exhibition catalogue: M. Kemp and M. Wallace, *Spectacular Bodies: The Art and Science of the Human Body from Leonardo to Now* (Berkeley, CA, and London: University of California Press and Hayward Gallery, 2000).

13. In the mid 1880s Freud studied at the Salpêtrière clinic in Paris with the psychologist Jean-Marie Charcot. Charcot was treating women hysterics with hypnosis. Beth B's piece *Hysteria* in 'Spectacular Bodies' (Hayward Gallery, London, 2000) was a multimedia installation relating to nineteenth-century definitions of hysteria, images of illness and the role of representation in the treatment of women. For an account of the staging of narratives of hysteria, see E. Showalter, *Histories, Hysterical Epidemics and Modern Culture* (London: Picador, 1997). For a general discussion of hysteria in relation to female sexuality see J. Rose, *Sexuality in the Field of Vision* (London and New York: Verso, 1986).

14. For instance: Jean-Antoine Houdon, *Écorché of a Standing Man*, bronze (1792), École Nationale Supérieure des Beaux-Arts, Département de Morphologie (cat. 141); William Hunter, *Écorché of Standing Man*, eighteenth-century polychrome plaster, Royal Academy of Arts, London (cat. 142).

'I think my medium probably is the ability to think about things. It's thoughtfulness. If I want to do something about that thoughtfulness, if I want to put it into the world or I want to de-privatize it then there are various mechanical methods or procedures which are to my taste and pass a kind of philosophical muster. I can argue for why they are done that way. But that isn't to say they couldn't be done another way.'

Richard Wentworth

KR: **You organized a big travelling exhibition called 'Thinking Aloud' [1998/9], which had a great variety of objects – sketches, models, maps, photos, the work of artists, architects, designers, as well as manufactured things.[2] There was none of your own work on display, but did you see the show itself as a piece of artwork?**

RW: I'm not very good about making distinctions between what's artwork and what isn't. That exhibition was borne of a very specific relationship with Roger Malbert[3] who was incredibly encouraging and imaginative on my behalf. In that sense, he was a classic curator. He saw that the exhibition was sitting around in me and he extricated the elements, one by one. But it was a speculative act; it never had a plan. Right at the end, I was still smuggling things in that I'd thought of the day before. Everybody commented on how it looked 'like me'.

KR: **Your work seems to come from a foraging process, often finding ordinary or unnoticed things which turn out to be extraordinary under the light you shine on them. I assume organizing the show was similar in that sense?**

RW: I don't have tidy strategies for making work. I'm not a nine-to-five studio artist. I was never good at that. Perhaps I'm not so keen on spending time with myself.

KR: **What do you feel is your relationship to the other artists whose work you presented?**

RW: I think it was very, very important that there was nothing of mine in the show. It would have been presumptuous. My work was in contacting people and persuading them, and, with only a couple of exceptions, getting more or less what I wanted, and then trying to make it work. I suppose that's a matter of taste and temperament and intellectual engagement. I felt the artists were relieved to be in a show with so little didactic posturing – but I had to wait to learn that!

KR: If you didn't know where the exhibition was going, how could you describe to an artist how their work might fit in? There must have been a great deal of trust.

RW: I said to people: 'This is a very open-ended show, these are some of the other people in it, and I can't say exactly where you'll be hung or how you'll be hung.' The only thing I did that caused a bit of a scene was I left a label on a Barry Flanagan piece that said, 'Flanagan'. It was a very wilful act. About two-thirds of the way through the show, Waddington's[4] found out and got very upset. I explained that they had sent me something and it had a label on it. I failed to remove it. The failure to remove it was a curatorial act. When I explained, it was fine with them, in the end. It was just a matter of restoring trust with Lesley [Waddington]. It was that beautiful stumpy elephant which looked the better for being 'named'.

KR: Why did the gallery object?

RW: They probably thought it was sloppy. In truth, I got lucky. Sculptures come with labels on them, they've got labels on them in auction rooms. If you go to somebody's studio you might look at a work that's still in a packing case. I wanted to touch upon those things. I don't suppose many people even noticed. I thought leaving the label on was slightly naughty but I didn't think it was a travesty. The spirit of the show was very open-handed. I wouldn't take anybody's work and try and diminish it. Artists usually do that verbally.

KR: Do you think an artist-as-curator brings something specific to organizing exhibitions?

RW: I don't like being called 'artist–curator–gardener'. I saw it as an opportunity that came at a certain moment, which I took. I'm someone who sort of 'encountered' all my ambitions, and noticed afterwards that I did them quite well. This current exhibition we're hanging at the Photographer's Gallery [Richard Wentworth/Eugène Atget: 'Faux Amis', Photographer's Gallery, London, 2001],[5] I don't quite know what I'm doing, and I'm extremely anxious about it. I don't know even how I want it, I just know it's got to be right. I'm not afraid of my judgement, but it can't be programmatic, or come solely from the head.

KR: So it's a very intuitive way of working.

RW: You back a horse. I think my instinct is quite good. I like the rhyming slang of it. In Thinking Aloud, there was a German model of how to make a ruin, you know, because the Germans think the world can be made in models. It was a very culturally charged thing, still shrink-wrapped in its box, and it was near a David Shrigley picture of a Norman Foster building, with a sign in front of it that said, *Ignore This Building*.

Image 8.2: David Shrigley, *Ignore This Building* (1998). Stephen Friedman Gallery, London.

I had been told that if I wanted to get Frank Gehry in the show, I should tell him that Norman Foster wasn't going to be in it! So when I saw that David Shrigley had made this piece of work, it was just a complete pleasure, at our moment of 'signature architecture', to be able to put it within hailing distance of Gehry.[6] I've never met Gehry, but it was like sending him a postcard. The show was full of that kind of thing, which didn't necessarily have to be detected but I think could be felt. Obviously some people knew who I was and what sort of mind I'd got, but lots of other people didn't. I've had a lot of fan mail saying things like: 'I do not normally go to art exhibitions, I went with my daughter, she thought it was wonderful, we have been four times.'

Image 8.3: Design Process Model of the Weatherhead School of Management, foam core, wood, paper, and plexiglass (30 October 1997). Courtesy Gehry partners.

KR: **Do you prefer the idea of a broad-based audience, rather than an 'art' audience?**

RW: Well, I think they're both interesting, but we are all components of a huge audience. The show was like a juggler or a circus out travelling in the world, pulling in very diverse publics. I think that's what's so amazing about national touring exhibitions, They'll deliver some Picasso etchings to a library in Wigan. And for one person in Wigan, that'll change their life. It probably won't do anything for the rest, but then culture works by seepage.

KR: **The idea that people made whatever narratives they wanted from your exhibition – you're quite happy for that to happen? Obviously, you didn't want a single response, but how important is it for people to 'get' your juxtapositions? The German make-your-own-ruin being next to the Gehry model, next to *Ignore This Building*. Or the irony of, say, the measuring instruments, the standards and rules and attempts to regulate everything, against the chaos of modern life.**

RW: If somebody had received the show in a schoolmasterly way, I would have minded. If they got it by sleight-of-hand or by humour, that's different. The show was built in a completely folkloric way. It was built out of meeting people whose conversation gave me ideas. I hope the show articulated that. People could somehow feel, say, that Francis Alÿs had come all the way from Mexico to London and handed me something, you know, that these things were not just borrowed from the Arts Council collection. I think there were a lot of things in it that didn't work, and things that were superfluous, but all shows are like that.

KR: **When I went around the exhibition I found myself looking for relationships between the objects all the time, different pathways through. I was never sure what was accidental and what was planned. I found that quite exciting.**

RW: Of course you do that when you walk down the street.

KR: **Yes. I guess that was what was strange about the exhibition. It was chaotic and cluttered enough that there was this feeling of walking down the street and making my own connections. But an exhibition is obviously a contrived thing. So knowing it was an exhibition gave me the feeling that meanings had been planted for me to find. There was a kind of oscillation back and forth between the two experiences.**

RW: That's what old museums were like, anyway. 'These things are interesting and I have put them in a room, and if you want to go, you can walk around anywhere you like.'

KR: **Cabinets of curiosities.[7]**

RW: Exactly. That's what people have compared it to, though I must say I knew very little about them. Innocence can be a great friend.

KR: **Who would you say you make your work for? Who is your audience, or who would you like it to be?**

RW: It's some imaginary community that's out there, a tribe dealing in ideas or thoughtfulness or energized thinking and doing. Making art is a way of making your own little paper dart with messages on it. You hope that it is out there flying around and landing and taking off again. One thing which is barely articulated in art schools is that eventually you don't have the audience of the art school. I have a feeling that those shared studios all over London are still full of people who are monasticized because no one suggested they were going to need something other than four plasterboard walls.

KR: **People sometimes take 'audience' literally, to mean who will be coming to the private view. What you are talking about is, I think, the deeper sense of audience – the whole field of ideas which might be receiving your work, which helps you to make it.**

RW: I suspect that as you grow as an artist, you have a sense of your effectiveness. Somebody who never gets a chance at being visible probably drops further and further behind this fictitious parapet, because there isn't any sense of conversation. Whereas if you have had the pleasure of some exchange, then you think, well I am not as inefficient and pointless as I feel. And of course when you meet other artists you think, 'phew, I am not completely alone in this foolish project'. The fact is that artists are lonely. How can we get any confidence? You have got to keep making the work and the work has got to tell you it is worth doing. It's not a complaint; I choose to do this thing, but it's not the way people think it is. It is both dangerous and foolish. But the predicament of overvisibility can be a problem. I don't know what I'd do with fame, how I'd use it. Art isn't to do with desiring celebrity, it's not a branch of the pop business.

KR: **John Updike, the American writer, once said 'fame is a mask that eats away at your face'. He was talking about his difficulty in later years in getting his work going, because his high visibility was doing something to his identity.**

RW: Exactly. And yet if you have no visibility at all, you can't move forward either. That's what I was trying to say about the importance of audience. As Updike was once a student at the Ruskin School of Art, perhaps his remark has a visual – literary complexity.

KR: **Does your work have a visual language and if so what does it consist of?**

RW: I have always imagined that artists don't want to have a visual language. They're fleeing from the idea of a visual language because a visual language would confine them, it would locate them. They have this fictitious idea that they can somehow be free. Fifteen or twenty years ago, I used to think that my work was very inconsistent, that it was justifiably, but slightly frighteningly, diverse. Now of course, I see it all as a horribly located language, and I'm disturbed by that. Maybe that's the prison of being an artist. After a while you find that you walk in your own footsteps and all your energies are spent trying to get out of your footsteps.

It's like when cab drivers ask 'What do you do then . . .?' If you're stupid you say 'I am a sculptor.' 'What do you work in?' And you think, this is not really the point, but in order to reply honourably it is safer to say 'wood'. 'Do you construct it or carve it?' they ask, and off you go down materials alley.

KR: **What is your medium, then, if it's not a particular material?**

RW: I think my medium probably is the ability to think about things. It's thoughtfulness. If I want to do something about that thoughtfulness, if I want to put it into the world or I want to de-privatize it then there are various mechanical methods or procedures which are to my taste and pass a kind of philosophical muster. I can argue for why they are done that way. But that isn't to say they couldn't be done another way.

What nobody ever wants to talk about in organizing exhibitions are the practical limitations. With this show we're hanging at the moment, the Atget photographs have to be at a certain lighting and a certain temperature and a certain humidity. You're hardly free to play with the images. You're constantly speaking to practicality or being expedient, or even just being diplomatic. On the curatorial courses it's discussed as if it's a series of intellectual acts. Show-making is a muckier thing than that.

KR: **Why do it then? What do you get out of it? The current show at the Photographer's Gallery is of your work, but what did you get out of curating 'Thinking Aloud'?**

RW: That's a really good question. I think it was a maturing thing to do. It was like going to my own funeral. I don't mean that it was a finale, but it involved so many friendships and so many connections, I think I became much less afraid of the world. People were so excited about the show that I felt valued in a surprising way. People are more cautious about expressing their feelings on individual artworks.

KR: **If they pass judgement on your work it's more likely to feel like a judgement on you. Whereas an exhibition is at one remove.**

RW: The other thing I got out of doing the show is something which is very difficult to talk about. I somehow exercised my taste without displaying it. I felt I was able to deal with things which I really like, or care about, or have strength of feeling for, without having to show that I own them. I didn't own most of what went in the show; I borrowed it. You can hear that impulse when people say 'my *own* work'.

KR: **So you could make a personal statement, but at arm's length, in a way. By 'taste' you mean what you find interesting?**

RW: I don't mean having matching bath towels. I do mean something big. I'd like to say my intellectual opinion, but it's terribly difficult territory. I wanted it to be like a masqued ball – with me at one remove. It's a strategy I use in a lot of my work.

KR: **But it *was* called 'Richard Wentworth's Thinking Aloud' . . .**

RW: The reason my name's in pale grey, not bold, on the catalogue is because I was shrieking down the telephone, 'Get my name off, get it off, get it off, get it off.' I didn't see the necessity of it. Susan Brades[8] had the wisdom to see that it needed to be located in a personality. But maybe there is an interesting question there to do with when you attribute something to an individual and when you don't.

KR: **It's about the idea of authorship, the feeling of one individual's eye and mind at work behind the scenes. As opposed to shows that are clearly the result of a huge collaboration.**

When we spoke before, I asked you what your medium was, and you said your medium was 'thinking'. Do you still see your medium as 'thinking'?

RW: That sounds rather smug! But yes, I do think it's what I do best. It's not good thinking, necessarily – it's a very 'unjoined-up' thinking. I'm slightly ashamed of that.

KR: **Don't you feel there's poetry in 'unjoined-up thinking'?**

RW: Maybe. When I was asked to do the Ruskin job,[9] at first I said no, I don't want to be in an art school. But I decided in the end to see it as a bucketful of possibility that's been handed to me. I think there's work to be done. Maybe one could join up some of the intellectual possibility of Oxford in a vivacious way. Somebody of my generation said to me, 'It's really great you're going to do it, because you think like an artist and you'll do it like an artist.' That was a great compliment, a real courage-giver.

KR: **What does it mean to 'think like an artist'? Are you happy with the category of 'art' and 'artist'?**

RW: It means a little area of the world which is freer, less fettered. Meeting artists is always a great pleasure, a sense, almost, of animal recognition.

KR: **Something about untidiness and making unpredictable links?**

RW: Yes, and speculating about things, using the imagination. Even speculating about something like September 11th. We've all been in situations, car crashes or

Image 8.4: Richard Wentworth,

San Francisco, 2001,

(photo ©: Richard Wentworth).[10]

Image 8.5: Richard Wentworth,

San Francisco, 2001

(photo ©: Richard Wentworth).[11]

Image 8.6: Richard Wentworth,

Caledonian Road, London, 2001

(photo ©: Richard Wentworth).[12]

whatever, where we were not in control as something unfolds. So it's natural to imagine how it was, or wasn't, for those people, and even to see the explosion of the towers as an astonishing, even beautiful, visual spectacle. Pornography of course. Maybe the fact that we speculate is a sign of how alive we are — it's a sign of our engagement with the possibility of being alive. What else are we going to do? It's a way of acknowledging that we are part of shared humanity.

But this question about 'art' and 'artist' . . . As all these pictures of mine have been delivered for the Photographer's Gallery, I've been thinking: how funny that a few of them are what Robert Malbert calls 'lecture slides', and some of them are images. And the two types actually need each other. There are some where the red is an object and the green is a place, and you immediately say 'the chair, keeping the door open'. You don't look at it strictly as a set of colours and tones. And then others are much more like an equation or a piece of algebra. I don't know which it's going to be when I make a photograph. The ones that I pour my greatest amount of belief into, at the act of making the picture, are often the least rich. The ones where I stop myself doing that, often tip over and become sort of iconic.

KR: Implying that those images are more complex?

RW: They're bigger embodiments of something, but less nameable.

KR: And is this what you see yourself doing that could be called 'art'?

RW: If you work in a territory for a very long time, you become a sort of authority on it without knowing it. I know all this stuff about how the world is organized and how it speaks. I've been staying in San Francisco. After three or four days, I knew things about the visual dialect of San Francisco.

Opposite:

Image 8.8: Exerpts from transcript of Helen Sharman on Radio 4, Peter Taylor, Tony Jolly, 'The New Curiosity Shop'. Courtesy of The Hayward Gallery, London.

KR: Visual dialect?

RW: Anywhere humans are engaged, my territory will show up in some way. Half of San Francisco is spent trying to find a way of being level. It's full of cars parked

Transcript of Helen Sharman on Radio 4
Peter Taylor, Tony Jolly - The New Curiosity Shop
Radio 4 1997/7?

. . .

There were three of us in the ?? capsule which is a very
small capsule that sits on top of the rocket. Really this
is just to get us to the space station that's going to be
much larger later on. The three of us sit side by side. I
say sit but its like sitting down but with the chair
flipped onto its back so really you're almost horizontal
but your knees are bent right up in front of you, your
elbows overlap. There's not much room. And you stay like
that for 2 hours before the launch, going through all
the checks you need to do. There's no real countdown,
either, in Russia. There's a clock that is counting down
in front of you, but there's none of this booming 10, 9, 8
of a voice crying somewhere in the distance. Bang on time
the rocket engines fire. You feel a bit of vibration. . .

As the gantry is released the thrust builds up as the
acceleration of course increases and you do start to feel
heavy and the more the acceleration builds up the heavier
you feel. . .

As soon as the final rocket stage is jettisoned you get
this wonderful glorious weightlessness that you have
experienced for a few seconds before in training but
never for very long.

First of all it's hey! Wow! Isn't this a novelty and then
it becomes annoying, you know, you can't keep the pages
of your book open because your book pages tend to float
and they turn over for themselves backwards and forwards.
Your pencil has to be attached to your book or otherwise
it drifts away and you lose it. . .

I think we've all seen pictures of the earth from space
and looking at it for real was everything I'd expected it
to be but so much more.

You've got this constantly moving picture. The blue that
everybody talks about is a blue that is so intense and so
deep. It's very very difficult to describe. I haven't seen
a blue really like that before I flew or since I've come
back.

The next thing that really catches your eye are the clouds and they are just so bright because the sunlight reflects from the top of the clouds back up to you in space, but it hurts your eyes to look at them for very long – it's that bright and I think the thing that amazed me too was the lack of greenness on the earth's surface.

You look through this hazy atmosphere full of an awful lot of water as well as an awful lot of everything else – the stuff that's come out of volcanoes, the stuff that we burn. I flew just after the Gulf war had finished. We could actually see oil wells burning – great big orange fires with plumes of smoke coming off so you're looking down through all this, and the only two parts of the earth that appear to be green were Northern Ireland or perhaps Ireland in general, and the North Island, New Zealand. The rest of the earth is either vegetation, a sage green almost a dull grey colour. There's an awful lot of barren land, brick red deserts, sandy coloured deserts and cities, of course, appear to be just a kind of dull grey brown which come to light, quite literally, at night time. The night view of the earth is spectacular, it really is. You see any fires that are burning, but the city lights are glorious.

In some ways it's quite frightening because you've got all of this light coming out into space it's this Electro magnetic radiation where is it going? Are we polluting space? We don't think about that. But at night you really can see where we live. The outlines of places like Australia, but people don't tend to live in inland Australia, but they live round the coast. The United Kingdom is light pretty much all over most of it, as does Western Europe. North America you see a predominance on the East Coast and West Coast. Japan and South eastern Asia – huge amount over there, but Africa and South America . . . you know you really do see where people have access to this modern electricity.

under houses. There are these incredibly elaborate topographies for getting off a sloping street, which makes the sidewalk into the most ludicrous landscape. There's dozens of ways of trying to keep water out of garages. Every San Francisco builder, anyone who's ever knocked up a bucket of sand and cement must know something about that. I don't suppose they speak to each other about it, it's just there in the parlance of the street. But I didn't go there thinking, 'In San Francisco, I'll look for what water will do.'

KR: How do you collect your observations, or develop any ideas that come from them?

RW: I've got hundreds of pieces of paper with little words and scribbles on them.

KR: Words rather than images?

RW: Words, yes. After the 11th, I just collected language – the language people used to talk about it. I think it's something to do with feeling extremely anxious about one's culture and what it's doing, especially in these last weeks.

KR: 'Thinking Aloud' had many references to the military and to territory that could be called political. The child's flak-jacket, the Romanian flag with the Soviet emblem ripped out, all the Second World War things. Even the written account of looking down at the earth from space was very politically charged. I got the feeling of a kind of 'anthropology of ourselves' going on, where these objects and artefacts are being dug up and presented for scrutiny and wonderment, like messages from another world. I was interested as well in the fact that the Helen Sharman piece was only words.

RW: I think a piece like that is incredibly visual, incredibly imagistic. I took it from the radio which is so much more pictorial than television. When I heard Helen Sharman[14] speaking on the radio, she was so eloquent, in a sort of naïve way, she said 'then you see Australia and you can see that nobody lives there, the continent is drawn by the electric light of the people living on the coast. And you see Africa's got no light at all, and then you see eastern America blazing, Western Europe blazing.' It's just so visually, politically, humanistically rich.

Richard Wentworth, excerpts from interviews by Karen Raney,

1998 and 2001

Notes

1. Richard Wentworth, *SF 2001*. This is fresh concrete crossed with shadows.

2. Richard Wentworth's 'Thinking Aloud' was a National Touring Exhibition organized by the Hayward Gallery, London, for the Arts Council of England, and curated by Richard Wentworth. It was at Kettle's Yard, Cambridge, 7 November 1998–3 January 1999, at Cornerhouse, Manchester, 9 January–28 February 1999, and at Camden Arts Centre, London, 9 April–30 May 1999. There is a catalogue of the exhibition (London: Hayward Gallery Publishing, 1998).

3. Roger Malbert, Senior Curator National Touring Exhibitions, was exhibition organizer for Richard Wentworth's 'Thinking Aloud'.

4. Waddington Gallery is a commercial gallery in London that represents the artist Barry Flanagan.

5. Richard Wentworth/Eugène Atget: 'Faux Amis', Photographer's Gallery, London, 2001. Wentworth's contemporary urban photographs and Eugène Atget's early twentieth-century photographs of Paris were exhibited in separate rooms.

6. The Canadian-born architect Frank Gehry works in Los Angeles. His most well-known recent design is of the Solomon R. Guggenheim Museum in Bilbao, Spain (2000). The British architect Norman Foster is based in London, and has designed many high-profile international projects. Recent ones include the Millennium Dome, London, and the Great Court for the British Museum, London. David Shrigley is a contemporary British artist based in Glasgow, whose work emerged in the 1990s. His work ranges from doodle-like drawings with text, to photographs and sculptures.

7. The 'cabinet of curiosities' was a private gentleman's collection of exotica from the lands being explored and colonized by Europe in the fifteenth and sixteenth centuries.

8. Susan Ferleger Brades, Hayward Gallery Director at the time of 'Thinking Aloud'.

9. The Ruskin School of Drawing and Fine Art is a department of the University of Oxford, England. Richard Wentworth was appointed 'Ruskin Master' from April 2002. (See W. J. T. Mitchell, Chapter 1, n. 7, p. 65, on Ruskin.)

10. Richard Wentworth, *San Francisco 2001*. US flag decal, venetian blinds.

11. Richard Wentworth, *San Francisco 2001*. This is a photograph of a garage door whose lower edge is shaped to the sloping contour of a San Francisco street. The pavement is divided to mark the double ownership of the garage.

12. Richard Wentworth, *Caledonian Road, London 2001*. This is a fake fireplace for sale on a London street.

13. Richard Wentworth, *London 1994*. This image is of a brick holding open a door.

14. The astronaut Helen Sharman described the experience of looking down at the earth from space. Richard Wentworth made a transcription of Sharman's words, which he heard on a radio interview. What was exhibited at the Camden Arts Centre version of 'Thinking Aloud' was this transcript, typed on A4 sheets of paper, which were pinned to the wall.

'One of the themes I've been writing about recently is memory, and I suppose photography has an obvious relationship to memory. In my case it may be I'm using the images as a kind of a ladder to walk up, and then I throw the ladder away, having got up there. But I certainly think images are becoming increasingly important to my writing.'

Sadie Plant

Previous:

Image 9.1: Sadie Plant, *Train* (1999).

(photo ©: Sadie Plant).

KR: How would you characterize yourself? Are you a writer, are you a theorist, are you an artist?

SP: I always choose to say writer, and that is definitely how I would like to be known. But if I say that, people often want to add 'and cultural critic' or 'and theorist' after it. I like to think of what I do in a practical way, especially now that I'm not teaching, I'm just concentrating on writing. I like to think of writing almost as a craft-type activity. It's the act of writing, not what you actually write about, that is the defining point.

KR: Can you say a bit about your background? How you got to where you are.

SP: I always wanted to be a writer, even when I was a tiny kid. Then I went to university, did my PhD in philosophy, and almost accidentally started teaching. I worked for a year at Queen Mary and Westfield College in London. Then I got the job that I had for five years at Birmingham, in the Department of Cultural Studies. After five years there I took a research fellowship at Warwick University, which was a very nice interdisciplinary role attached to the Philosophy Department. I'd always had an eye to leaving the academy – it wasn't my big ambition to go into it in the first place, although I enjoyed the teaching – and as soon as it became possible for me to work freelance and survive by writing I decided to do it.

KR: You've recently finished a book called *Writing on Drugs*.[1]

SP: Yes. That's a book that I first had the idea for quite a few years ago, before I started working on the previous book. It was in my mind for a long, long time and I put it all on one side to write *Zeros and Ones*.[2] *Writing on Drugs* was the first big project that I did in my new freelance capacity.

KR: And your next book?

SP: The next book isn't quite formulated yet. I've been doing a lot of writing and collecting of material over the last few years, and I've done a lot of travelling since I stopped teaching. I'm hoping all that will come together in this new book, which I think will be something more fictional than I've done in the past.

In all three of my books there's almost a fictional undercurrent, or something that wanted to be a bit more fictional but was kept within the confines of a scholarly type of book. I'd like to let that fictional twist run a bit more. I've done a lot of travelling in the Middle East and Islamic countries, and a lot of thinking about cities, and about so-called globalization. Those are just two of many of the elements that I hope will get into the book.

KR: **In _Zeros and Ones_ you have a lot to say about the deficiencies of the written word. It's hierarchical, it's static, and so on. I find it interesting that you are a writer and yet you seem to be mistrustful of words. What have your strategies been in relation to that? Do you see it as a contradiction?**

SP: Well I certainly see it as a paradox. I've decided that life is full of paradoxes and there's no point in trying to iron them all out. It's a really good thing to pick up on, because I do sometimes feel that if I could begin again and choose a particular medium to work in, I would choose something else, maybe film or music. I feel a bit landed with writing. It is what I do, but it's not a matter of choice. I say music or film – or maybe architecture – because there are people that I admire who work in those fields, and it seems to me that their work can be a lot more immediate than writing.

The thing I find unsatisfactory about writing is that it's always in danger of remaining a kind of secondary activity, always in relation to something else. But although that's a criticism of writing and a disadvantage of it, it's also what can make it a worthwhile thing to do. What you try to do when you write is to overcome that distance. Your job is to try to make writing as immediate as I would say a piece of music or an image is. That's what you are aiming at. Writing is a difficult thing to do, but it is precisely the obstacles and difficulties it presents, that makes it so compelling. In *Zeros and Ones* and *Writing on Drugs*, even though they're very, very different books, there are moments in each of them where they manage to make the jump. When the drugs book is dealing with a certain drug, there are moments when it succeeds in conveying something about the effects of that drug in an immediate way.

KR: *The Most Radical Gesture*[3] **was a more or less straightforward academic book, while *Zeros and Ones* you've divided into small sections that seem as if they could be read in any order.**

SP: In principle it can be read in different orders, though obviously it's still a book, it's still a linear text.

KR: I presumed that was your way of trying to get out of the straitjacket of normal writing.

SP: Yes, very much so. I suppose with that book I was trying to learn some of the lessons from the new media but to make it in an old medium. How can those changes feed back and affect the old world of the book? I love experimentation but I'm always wary about being gimmicky. There's a danger that the style will take over and then you've lost the whole point of it. So the experimentation is quite understated in that book.

KR: As well as being able to read the sections in a different order, underneath each heading there is this loose arrangement of ideas that are linked, it seems to me, in the way that poetry links ideas. Would you use that word 'poetic' for what you do?

SP: I'm flattered when people say that. It's not necessarily a word that's in my mind, but yes, I hope it is poetic in the sense that it's suggestive, evocative. That book came out of an academic context, and I was trying to do something that would be informative but not educational in the sense of being teacherly. I think you can do a lot just by example and by suggestion and by the way that you put things together. Hopefully you allow other people to do that for themselves.

KR: **Poetry invites people to use their imaginations.**

SP: Yes, exactly. I'd like to inspire people to use more imaginative ways of thinking and organizing ideas about anything. So I think that book has some implicit messages, which I am pleased that people seem to have got from it. With a subtle shift of perspective it's possible to put together prosaic elements of the world and make something very different out of them.

KR: **Were you trying to do something like the 'weaving with words' that you write about?**

SP: Yes, to some extent I tried to make that happen in the text. I'm always trying to make the content and the mode of expression synchronize.

KR: **Can I ask who you feel that you write for? Who is your audience?**

SP: I honestly don't know how to answer this. In terms of the literal sense of an audience, I hope it is possible to write a book which can be read by a wide range of people coming from such different backgrounds that they might each effectively be reading a different book. I like to think that you don't have to be an intellectually-minded person to appreciate my work. I tend to use my dad as a reader, because he's a very bright guy, an engineer, who left school as a teenager. If it gets past him I feel reasonably satisfied that somebody who is interested but has no academic knowledge or background can get something from my work. I think to some extent I do achieve that. When I meet people who have read one or all of the books, I get the sense that I have quite a wide audience, and that really pleases me.

But having said that, when I am actually writing, I'm not thinking about the people who are going to read it. If I'm really honest, I don't know why I'm doing it. In the moment I don't think I'm writing for anybody.

KR: Can you talk about the genesis of *Zeros and Ones*, or any of your writing.

SP: They all have quite different beginnings. For years I steered clear of writing anything about feminism, sex, sexuality, mainly because I'd spent most of my time as a graduate student in the Philosophy Department. There still weren't many women in the philosophy department I was in at that time, and there was the expectation that because you were female you would be writing feminist philosophy. That made me run in the opposite direction. I vowed never to write about women and anything.

But when I was teaching at Birmingham I got interested in new technology, and became frustrated by the fact that at the time there seemed to be this ridiculous masculine flavour to it all. Female students who were more than capable of dealing with the Internet, which was then new, were elbowed out or somehow made to feel that it wasn't for them; the boys were hogging the machines. So I started casually hunting for things that might upset that apple-cart a bit, and I came across the Ada Lovelace story. Then I started finding all these other bits of women's history which I wasn't really looking for. I was looking for ammunition to point out how unnecessary this gendered approach to technology was. So the starting point of *Zeros and Ones* was practical concerns that had come up through my teaching. But when I discovered the Ada Lovelace story it began to develop into a more positive thing, and that's when it started to become a book.[4]

KR: Does the visual image come into your writing?

SP: It does so more now than it ever has done. I've noticed this since I've been writing somewhat more fictional things. I am really interested in photography, very much as an amateur, and I find that inspiring for writing. And I'm learning to draw as well. So at the moment, I often find myself using images as springboards for texts.

KR: An image will capture your imagination, and you live with it for a while and write around it? Or will you use an image directly as part of a narrative?

SP: One of the themes I've been writing about recently is memory, and I suppose photography has an obvious relationship to memory. In my case it may be I'm using the images as a kind of ladder to walk up, and then I throw the ladder away, having got up there. But I certainly think images are becoming increasingly important to my writing.

KR: I'm interested that you're learning to draw. What prompted that? How do you find drawing in relation to writing?

SP: I can't remember exactly why I decided to give it a shot, but the pleasure I've discovered in it is very much thanks to the classic *Drawing on the Right Side of the Brain* book, by Betty Edwards.[5] Drawing has really changed my perceptual parameters – I see the difference all the time. And I do find that it has a wonderful relationship to writing, especially when both involve pen and ink. While I use and enjoy photographs as finished images, drawing is far more about the processes involved: one sees, thinks, dreams, disappears while drawing just as (sometimes!) this happens as one writes. And in many ways drawing and writing present the same limits and the same challenges: what can be said or done with the minimum of lines?

KR: Some artists produce very 'visual' works and yet they avoid doing the groundwork through their dominant medium. For instance, the video artist Bill Viola prepares the ground for his works mostly through writing, rather than, say sketching. I wondered if there's a common theme here about reaching across to other modalities for inspiration. A video artist

who develops work through words, a writer who mistrusts words and starts instead with images.

SP: Perhaps you do tend to look to other areas for your raw material.

KR: **Is it so you can then make a transformation of the 'foreign' material into your own medium? Both Viola and the architect Hani Rashid talked in a slightly suspicious way about 'the visual'. It's either too seductive and it tricks you, or it's not enough on its own . . .**

SP: I wonder if it's familiarity that produces that kind of love–hate thing. The more you know about a medium the more you see its traps and limitations.

Image 9.2: Sadie Plant, *Desert*
(1999). (photo ©: Sadie Plant).

KR: **Whereas someone else's medium seems easy, direct, immediate?**

Image 9.3: Sadie Plant, *Lagoon* (2002). (photo ©: Sadie Plant).

SP: It looks like a wide-open road. But still, perhaps that's why other media are inspiring to your own, because you can look at them almost innocently. You can take what you need from them. To be honest, a lot of these processes are entirely mysterious to me. I don't know how any of it works. I don't know why I do what I do and I don't know what it's for. That's the real truth. You just have to trust it and do it.

KR: **Rashid said, about architecture, that he doesn't know the origin of it. I think about architecture as being one of the more deliberate of the arts. It's collaborative and it requires huge amounts of very deliberate preparation, but I suppose he's working on the more abstract end of it – starting from a sound, and making a building grow out of a sound, that**

sort of thing – rather than on the 'nuts and bolts' end that figures out how you fit the staircase into the building.

SP: By the same token, I like the fact about architecture that no matter how theoretical it gets, it's got some tangible engagement with reality.

KR: **You have to be able to open the doors and get in and out.**

SP: Exactly. I think that gives architecture an edge because it can't go too far off this engagement with the grit of reality.

KR: **Does the phrase 'visual literacy' mean anything to you?**

SP: I assume that what people mean by visual literacy is that you've acquired a certain amount of skill in how you use your eyes. But I don't really like the phrase because I don't think you read a picture, and I don't think looking is about being literate.

I've always been very sceptical about this semiotic tendency to say that people, fashion, the unconscious, capitalism, images are readable, or legible. I think it is the wrong vocabulary, at the very least, and possibly has completely the wrong set of ideas behind it as well. Your clothes are clothes, they're not a text. I think you can lose what is special about clothes, for example, by superimposing the concept of text onto them. A lot of literature about cities is like this, and architecture too: supposedly you can read a building or you can read a city. I don't think you can.

KR: **Is it that skills that are applicable to words are not applicable to images or objects?**

SP: Yes, and it's the whole philosophy behind it – that reality is composed on language and it's all a matter of different kinds of language. I don't like where that's coming from either. It was developed as a kind of anti-humanist philosophy, but I think it's in fact far too humanist, because it puts everything in terms of a very human skill. What excites me about a city like Birmingham is that it's a convergence of different kinds of flows of material – the traffic, the pollution, the sewage system, the power supplies, the waste disposal, and all the images and the culture and the people. I think you need different approaches to each of those material processes, and that they are processes that are above and beyond, or below and beyond, our human perspectives on them. Sure, you can read the sewage system, but I don't think it's going to get you very far in understanding how it works or, more importantly, how it fits in with the composition of a city.

KR: I suppose the idea of applying linguistic metaphors to everything had a radical edge when it started – trying to say that the visual world is as charged with culture as language is.

SP: I couldn't possibly argue against making that move, but I think the danger is the implication that the prime purpose of these things that you're busily reading is to be there for somebody to perceive them.

KR: And decode them. Make them have meaning.

SP: And decode them, exactly. Obviously you can do that, but it's not their own purpose in life. You can end up with this kind of self-reflexive, closed-loop thing going on between you and the world.

KR: Because of the instruments you bring to it, you're going to find what you went looking for, something in relation to yourself?

SP: I concede that semiotics is a useful way to look at things up to a point, as long as it's not taken too far and to the exclusion of other approaches. In the academy, you often do need to get behind a position and go for it. But I think if you're interested in how things really work rather than the political dynamics of the intellectual world, it's often a lot more complex than that.

KR: You're very optimistic, aren't you, about the potential of digital technologies to be subversive? And you think the way they work is like a kind of thinking that you identify as feminine. Is that right?

SP: Yes. Though that might be a bit positive on the feminine side. As I was saying earlier, the origin of this book was very much trying to find things that were not masculine, rather than things that were positively feminine. But then I started thinking that in many ways what is feminine is defined as the left-overs from the masculine, and there is a certain value in gathering that all together and making it into a positive thing. It's become very clichéd by now, but I do think there are certain structural or systemic elements of digital technology that are antithetical to hierarchical, patriarchal social structures. That cannot fail to be interesting to anybody who wants to undermine or change those structures. So I do feel vindicated about some of the material I've written, my ideas about where things might go and the changes that the technology can produce.

Recently I've been doing some research about mobile phone technologies and their social take-up. That is a good example of how digital technology is finding its way into people's hands in the most unlikely parts of the world. Certainly when I wrote *Zeros and Ones*, I thought I was being optimistic to think that this would happen. But small developments like the mobile can make some enormous differences to people who would otherwise be marginalized or excluded from new technologies.

KR: Do you think the nature of digital technology will allow it to evade the powers that want to control it?

SP: Well, we'll have to see. Certainly I think it can put up a good fight. If you take the Internet, that's the classic case, obviously there are hundreds of attempts to police it, to control it, to centralize it, to turn it into television really, in one form or another, and to some extent those efforts have been successful. But on the other hand, there is something implicit in the system that makes it very difficult ever entirely to do that. It's analogous to a city where the bulk of that city gets taken up by

McDonalds and Gap, but there's still all the underground back-street stuff going on as well. So even in the worst-case scenario, I think the Net would remain like that, even if it's just the periphery that is able to evade the centralizing tendencies.

I think the mistake we all make is to get too invested in a particular kind of technology. If the Internet does prove to be too easily taken over by corporate and state interests, then the hope is that some other system would emerge, or some other change would happen that would pick up on this tendency once it's been set in motion. The crucial thing is that the battle keeps going. You don't have to win it in a revolutionary sense, as long as there is still that dynamism that is capable of operating in a different way to the centralizing authority. The mobile phone thing has produced some very interesting effects in some parts of the world. For example in the Philippines, when Estrada was ousted in January, that was a kind of mobile phone revolution. All the demonstrations and the meetings and the news was passed around through text messages. It's a very interesting scenario. Obviously the technology didn't make the revolution happen, but it certainly affected how it was possible to have that kind of grass-roots mobilization very much without a centralized information source. So I think there is some truth in this idea that information flows like water and tries to find outlets for itself. I think more than the desktop computer, the mobile phone with Internet access has the potential to be a culturally significant technology, and perhaps to fulfil some of the optimism that, as you say, I do have in *Zeros and Ones*.

KR: Is there a side to the new technologies that worries you, or ramifications of it that you think are troubling or sinister?

SP: Oh, I think it's all quite worrying! It almost goes without saying that the technologies are rarely produced with benign social intentions. I think the trick is finding what you can do to undermine that. It is very much about unanticipated effects and unintended consequences. You can portray the whole digital enterprise as the epitome of a classically patriarchal dream of total control – now we can finally play God. And yet as we know, both in terms of theory and practical consequences,

Image 9.4: Sadie Plant, *Dubai*

(2001). (photo © : Sadie Plant).

Image 9.4: Sadie Plant, *Dubai* (2001). (photo © : Sadie Plant).

it has introduced far more chaos and disorder than control into the world. If you read 1950's and 1960's literature about computerization, it is shot through with this dream of everything running like clockwork. As we know the result is very far from that. There are other processes going on that we just don't see until they actually happen. So it's another lesson about the limits of our ability to either comprehend the whole picture or to control it.[6]

KR: And that is very optimistic.

SP: Well, it can be either very optimistic or very pessimistic. It depends on your attitude to control. But I find it optimistic because I think, for all the dangers it throws us into, it does at least mean that there's always some room for manoeuvre. This happens with computer technology more than any other technology, simply because the computer is such a complex thing, and it's by definition a multipurpose machine. So you're bound to get this chaotic effect coming out of technological change. Even if that throws an element of uncertainty into everything, at least it means it's not all a pre-programmed, pre-scripted future. When you see how people use technologies in ways that are so far from what the original intention was, I think it does give cause for enormous optimism.

KR: Are there artists that you admire now who are using digital technologies?

SP: When I was writing *Zeros and Ones* I was very much encouraged by several women artists, mostly Australians, in particular Linda Dement and the four women that made up VNS Matrix.[7] They were doing then what a lot of people are doing now: looking at multimedia to see what you could do that you couldn't do in an old medium. That's what I admire in the ways people use the new media in relation to art. The thing that can be a bit depressing about contemporary uses of new technology is when it reproduces things that could have been done in some older format.

KR: Artists or writers often want to use the so-called interactive aspect of digital technology. You have these interactive novels with alternate endings, or with endings you can write yourself. And artworks on the Internet where the audience helps make the work. What's your feeling about that in relation to what an artist or a writer does?

SP: Well, two things. Obviously, it does present a whole new world of possibilities, some of which I would be interested in exploring without being too committed to anything. But I think there are difficulties with the kind of interactivity where things are infinitely open-ended or changeable or chosen by the reader. There is value in being presented with something which is a more or less bounded object or entity. As the audience, you don't necessarily want to be called upon to be producing the thing. There are circumstances where you want to be in a passive mode, you don't want to participate. Film is perhaps a good example. The most recent film I saw that had this effect on me was the Claire Denis film, *Beau Travail* [1999]. I thought it was really fantastic. But you know, if there had been any point where I had had to make a decision, I would have been horrified. You just want to let it invade you.

KR: But that's not really out of laziness or passivity, is it?

SP: No, not at all. It's out of the experience. It's like a long bus journey, where you don't really know where you're going or where you are. You are in a process, and you're not in control of it. Were you to be called upon to start deciding which road the bus took it would be a very different experience.

KR: **What if one of your books had been produced in such a way that people could change any aspect of it. Would you mind that?**

SP: I'm quite open to it, really. *Zeros and Ones* doesn't really have an end or a beginning; in principle you could almost infinitely add other sections to it. But I think certain limits can be good: there needs to be a sense in which you're providing the parameters, so that you're offering something.

KR: **You could say that reading a traditional novel could be just as interactive as something digital that seems interactive but it's only in quite limited ways.**

SP: Yes, definitely. I think one of the more interesting implications of digitization is that it can give you a new perspective on what was happening in older media, or older historical periods. You can look back at certain books and see what we now talk about in terms of interactivity. It's just that we didn't have the vocabulary for it before.

KR: **By opposing the new to the old, you end up seeing how they're similar.**

SP: That's one of the disconcerting effects of new technology and one of the reasons why it causes a lot of interest in the art world. Take a very simple but huge question, like the one about creativity and originality. On the one hand, you can say the computer completely undermines all that, or puts a different perspective on it. But that very thought requires you to question the whole history of art. When you start looking for the 'original' work – where are the people who supposedly thought they were small gods making art? You start looking back over the canon, and suddenly the canon isn't there any more. That's one of the reasons why I think we went through this supposed postmodern crisis. The rug does get pulled out from under your feet. It's not just that something changes now, it's that it changes how everything seemed in the past as well. Any big change rewrites history. You do really get this sense of vertigo.

KR: **And also, the idea of language being fixed and hierarchical is a simplification. There are poles of fixity or say fluidity, within any medium. Griselda Pollock talks about the pole of language which tries to be as clear and direct as possible, saying only what it wants to say, like a legal document. And then the other extreme, moving towards literature and poetry, is something much more chaotic and non-linear and troubled by bodily experience, fantasy. Something ambiguous and layered and contradictory. But when we talk about language, especially in relation to visual forms, we usually focus on that first function. Words are fixed, images are not.**

SP: I think one of the things about writing that I find most engaging is that most people write in some way, even if it's only the shopping list. You can't say that about painting or sculpture. It's interesting to focus on something that most people do, to some extent, whether they're writing letters or, as you say, legal documents. It gives you a very clear sense of what it is that you need to do to be a writer, and makes you focus on why what you're doing is different from making a shopping list.

KR: **Getting back to the question of audience participation in works. Do you think a work of art has to be a bit self-sufficient and impermeable? It's whole enough to resist actual participation, and because of that it can invite imaginative participation.**

Then I wonder if there might be almost a moral side to it. In fiction you are trying to create worlds where certain things happen and there

are consequences of one's actions. **If someone makes this kind of decision, this is what happens. Writers make you try these things out in your mind and see what happens. If you could change what happens –**

SP: You'd have happy endings everywhere.

KR: **Or unhappy endings, but you wouldn't have that sense of the irreversibility of life.**

SP: Perhaps the issue isn't so much whether or not something is done in an interactive way, but as you're saying, whether it is capable of creating and sustaining a world, producing a particular atmosphere or a particular scenario. I am not hostile to experimentation with non-linearity and interactivity because I think those things are fascinating. I haven't seen anything that I think is a mind-blowingly brilliant use of this potential, but I'm in no position to criticize because I haven't made any attempt to do it either. I suppose I am at the moment content with experimenting to the extent that I do, within the form of paper and print. I do play with other stuff, but the next project is still going to be something published by a publisher. I would be interested in doing something in the future that is slightly more multimedia and on the screen, but I would want to be extremely clear and careful about what I did.

KR: **Multimodality is another feature of digital technologies. You can combine visuals and sound and text . . .**

SP: That does very much appeal to me.

KR: **Yet none of your books have images in them.**

SP: No, there are no illustrations.

KR: **Did you ever consider using images?**

SP: Fleetingly, perhaps, but not seriously so far. There were occasions in both books where an image probably would have been a very good idea, but to me it would have felt like a bit of a short cut, cheating almost. I don't like images just to be illustrations of a text. I want everything to be crucial or not there at all. So if I did do something with images, the images would have to be absolutely vital and not just a matter of making the book look attractive.

But much as I can feel myself going in this multimedia direction, I think I will always be a word person at the end of the day. I notice, to my shame, that whenever I go to an art gallery I am one of those people who is as interested in reading the captions as in looking at whatever it is I'm looking at, although this is changing as I learn to draw. I'm quite critical of people who do that, but I notice myself doing it. Left to my own devices, I immediately want to know: What's the title? Who did it? What's it made of? I want to read about it, to place it.[8]

KR: **Is it because we're so used to getting our information through words?**

SP: Maybe that's it. But I wonder if that is really the case? We're also used to having images flashed in front of us. We're used to television and film. It's an interesting question. I've always assumed that in my case it was a sign I was just interested in words more than the images. But it could also be my proletarian insecurity!

KR: **In The Most Radical Gesture you wrote that 'History is not dead but sleeping.' And you wrote about postmodernism being to a large extent passive and rather cynical, not interested in action, in making change. I wonder if you think that has shifted in the last ten years. Has history woken up since 1992? Or maybe it's not an area you're thinking about a great deal now.**

SP: I do think about it, actually. There are lots of issues around so-called globalization that I think fit in with these sorts of questions. To be really honest, I don't know what I think at the minute, and it is bugging me a bit. It's funny you should bring this up because I have been having a lot of conversations recently, and

I honestly can't decide what's going on on these fronts. I'm not sure there is the advent of a new kind of activism around these issues, or how coherent it is. I don't know whether to think on the more pessimistic side, that history is still in hibernation, or if there is perhaps the return of an older notion of history. You'll have to get back to me on this one.

KR: I respect those kinds of answers.

SP: The kind you'd never get off a politician.

KR: Do you think it's because things are unclear at the moment? Or is it also that the kind of work you're moving towards is not so academic or analytical, so you're thinking in a different way?

SP: That may be true, although I find it difficult to turn off the part of my brain that endlessly analyses the minutiae of things. I've exposed myself to a lot of new things in the last twelve months that are relevant to these questions, but I feel I haven't processed it all yet. I'm waiting for a few things to become clearer.

To give you an example, I'm quite exercised by all the issues around globalization. The atmosphere around race and asylum-seekers at the moment makes me extremely uncomfortable. I want to argue for more globalization, which is about the most unfashionable thing you could say. The critics of globalization look at the situation and quite rightly they see that money can move and goods can move, but people can't, not so freely anyway. So their response to that is to argue against the free movement of goods and money. But I want to argue in favour of the free movement of labour. I think that would be an extremely subversive point to make, that there isn't enough free movement of people. I've been in close contact with many refugees in the last twelve months, so I suppose that's what's made me particularly aware of the fact that there is very little free movement for most people and that's where I think the flaw lies. It's a point that you very rarely see made. So I would quite like to intervene in all this and maybe I am slowly building up to saying something about it, but I haven't quite got around to it yet.

KR: You've written a book on the Situationists,[9] one on women and technology and one on drugs. And one in the offing that may be about globalization. How related are these to one another? I'm trying to piece together your different routes of enquiry.

SP: It's funny. It makes such sense to me, but I know it must look so eclectic to other people. In my mind the three existing books have got several things in common. The most relevant one is that they all take either a theme or a period of history that has an established orthodox account, and they're all looking for a hidden history. In the case of the Situationist book, it was the hidden history of the 1968 thing and postmodern theory. In *Zeros and Ones* it was Ada Lovelace's margins-and-footnotes story within the history of technology. In the drugs book, it's very much the same idea – that a lot of our supposedly mainstream, sober, anti-drug culture, has been informed by the use of substances that are now regarded as completely unacceptable.

These histories are not really hidden. I very rarely go to interview people or make a real effort to dig up some lost text. I pride myself in using very easily available materials. It's all there, it's just a matter of how you put it together.

So all three books look for hidden histories and they come up with a slightly different picture of their subject, as a consequence. A long time ago I thought about doing the drugs book and the technology book as one book. They seemed very much two sides of the same coin, largely on the basis that they're both material things. I'm always looking for the material that has informed a supposedly immaterial history, and obviously drugs is a classic case. If you look at, say, Freud using cocaine, and how that may or may not have influenced the development of his psychoanalytic theory, it's a perfect instance of how this handful of chemical dust has perhaps had an enormous impact on a history of ideas. You could say very similar things about technology, because it's, again, material processes inducing what are often seen as idealist changes of attitude or social structure. So I suppose at heart I'm a Marxist. I do believe in economic and technological and tangible material processes being if not determining then at least extremely significant in the whole of our cultural life.

KR: **Do you take the view that the technology arises first and wreaks its changes, or do you think that technology arises as a consequence of other, less tangible factors?**

SP: Well obviously it does do the latter. I'm not a technological determinist,[10] but I do think there's a tendency to run too far in the other direction. It's not that technology on its own makes things happen. But I do think that if you change the ways in which things are done in a practical way, then almost inevitably society does shift. It doesn't have to be a black and white causal thing, but certainly I think it's a very important influence.

Zeros and Ones very speculatively talks about the history of feminism in relation to technological change, and I do think there's significant mileage in it. It's the same idea really: if you change the processes of production or distribution or communication or whatever it might be – things crucial to a society – you will encourage and often accelerate certain social changes. If you look at what happened to the family and the role of women in the industrial revolution, or at any point after it, I think you can say that technology was hugely significant. And in terms of studying culture, it is a useful place to start – tracking the development of technology and the changes associated with it.

Sadie Plant, interviewed by Karen Raney,

May 2001

Notes

1. Sadie Plant, *Writing on Drugs* (London: Faber & Faber, 1999; New York: Farrar Straus and Giroux, 2000).

2. Sadie Plant, *Zeros and Ones: Digital Women and the New Technoculture* (London: Fourth Estate, 1996; New York: Doubleday, 1997).

3. Sadie Plant, *The Most Radical Gesture: The Situationist International in a Postmodern Age* (London and New York: Routledge, 1992).

4. In *Zeros and Ones*, Plant tells the story of Ada Lovelace, a woman who worked in the margins of a nineteenth-century research text by L.F. Menabrea, 'Notes to Sketch of the Analytical Engine invented by Charles Babbage Esq.' Her indices, prefaces and footnotes were seen as subordinate to the main text, when in fact they provided the crucial means of locating the work socially and historically.

5. B. Edwards, *Drawing on the Right Side of the Brain* (Los Angeles, CA: J. P. Tarcher, London: Souvenir Press, 1979).

6. See Francis Fukuyama, *Our Posthuman Future: Consequences of the Biotechnology Revolution* (New York: Farrar Straus & Giroux, 2002). Also Paul Virilio, *The Open Sky* (trans. Julie Rose) (London: Verso, 1997).

7. Linda Dement is an Australian artist with a background in fine art, photography, writing, animation and film. Her CD-ROMS include *Cyberfesh Girlmonster*, *Typhoid Mary* and *In My Gash*. VNS Matrix is a group of Australian women artists. Their aim is 'to investigate and decipher the narratives of domination and control which surround high technological culture, and explore the construction of social space, identity and sexuality in cyberspace' (VNS Matrix website).

8. W. J. T. Mitchell talks in his interview about this tendency to rely on labels in museums. 'Robert Morris says the labels are like lifelines and you go reeling yourself over to them because you're afraid you're going to drown in the image.'

9. Situationist International was a leftist student movement with Marxist roots, operating mainly in France in the 1960s. Its self-proclaimed leader was Guy Debord, who wrote a now classic text on modern-day capitalism and cultural imperialism, *The Society of the Spectacle* (1973; New York: Zone, 1994).

10. 'Technological determinism' refers to a view of the relationship of technology to society in which technologies, discovered by an independent scientific process, are the cause of social change and progress. See W. J. T. Mitchell, Chapter 1, n. 8 (p. 65).

Biographies

Note that full details are given only for works not cited in the Bibliography.

W. J. T. Mitchell is Gaylord Donnelley Distinguished Service Professor of English and Art History, University of Chicago. Editor of the interdisciplinary journal, *Critical Inquiry* since 1978, Mitchell is a scholar and theorist of media, visual art and literature, associated with the emergent fields of visual culture and iconology (the study of images across the media). His authored and edited books include: *The Last Dinosaur Book: The Life and Times of a Cultural Icon* (Chicago, IL: University of Chicago Press, 1998); *Picture Theory; Art and the Public Sphere; Landscape and Power* (Chicago, IL: University of Chicago Press, 1992); *Iconology: Image, Text, Ideology; Against Theory: Literary Studies and the New Pragmatism* (Chicago, IL: University of Chicago Press, 1985); *The Language of Images* (Chicago, IL: University of Chicago Press, 1980); *On Narrative* (Chicago, IL: University of Chicago Press, 1981); *The Politics of Interpretation* (Chicago, IL: University of Chicago Press, 1983), and *Blake's Composite Art* (Princeton, NJ: Princeton University Press, 1978).

He is the recipient of numerous fellowships and awards, including the Guggenheim Fellowship, the Berlin Prize, the Gordon E. Laing Prize from the University of Chicago Press, and the Charles Rufus Morey Prize for a distinguished book in art history from the College Art Association of America. His current projects include two books: *What Do Pictures Want? Essays on the Lives of Images* and *Totemism, Fetishism, Idolatry.*

Bill Viola is widely recognized as the leading video artist on the international scene. Since 1972 he has created videotapes, architectural video installations, sound environments, electronic music performances and works for television broadcast. Viola's single-channel videotapes have been broadcast and presented cinematically around the world, while his writings have been published and anthologized for international readers. Viola uses video to explore the phenomena of sense perception as an avenue to self-knowledge. Clearly at odds with the cynicism of his age, his works focus on universal human experiences – birth, death, the unfolding of consciousness – and have roots in both Eastern and Western art, as well as Islamic Sufism, Christian mysticism and Zen Buddhism.

In 1995 Viola was selected to represent the United States at the 46th Venice Biennale with an exhibition entitled 'Buried Secrets'. In 1997 the Whitney Museum of American Art in New York organized 'Bill Viola: A 25-Year Survey Exhibition' that toured the United States and Europe from 1997 to 2000. In 1998 Viola was a scholar-in-residence at the Getty Research Institute for the History of Art and Humanities at the Getty Center, Los Angeles. He works at his studio in Long Beach, California, where he lives with his wife and manager Kira Perov and their two children.

Okwui Enwezor, born in Nigeria, was the Artistic Director of Documenta 11, in Kassel, Germany (2002). He was also the Artistic Director of the 2nd Johannesburg Biennale (1997). Until recently Enwezor held a position as the Adjunct Curator of Contemporary Art at the Art Institute of Chicago. Enwezor's curatorial projects include: 'In/sight: African Photographers, 1940–Present', at the Guggenheim Museum, New York; 'Mirror's Edge' (Bild Museet, Umeå; Castello di Rivoli, Torino; Vancouver Art Gallery and Tramway, Glasgow, 1999–2001); 'Stan Douglas: Le Detroit' at the Art Institute of Chicago (2001); 'Global Conceptualism' (Queens Museum, New York, 1999); 'The Short Century: Independence and Liberation Movements in Africa, 1945–1994', at the Museum Villa Stuck, Munich, which travelled to Berlin, Chicago and New York (2001).

A poet and critic as well as a curator, Enwezor has written extensively on contemporary African, American and international art and artists. He is the publisher and founding editor of *Nka: Journal of Contemporary African Art*, a critical art journal co-published with the African Studies Center at Cornell University. Enwezor is a correspondent for *Flash Art*, consulting editor to *Atlantica* (a bilingual art and culture publication of the Museo Centro Atlantic de Arte Moderno, Canary Islands), editor-at-large of *aRude* and a regular contributor to *Frieze*, *International Review of African-American Art*, *Third Text*, *Index on Censorship*, *Glendora Review*, *Africa World Review*, *African Profiles International* and *SIKSI*. He divides his time between New York and Kassel.

Barbara Kruger was born in Newark, NJ, and educated at Syracuse University, New York, and Parsons School of Design, New York City. She lives in New York City and Los Angeles, CA. Her work is represented by the Mary Boone Gallery in New York City.

Recent solo shows include: South London Gallery, London, England (2001); Whitney Museum of American Art, New York (2000); Galerie Yvon Lambert, Paris (1999); Museum of Contemporary Art, Los Angeles, CA (1999). Recent public projects include: banner billboards at Eighth Avenue/42 Street and Washington Street/West Side Highway, co-produced by the Public Art Fund and the Whitney Museum of American Art, New York (2000); New York City/Queens Transit Line bus wrap, Public Art Fund, New York (1997); Design for outdoor theatre, North Carolina Museum of Art, Raleigh, North Carolina (collaboration with Smith-Miller & Hawkinson and Nicholas Quennell) (1995); editorial feature, *Harper's Bazaar* (1994); design for train station, Strasbourg, France (1994). *Thinking of You* is the comprehensive catalogue of Kruger's first retrospective exhibition at Los Angeles Museum of Contemporary Art, CA (1999).

Griselda Pollock is Professor of Social and Critical Histories of Art and Director of the AHRB Centre for Cultural Analysis, Theory and History at the University of Leeds. Co-founder and director (1986–2000) of the Centre for Cultural Studies (1986), she is also the Director of the Programme in Feminism and the Visual Arts which combines theory, history and practice. She is known for her work on nineteenth- and twentieth-century European and American studies and for her long-term project to develop feminist interventions in art's histories. Her current interests include psychoanalysis and aesthetics, studies in trauma and cultural memory with reference to the Holocaust and a major study of Charlotte Salomon.

Recent publications include: *Generations and Geographies in the Visual Arts: Feminist Readings*; *Mary Cassatt: Painter of Modern Women* (London: Thames & Hudson, 1998); *Differencing the Canon: Feminist Desire and the Writing of Art's Histories*; *Looking Back to the Future: Essays on Life, Death and Art*. Forthcoming: *The Case against Van Gogh*; *Cities and Countries of Modernism*.

Hani Rashid is an architect based in New York City. In 1988, with his partner Lise Anne Couture, he founded a design, architecture and research practice, Asymptote Architecture, now a highly accomplished practice with international recognition. Asymptote is working at the forefront of a new discipline: the design of interactive architectural environments intended for the space of the computer. Asymptote's design of the virtual trading floor for the New York Stock Exchange and the design of the Guggenheim Virtual Museum are two undertakings which are expanding both the realm of architecture and that of interactive digital media.

In addition to building designs and urban proposals, Asymptote has also received acclaim for several of their art-scaled projects which range from large public works to smaller gallery installations. Representing the United States at the 2000 Venice Biennale in Architecture, Hani Rashid exhibited four installation pieces each exploring digital technologies and their interface with the built environments, resulting in hybrid works that are at once art, technology and architecture. The work of Rashid and Couture has been featured in over 200 publications.

Martin Kemp was trained in Natural Sciences and Art History at Cambridge University and the Courtauld Institute, London. He is currently Professor of the History of Art at the University of Oxford, having spent most of his career in Scotland (Universities of Glasgow and St Andrews). He has extensively researched the art, science and technology of Leonardo da Vinci, resulting in his first monograph, *Leonardo da Vinci. The Marvellous Works of Nature and Man* (London: J. M. Dent, 1981), winner of the Mitchell Prize, and in the major exhibition, 'Leonardo da Vinci', at the Hayward Gallery, London (1989).

The continuing theme of his research has been the relationship between scientific models of nature and the theory and practice of art. The culmination of the optical researches is *The Science of Art: Optical Themes in Western Art from Brunelleschi to Seurat* (New Haven, CT: Yale University Press, 1990 and 1992). With Marina Wallace, he curated a major exhibition in 2000–1, 'Spectacular Bodies: the Art and Science of the Human Body from Leonardo to Now', at the Hayward Gallery, London. Together they have founded the exhibition-making and consultancy company, Wallace Kemp/Artakt, specializing in mounting art–science events, including the first ever exhibition in the Abbey of Mendel in Brno in the Czech Republic (2002).

Richard Wentworth is a British artist who lives and works in London. He exhibits internationally and is represented by the Lisson Gallery, London. Recent exhibitions include: Galerie Weisses Schloss, Zurich (1998); Gallery Wang, Oslo (1999); Lisson Gallery, London (1999); Galerie Margaret Biedermann, Munich (2000); 'Point de Vue' [Point of View], Musée des Beaux-Arts et de la Dentelle, Calais (2001); Sao Paolo Bienale (2002); The Fluxus Memorial Exhibition, 40 Jahre: Fluxus und die Folgen, at Kunstsommer, Wiesbaden (2002).

Other recent projects include: the design of external public space at the New Art Gallery, Walsall, in collaboration with Caruso St John architects (2000); 'Richard Wentworth's Thinking Aloud', national touring exhibition (Hayward Gallery) Kettle's Yard, Cambridge, touring to Cornerhouse, Manchester and Camden Art Centre, London (1998–99); 'Faux Amis' (Richard Wentworth and Eugène Atget), Photographer's Gallery, London. From April 2002 Wentworth was appointed Ruskin Master at Ruskin School of Art, Oxford. His project commissioned by *Artangel: An area of Outstanding Unnatural Beauty*, took place September to November 2002 in King's Cross, London.

Sadie Plant was born in Birmingham and studied Philosophy at the University of Manchester, where she gained her PhD in 1989. She has published three books: *The Most Radical Gesture: The Situationist International in a Postmodern Age*; *Zeros and Ones:*

Digital Women and the New Technoculture; and *Writing on Drugs*. She has recently published *On the Mobile*, a report on the international cultural implications of mobile phones, commissioned by Motorola in 2001. After spending much of the 1990s in the academic world – as Lecturer in Cultural Studies at the University of Birmingham until 1995, and Research Fellow at the University of Warwick until 1997, Sadie is now writing full-time from her base in Birmingham.

Select Bibliography

Arnheim, R. (1969) *Visual Thinking*, Berkeley, CA: University of California Press.

Bal, M. (1994) *On Meaning-Making: Essays in Semiotics*, Sonoma, CA: Polebridge Press.

Barlow, H., Blakemore, C. and Weston-Smith, M. (eds) (1990) *Images and Understanding*, Cambridge: Cambridge University Press.

Barthes, R. (1977) 'The Rhetoric of the Image', in *Image, Music, Text*, ed. and trans. Stephen Heath, London: Collins/Fontana.

——(1957; 1993) *Mythologies*, London: Vintage.

Benjamin, W. (1936; 1992) 'The Work of Art in the Age of Mechanical Reproduction', in W. Benjamin, *Illuminations* (London: Collins/Fontana), pp. 211–44.

Berger, J. (1972) *Ways of Seeing*, London: BBC Books and Penguin.

Berman, M. (1983) *All that is Solid Melts into Air*, London: Verso.

Bryson, N., Holly, M. and Moxey, K. (eds) (1991) *Visual Theory*, Oxford: Polity Press and Basil Blackwell.

Campbell, S. and Tawadros, G. (eds) (2001) *Stuart Hall and Sarat Maharaj: Modernity and Difference*, in IVA annotations series. London: Institute of International Visual Arts.

Danto, A. (1986) *The Philosophical Disenfranchisement of Art*, New York: Columbia University Press.

Deleuze, Gilles and Guattari, Felix (1998) *A Thousand Plateaus: Capitalism and Schizophrenia*, London: Athlone Press.

Druckrey, T. (ed.) (1996) *Electronics Culture: Technology and Visual Representation*, New York: Aperture Foundation Books.

Enwezor, O. (ed.) (2000) *The Short Century: Independence and Liberation Movements in Africa 1945–1994*, Munich and London: Prestel.

Enwezor, O. and Oguibe, O. (eds) (1999) *Reading the Contemporary: African Art from Theory to the Marketplace*, London: Institute of International Visual Arts.

Enwezor, O., Oguibe, O. and Zaya, O. (eds) (1996) *In/Sight: African Photographers 1940 to the Present*, New York: Guggenheim Museum.

Ferguson, B., Greenberg, R. and Nairne, S. (eds) (1996) *Thinking about Exhibitions*, London: Routledge.

Fernie, Eric (1995) *Art History and its Methods: A Critical Anthology* (selection and commentary by Eric Fernie), London: Phaidon.

Foster, H. (1996) *Return of the Real: The Avant-garde at the End of the Century*, Cambridge, MA, and London: MIT Press.

Foucault, M. (1972; 1995) *Discipline and Punish: The Birth of the Prison*, London: Vintage.

——(1972) *The Archaeology of Knowledge*, London: Tavistock.

Fukuyama, F. (2002) *Our Posthuman Future: Consequences of the Biotechnology Revolution*, New York: Farrar, Straus & Giroux.

Gardner, H. (1993; 2nd edn) *Frames of Mind: The Theory of Multiple Intelligences*, London: Collins/Fontana.

Gilman, S. (1985) *Difference and Pathology: Stereotypes of Sexuality, Race, and Madness*, Ithaca, NY, and London: Cornell University Press.

——(1995) *Health and Illness: Images of Difference*, London: Reaktion Books.

Gombrich, E. (1959) *Art and Illusion: A Study in the Psychology of Pictorial Representation*, Oxford: Phaidon.

Hanfling, O. (ed.) (1992) *Philosophical Aesthetics: An Introduction*, Oxford and Milton Keynes: Blackwell and the Open University.

Harris, J. (2001) *The New Art History: A Critical Introduction*, London: Routledge.

Harrison, C. and Wood, P. (eds) (1992) *Art in Theory, 1900–1990*, Cambridge, MA, and Oxford: Blackwell.

Hausman, C. (1991) 'Figurative Language in Art History', in Kemal and Gaskell (eds), 1991, pp. 101–27.

Innis, R. (ed.) (1985) *Semiotics: An Introductory Anthology*, London: Hutchinson.

Jantjes, Gavin (ed.) (1998) *A Fruitful Incoherence: Dialogues with Artists on Internationalism*, London: Institute of International Visual Arts.

Jay, M. (1993) *Downcast Eyes: The Denigration of Vision in Twentieth-Century French Thought*, Berkeley, CA: University of California Press.

Jones, A. and Stephenson, A. (1999) *Performing the Body/Performing the Text*, London: Routledge.

Kemal, S. and Gaskell, I. (eds) (1991) *The Language of Art History*, Cambridge: Cambridge University Press.

Kemp, M. (1990) *The Science of Art: Optical Themes in Western Art from Brunelleschi to Seurat*, New Haven, CT, and London: Yale University Press.

——(1994) 'Coming into Line: Graphic Demonstrations of Skill in Renaissance and Baroque Engravings', in J. Onians (ed.), *Sight and Insight: Essays on Art and Culture in Honour of E. H. Gombrich at 85*, London: Phaidon.

——(1997) *Behind the Picture: Art and Evidence in the Italian Renaissance*, New Haven, CT, and London: Yale University Press.

Kemp, M. and Wallace, M. (2000) *Spectacular Bodies: The Art and Science of the Human Body from Leonardo to Now*, Berkeley, CA, and London: University of California Press and Hayward Gallery.

Krauss, R. (1993) *The Optical Unconscious*, Cambridge, MA, and London: MIT Press.

Kress, G. and van Leeuwen, T. (1996) *Reading Images: The Grammar of Visual Design*, London: Routledge.

Kruger, B. (1999) *Thinking of You*, Los Angeles, CA: Museum of Contemporary Art.

Lanham, R. (1993) *The Electronic Word: Democracy, Technology and the Arts*, Chicago, IL: University of Chicago Press.

Lichtenberg-Ettinger, B. (1995) *The Matrixial Gaze*, Leeds: Feminist Arts and Histories Network.

Livingstone, M. (2000) 'Bill Viola' in R. Morphet, *Encounters: New Art from Old*, London: National Gallery.

Lyotard, J.-F. (1984) *The Postmodern Condition: A Report on Knowledge*, Manchester: Manchester University Press.

Maharaj, S. (1994) 'Perfidious Fidelity: The Untranslatability of the Other', in J. Fisher (ed.), *Global Visions: Towards a New Internationalism in the Visual Arts*, London: Kala Press in association with Institute of International Visual Arts.

McLuhan, M. and Powers, B. (1989) *The Global Village: Transformations in World Life and Media in the 21st Century*, New York and Oxford: Oxford University Press.

Merleau-Ponty, M. (1962; 1986) *The Phenomenology of Perception*, trans. Colin Smith, London: Routledge & Kegan Paul.

Messaris, P. (1994) *Visual Literacy: Image, Mind, Reality*, Oxford: Westview Press.

Mitchell, W. J. T. (1986) *Iconology: Image, Text, Ideology*, Chicago, IL: University of Chicago Press.

——(1993) interview with Barbara Kruger in *Art and the Public Sphere*, Chicago, IL: University of Chicago Press.

——(1994) *Picture Theory: Essays on Verbal and Visual Representation*, Chicago, IL: University of Chicago Press.

——(1996) 'What Is Visual Culture?' in I. Lavin (ed.), *Meaning in the Visual Arts: Views from the Outside – A Centennial Commemoration of Erwin Panofsky*, Princeton, NJ: Princeton University Press.

——(1996) 'Word and Image' in Nelson and Shiff, 1996, pp. 47–57.

Moxey, K. (1994) *The Practice of Theory: Post-structuralism, Cultural Politics and Art History*, Ithaca, NY, and London: Cornell University Press.

Nelson, R. and Shiff, R. (eds) (1996) *Critical Terms for Art History*, Chicago, IL: University of Chicago Press.

Owens, C. (1983) 'The Discourse of Others: Feminists and Postmodernism', in H. Foster (ed.), *Postmodern Culture*, London: Pluto Press.

Plant, S. (1992) *The Most Radical Gesture: The Situationist International in a Postmodern Age*, London and New York: Routledge.

——(1996) *Zeros and Ones: Digital Women and the New Technoculture*, London: Fourth Estate.

——(1999) *Writing on Drugs*, London: Faber & Faber.

Pollock, G. (1988) *Vision and Difference*, London: Routledge.

——(1999) *Differencing the Canon: Feminist Desire and the Writing of Art's Histories*, London: Routledge.

——(2000) *Looking Back to the Future: Essays on Life, Death and Art*, London: Routledge.

——(ed.) (1996) *Generations and Geographies in the Visual Arts: Feminist Readings*, London: Routledge.

Preziosi, D. (1998) 'The Art of Art History' in D. Preziosi (ed.), *The Art of Art History*, Oxford: Oxford University Press.

Raney, K. (1997) *Visual Literacy: Issues and Debates*, London: Middlesex University and the Arts Council of England.

——(1999) 'Visual Literacy and the Art Curriculum', in *Journal of Art and Design Education*, 8.1.

——(1999) 'Art Education and Talk: From Modernist Silence to Postmodern Chatter', with Howard Hollands, in J. Sefton-Greene and R. Sinker (eds), *Evaluating Creativity*, London: Routledge.

Rashid, H. and Couture, L. A. (1995) *Asymptote: Architecture at the Interval*, New York: Rizzoli International.

Sarup, M. (1988) *An Introductory Guide to Post-structuralism and Postmodernism*, Brighton: Harvester/Wheatsheaf.

Sim, S. (1992) 'Structuralism and Post-structuralism', in O. Hanfling (ed.), pp. 405–39.

Sontag, S. (1977) *On Photography*, London: Penguin.

Vidler, A. (2000) *Warped Space: Art, Architecture and Anxiety in Modern Culture*, Cambridge, MA and London: MIT Press.

Viola, B. (1995) *Reasons for Knocking at an Empty House: Writings 1973–1994*, ed. R. Violette, London: Thames & Hudson and Anthony d'Offay Gallery.

——(1997) *Bill Viola: a Twenty-Five Year Survey*, texts by Lewis Hyde, Kira Perov, David A. Ross and Bill Viola. New York: Whitney Museum of American Art; Paris: Flammarion.

Virilio, P. (1997) *The Open Sky* (trans. Julie Rose), London: Verso.

Warner, Marina (1993) *Richard Wentworth*, London: Thames & Hudson in association with the Serpentine Gallery.

Wentworth, R. (1993) 'Parade: Twenty-one Non-sequiturs', in N. Cummings (ed.), *Reading Things, Sight Works*, Vol. 3, London: Chance Books.

Wentworth, R. (1998) *Richard Wentworth's Thinking Aloud*, London: Hayward Gallery.

Williams, R. (1975) *Television: Technology and Cultural Form*, London: Routledge & Kegan Paul.

Wolff, J. (1993) *Aesthetics and the Sociology of Art*, 2nd edn, London: Macmillan.

Index

References to images are given in *italics*, notes are marked by 'n', and main text is in **bold**.

Henrietta of Lorraine (van Dyck)   35n.15

Hirschhorn, Michelle   157n.13

Hirschhorn, Thomas   102–3, 112n.11, 126–7, *126*

Hirst, Damien   212n.9

Hollein, Max   177–8

Horkheimer, Max   103–4, 112n.13

Houdon, Jean-Antoine   206, 213n.14

Hugonin, James   198

human genome project   80

Hunter, William   206, 213n.14

hybridization   12, 211

I

iconoclasm   54

Iconology (Mitchell)   51

iconophilia   93–4, 96

iconophobia   54–5

Igbos, the   97–8

Igloolik/Isuma Productions   98, 111n.5

Ignore This Building (Shrigley)   *218*

image-text   2, 52–4

image/text   2, 53–4, 57

imagetext   2, 52–4

Imperfect Utopia (exhibition), *see* exhibitions

Inscriptions of the Feminine (module)   132–3

institutional ethics   93–4

Interim, Part 11 (Kelly)   *150*

International Visual Literacy Association   65n.11

interpretations   189

Inuit culture   17

Irigary, Luce   156n.1

Isaacs, John   213n.12

Islamic culture   73–4, 94

It's Our Pleasure to Disgust You (Kruger 1991)   12

J

Jantjes, Gavin   37n.36

Jay, Martin   36n.27, 89n.2

Jones, Amelia   37n.40–41

Journal of Contemporary African Art (Enwezor)   93

K

Kant, Immanuel   51, 65n.3

Kelly, Mary   149–50, *150*, 157n.10,15

Kemp, Martin

  introduction   5, 14–16, 23–4, 29–30, 32, 50

  interview   **183–211**

  images   *182, 207*

  notes   36n.21, 65–6n.8, 212n.1&2, 212n.9,10&12

Kennedy Roger   65n.5

Koolhaas, Rem   109, 112n.20, 176, 181n.10

Krasner, Lee   21, 141

Krauss, Rosalind   4, 34n.7, 89n.2

Kress, Gunther   36–7n.30

Kristeva, Julia   15, 132–3, 135–7, 143, 156n.4–5

Kruger, Barbara

  introduction   3–6, 11–12, 17, 24, 32

  interview   **115–27**

  images   *48, 114, 117, 119*

  notes   34n.9, 112n.16,128n.5

Kunuk, Zacharias   111n.5

L

Lacan, Jacques   2, 25, 47, 65n.5–6, 66n.13, 111n.8, 139, 156n.6

Lagoon (Plant)   *245*

Landscape and Power (Mitchell)   30

Lang, Gerhard   213n.12

Le Corbusier   171, 181n.6

Lee Krasner at work (Haas)   *130*

Leeds University   132

Lelli, Ercole   205

Lessing, Gotthold Ephraim   51

Let Us Now Praise Famous Men (Evans)   11, 95

Levine, Sherry   66n.15, 111n.3&9

Libeskind, Daniel   176, 181n.10

Linker, Kate   34n.5

London 1994 (Wentworth)   *229*

London University   238

Love is Something You Fall Into (Kruger)   121

Lovelace, Ada   27, 242, 257

Luddites   181n.9

DATE DUE